THE DYNAMICS OF ART AS THERAPY WITH ADOLESCENTS

ABOUT THE AUTHOR

Bruce L. Moon is the director of the Marywood University Graduate Art Therapy Program in Scranton, Pennsylvania. He holds a doctorate in Art Therapy with specialization in the Creative Arts. Dr. Moon's clinical practice of art therapy has spanned over twenty-four years and has been heavily focused on children and adolescents. He has lectured and led workshops at many sites in the United States and Canada.

Bruce is an active painter and folk musician. He and his wife Cathy and their two children, Jesse and Brea, live in the mountains outside of Scranton.

Author of four other texts, *Existential Art Therapy: The Canvas Mirror, Essentials of Art Therapy Training and Practice, Introduction to Art Therapy: Faith in the Product,* and *Art and Soul: Reflections on an Artistic Psychology,* he brings to the profession a rich tradition of training in art, education, theology, and art therapy. The integration of these with his interests in existential philosophy, depth psychology, music, and clinical work provides an engaging poetic and theoretical approach to art as therapy with adolescents.

The Dynamics of Art as Therapy With Adolescents

By

Bruce L. Moon, Ph.D., A.T.R.

CHARLES C THOMAS • PUBLISHER, LTD.
Springfield • Illinois • U.S.A.

Published and Distributed Throughout the World by

CHARLES C THOMAS • PUBLISHER, LTD.
2600 South First Street
Springfield, Illinois 62794-9265

© *1998 by* CHARLES C THOMAS • PUBLISHER, LTD.
ISBN 0-398-06923-9 (cloth)
ISBN 0-398-06924-7 (paper)

Library of Congress Catalog Card Number: 98-37400

Printed in the United States of America
CR-R-3

Library of Congress Cataloging in Publication Data

Moon, Bruce L.
    The dynamics of art as therapy with adolescents / by Bruce L.
Moon.
        p.   cm.
    Includes bibliographical references.
    ISBN 0-398-06923-9 (cloth). -- ISBN 0-398-06924-7 (pbk.)
    1. Art therapy for teenagers. I. Title.
RJ505.A7M66 1998
616.89'1656'0835--dc21   98-37400
                                                                                    CIP

FOREWORD

Who would be born must first destroy a world
Hermann Hesse

It is an honor to introduce Dr. Bruce Moon's latest writings on the therapeutic uses of art with one of the most taxing, yet rewarding populations—that of adolescents. This is an eminently readable and accessible guide to eliciting art from disturbed teens. Moon's method lies in the great oral and visual tradition of American story tellers—from Mark Twain to Thomas Hart Benton. Speaking in reverent and almost poetic tones, Moon's clinical stories capture the exasperation that is adolescence.

Many therapists avoid working with adolescents, given their propensity to be defiant, hurtful, ungrateful, and impossible to reason with. Clinicians often consider adolescence to be a state of "naturally-occurring" madness, whose hormone-driven and impulsive behavior mimics many a psychopathology. Adolescence is the last great developmental milestone, as negotiating its many pitfalls may take a person a full third of their lifetime. Defenses are rigid, fragile and often impenetrable. Emotions are often volatile. The potential for insight is limited. Relationships center upon seeking immediate gratification, and often remain impoverished and exploitive.

Yet Moon is somehow able to form alliances with these difficult children. Practicing in the "artist-as-therapist" tradition, Moon comes to his sessions bearing tantalizing gifts. As the teens enter his studio, they are immediately surrounded by an array of intriguing images created during the art therapy sessions. Displayed also are the evocative pictures painted by Moon himself. An inviting buffet of paint, gesso, canvas and other media are laid out, stimulating even the most recalcitrant teen to imbibe their senses. The atmosphere is one of "infectious" passion and creativity.

Moon sets the stage for such creative license in part, by making art along side of clients in the art therapy studio. Here, the children can

v

safely view his own struggles, uncertainties, as well as the wonders of artistic exploration. By modeling ways in which the teens can metaphorically "dialogue" with their own "daemons," Moon bypasses the two most daunting and ubiquitous issues of adolescence—that of power and authority. Instead of simply confronting defiance and meting out consequences for antisocial behavior, Moon provides a "corrective experience" that is firmly within the object relations tradition. With his quiet presence, he creates a sanctuary where these troubled children can exorcise their rage, despair, and emptiness within a space that is gently facilitating—a version of the benignly supportive "holding" environment conceived by Winnicott. As the steward of this sanctuary, Moon provides "safe anchorage" in the Mahlerian sense, whereby, even the most alienated and resistant teens seem to relax their defenses and begin to develop what Moon considers the most important objective in therapy—the capacity to form "quality relationships."

Moon's techniques are deceptively straightforward. Rather than presenting as the high-brow clinician, Moon's demeanor lies within the fold of Midwestern hospitality. For instance, he greets each child in the same ritualized manner, uses corny buzzwords, sings folk songs, and maintains an unfailingly up-beat demeanor, which, all tolled, might seem quaintly old-fashioned to a nose-pierced, hardened adolescent. Yet for such emotionally raw and damaged children, the disillusionment over their parents' own divorced relationships, substance abuse, and self-indulgence, has resulted in almost appropriate disrespect for their elders. As an antidote to nihilism, Moon's gentle homespun sensibility must be unfailingly predictable, reassuring and comforting.

It is always interesting to me how Moon's down-home pastoral sensibility masks the sophisticated existentialist. He remains unprovoked by adolescent rage, manipulation and defiance. He doesn't take it personally when his teens attempt to enrage or wound him—a therapeutic stance which few therapists (including this one) can maintain. Viewing their provocations as a kind of dramatic reenactment of past adult conflict, Moon remains at once dispassionate yet emotionally available. Although he is fully present with the children and their pain, he is in no way preoccupied with "making the children feel better." Suffering, in Moon's existential/Protestant ethic, is not something in which to escape and replace with "feel good" gambits that are so prevalent in our "quick-fix" culture. Instead, the elements of hardship and struggle are approached as a Zen-inspired way of "being." Suffering gives life its rich contrasts, its substance and a freshness of perspective.

This is a timely, relevant work which is sorely needed by the field and, indeed, by our culture. For never before has the passage from childhood to adulthood been fraught with such uncertainty and conflict. As I muse over this essay, I am seated in Edith Kramer's NYC loft, watching her go about her business of a lifetime, lovingly painting "the horrors and beauty of the world." As art therapy history quietly and unassumably unfolds before me, I say something about Moon's ideas on the curative powers of art with regard to adolescents. Looking up from her easel, she sighs, that, for eons, culture has assisted children in making the transition between childhood and adulthood by providing challenging yet satisfying rituals. She cited those premodern cultures, such as the American Indian tribes, who sent their boys naked into the wilderness to embark upon a "vision quest," or in the case of girls, the magical rites of dance or body-adornment that helped shepherd them from pubescence to womanhood. Each provided the necessary support, structure and aesthetic sensibility during a time of critical vulnerability and volatility. I remarked that, in contemporary Western culture, such rites of passage have all but atrophied. Consequently, the children have been left to invent their own harrowing rites of passage. They flock to popular media as a means of vicariously experiencing the "thrills" of gratuitous violence or sexual conquest, while learning nothing about the forming of loving relationships. Gang initiations, hazing or other peer-pressured substance abuse, are all misguided attempts on the part of the adolescent to create his or her feats of courage and accomplishment. In the most dreadful of instances, drive-by shootings and random shooting sprees aimed at schoolmates and parents all bespeak of a culture gone mad. Sadly, we continue to fail our children in their bid to meet their developmental needs.

Kramer has written that to channel children's energies without destroying their spirit remains an endless task of the therapist. For this is the same delicate balance explored by Hesse in his novel *Damian* — story of a child's awakening to self-hood.

In this volume, Moon has struck such a balance between accepting the self-sabotaging and destructive tendencies of his lost-children, while harnessing their resilient energies towards self-discovery and growth. In remaining true to the art process, Bruce Moon remains a standard-bearer for those who believe in intrinsic therapeutic power of art. This book represents a means by which can begin to restore"soul" to both our children and the culture in which they continue to struggle.

DAVID HENLEY, A.T.R.
New York City

INTRODUCTION

People often ask me why I like working with adolescents, particularly difficult adolescents. My usual reply is something like, "They keep me honest." I am seldom able to adequately explain the complexities of the relationships that form in the learning environment with students, despite the fact that I'm constantly reexamining my work and daily interactions as a special education teacher. It was a surprise and a pleasure then, to read Bruce Moon's book on Adolescent Art Therapy, because in it I find so much commonality with my own experience in the classroom. Reading this book was like having lived in a foreign country for a long time and then finally talking with someone who speaks my language.

I have been an educator for the last 25 years, working primarily with emotionally disturbed and learning disabled adolescents. I've studied many approaches to teaching, most of them mechanistic and focusing on modification of behavior. In addition to my training for special education, I studied art as an undergraduate and have incorporated art in my teaching. The incorporation of art and the use of imagery in my work has been an important vehicle for personal development for both me and my students. The approach to using the creative process with adolescents Moon describes in this book is, in my view, eminently effective in generating change and growth, and in establishing a trusting relationship between the therapist (teacher) and the adolescent. In addition, the creative process as described in the text aids the adolescent. In addition, the creative process as described in the text aids the adolescent in developing a new relationship with his or her inner self.

There is a concept in education that teaching ought to be personality-independent; in other words, anyone should be able to take a structure and curriculum and "apply" it to a group of students. It is alarming to me that so many people subscribe to this idea. In Moon's book, I found descriptions of the art therapy process that are akin to the effective practices I utilize in my classroom. Who would have thought a book about art therapy would speak so profoundly to an educational ear?

Anna Freud's description of adolescence as a period of "normal psychosis" is quoted early in *The Dynamics of Art As Therapy With Adolescents.* I don't necessarily agree with this (and neither does Moon), but one of the sections of the book that most attracted me was titled "The Hard Work of Treating Adolescents." He includes descriptors of adolescents which ring true in my experience. . "[they] do not sit passively, they do not behave predictably, they are seldom grateful, they are never satisfied...they can often be mean, demanding, moody, destructive, self-absorbed, hostile, provocative, manipulative, seductive, and inconsistent." The way he views these behaviors, though, is especially meaningful. He describes them as "performance art enactments," as outward, though often disguised, expressions of the inner workings, conflicts, pain, and chaos that the adolescent is feeling. To me, this view helps to remind me that the behaviors don't have to be translated as personal attacks. I can be more helpful and useful to the student if I step into the audience (a la, the Living Theater of the '60s and '70s) and not get caught up in the student's whirlwind of emotions.

Moon uses the terminology "artist as therapist" and "responsive art making" throughout this work. The phrases speak to his view that the ongoing process occurring between artist|therapist and client is the arena where healing takes place. He articulates this view through his clinical discussion of the aspects of therapeutic relationship and through clearly drawn, realistic narratives about patients. Additionally, his faith in art making as an essential curative modality for the client is displayed repeatedly throughout this book. The artist/therapist, working within an understanding of the developmental issues of adolescence and the phases of engaging (and resisting) involvement in the therapeutic process, is the guide and mentor who assists in making this powerful tool accessible to the adolescent.

Moon views art as the window into the inner life of a person. He presents a model whereby the artist/therapist uses his or her own experiences in an observable way, modeling the healing possibilities by engaging in art-making alongside the adolescent. The potential for this way of working to be effective would seem to be true of all creative therapies. Since the adolescent who is in psychological pain is frequently suspicious and distrustful of adults, it is particularly important that the therapist establish rapport, and the therapist's own artwork can be an effective vehicle for doing so. The artist/therapist's work also serves as a model, in very explicit terms, of how to use art as a medium for understanding, interpreting, accessing, expressing, and resolving emotional turmoil.

Moon writes about the idea that "feeling good" is not the point of therapy, at least not initially. There is the hope that the development of an understanding of inner workings will help students and clients lead a more contented and satisfied life, but the path to that goal is fraught with difficulties, pain and confrontations of all kinds. My own students sometimes accuse me of not being "supportive"; my program is identified as "Emotional Support," after all! It is difficult for them to understand that support doesn't always mean making them happy. Rather, it is supportive to assist them in having a deeper relationship with their inner selves, to help them learn how to accept and give feed back about their behavior, and to demonstrate that their actions affect others, sometimes profoundly .

Moon's comfort level with "not knowing" what to expect fits with his existential approach to therapy. He makes it clear that interpreting patients' work has very limited, if any, value in helping the patient to grow. In fact, he makes the point that interpretation can interfere significantly with establishing a trusting relationship with an adolescent. He does not need to hide behind the "expert" mask in the relationship with adolescents, which bespeaks his years of experience, his deep understanding of himself, and his understanding of his patients. He says, "Now I stand before their images (and my own) in an attitude of wonder at their power and charm." This sentiment is reiterated again and again, and allows the reader to have a feeling for the deep compassion and respect Bruce holds for the young people he works with and for their images.

Particularly useful to me and, I would suspect, to other educators, is Bruce's description of the four phases of Adolescent Art Therapy. I have seen these processes unfold over and over in group and individual work with adolescents who are struggling with their own internal demons. The phases he describes are: Resistance, Imagining, Immersion, and Letting Go. The resistance phase is magnificently communicated, both in terms of clinical process and examples from his work with adolescents. I can easily recall from my own work, instances of dealing with the "Rebel," the "I'll Do Anything You Want" kid, the "Catch Me if You Can" kid; the "You are the Only One Who

Understands" kid. How easily we can get sucked into the dance around these dramas. But again we are reminded of the "performance art enactment" and given ideas about how to work with the behavior in order to move on to the next phase of treatment. The "Imagining" phase is described as the period during which the adolescent can begin to let go of her denial and to trust the adult. "Immersion" is the phase in which the hardest work is done by the adolescent, when behaviors and old images of the self are discarded and the adolescent begins to form a more realistic view of herself. The last phase, "Letting Go," is the separation phase in which the patient deals with the loss of the therapist, but it is also the phase where consolidating and internalizing the growth work happens most clearly.

In my own experience, these phases happen repeatedly during the time I am working with my students. As students confront aspects of their own conflicts, they can reenter resistance, imagining, and immersion. I observe this movement into and out of phases of growth partly because of the length of time I work with students. In the program where I teach, students could conceivably be with me for four years. We have a four-year curriculum of integrated and thematic academic work, and the therapeutic aspects of the program are ongoing and evolving as the needs of the group and individuals within the group change.

A most memorable experience for me was with Susan, a young woman who came to the program in 10th grade. She was an angry, self-destructive person with serious learning disabilities which, despite her superior intellectual capacities, made the school experience a nightmare for her. Susan was an intense and creative student who was interested in learning and was able to flourish with the atmosphere of acceptance and safety in the program. She really learned to spread her wings in this environment. However, during the midpoint of her senior year, I saw every problematic behavior she had evidenced during our first year together reemerge with a vengeance. It was through continued assurances on many levels, symbolic and material, that Susan was able to trust again in her own abilities, to understand that the relationships she had formed here would be sustainable, if only through memory, and that I and her fellow students would not abandon her during this difficult time. She began to move into the letting go phase and was able to move on.

The chapter titled "The Structure of the Therapeutic Arts Studio" also hit a sympathetic chord. Bruce discusses the importance and meanings of space and the messages a physical setting conveys. In college, I had a printmaking instructor who insisted that students "take in" the s-pace in the printing studio (the posters, artwork arrangement of tools and furniture, etc.) as a way of getting to know him. It was the first time that awareness of the importance of place was ever brought to my attention. Since then, I have been attuned to such issues, both intuitively and consciously, and use it in my own classroom. Many of the points made in Moon's chapter on structure and space are important for educators to attend to: the issues of safety (psychological and physical); the importance of keeping rules simple, consistent and easy to enforce; the modeling of behavior by the therapist teacher; and the establishment of ritual in the day-to-day interactions and working of the group.

Another particularly valuable issue raised in this section of the book is the powerful impact of the therapist's attitude toward the patient in establishing a working relationship. Even if a negative attitude is not explicitly expressed, the adolescent will know through nOnverbal cues how the therapist feels. This is, in part, what I referred to when I stated that work with adolescents keeps me honest. Adolescents seem to have an uncanny ability to "zero in on" the hypocrisy and pretense that a person holds.

In my own work, I consider the physical and psychological safety of a student to be a basic need, which is attended to in a variety of ways.

In Maslow's hierarchy of needs, the issue of safety is second only to the physiological need of food and shelter. Therefore, I believe it is important to guard against my students feeling threatened or insecure about their own safety and ability to be present, in mind and body. I agree with Moon that taking care of the space in which one meets with adolescents is, in fact, taking care of the adolescent. It is one of the few areas in which the professional can have some control.

To some individuals reading this introduction, it may be considered a "stretch" to compare the art therapy model of Bruce Moon with the educational process, but I contend that in a classroom, as in the art therapy studio, there is substantial, deep work being done by the adolescent. If important and specific conditions exist in the classroom, the possibilities for growth are significant. The conditions include: the teacher, like Bruce's artist/therapist, brings an attitude of respect, positive regard, and acceptance to the relationship with the adolescent;

the classroom space is maintained in a safe, consistent and predictable manner; and lastly, the teacher is willing and able to be a positive model—a real human being.

My own thoughts and feelings have been stirred by this book. Bruce's writing is clear and readable, his sense of humor endearing, and his arguments compelling (though I admit to a bias in the direction of humanistic/existential philosophy). Particularly affecting are his word portraits of the adolescents and his interactions with them. These vignettes are moving and heartfelt, and exquisitely display the range and depth of Bruce's compassion, empathy and true affection for his patients. I fear that this methodology is being overtaken by the forces of managed care and "the bottom line," and hope that books like this will inspire therapists, educators and anyone working within an adolescent population to explore this very effective and affecting approach.

SANDRA SCHOENHOLTZ, M.ED.
Philadelphia, Pennsylvania

PREFACE

For most of my professional life as an artist-therapist, I have worked intensely with adolescents who are suffering severe emotional and mental disturbances. I confess, I love the work. This book is my effort to share what I consider essential philosophic, technical, pragmatic and ethical aspects of practicing art therapy with adolescent people. This book is an act of love.

Hurting adolescents present artist-therapists (therapists of any kind for that matter) with a host of particular struggles and difficulties that make art therapy very complicated. The anguish of adolescents often manifests itself in intense and conflicted feelings about their parents, other family members, teachers, and authority figures of any kind. These conflicts often revolve around issues of identity, dependency, autonomy, self-control, self-expression and existential concerns. The conflicts are, by necessity, acted out in the therapy context. What follows reflects my point of view on art as therapy in the treatment process with adolescents who are suffering. It provides an in-depth understanding of the central role art plays in the successful treatment of adolescent patients and of the course and natural history of art as therapy with adolescents. The book reflects the progressive development of my artistic and therapeutic thinking as my clinical experience and understanding of the application of dynamic artistic and therapeutic principles has evolved. This book will provide its readers with a picture window into this author's professional growth and development related to the complexities of the subject.

Many art therapy colleagues have urged me to do a book about my work with adolescents. I have made a very conscious effort to describe poetically, and in detail, the central role art making plays in the successful treatment of adolescents. I am thankful to Charles C Thomas, Publisher, for giving me the opportunity to do so. I am also grateful to my former colleague, Marcel Hundziak, M.D., who organized and opened the first Adolescent Unit at Harding Hospital, and to Carol

Lebeiko, M.D., Donald Brown, M.D., Robert Huestis, M.D., Larry Simpson, M.D., and Russell Newman, Ph.D. who taught me much of what I know about adolescents and psychotherapy. To Don Jones, H.L.M., A.T.R., goes acknowledgment for serving me as a role model and inspiring me to pursue a career in art therapy. A debt of gratitude is owed to Edith Kramer, Cathy Moon, Debra DeBrular, Pat Allen, Ph.D., Shaun McNiff, Ph.D., Donald Rinsley, M.D., Viktor Frankl, M.D., and Viktor Lowenfeld, whose disparate influences have swirled together to form the foundation of my clinical work with adolescents. I am also indebted to Barry Heermann, Ph.D., who shepherded my development as a scholar as I pursued research into the artist as therapist approach during my doctoral studies. I also am deeply thankful to Robin Lawrie, A.T.R., who served as a first reader and to Ellie Jones who contributed final editorial revisions. To the many art therapy, music therapy, recreation therapy, social work, nursing, and psychology colleagues who worked in the Child and Adolescent Division of Harding Hospital, I express my deep appreciation.

Finally, others too numerous to name have in various ways contributed to the ideas presented here. Most significant have been those many profoundly suffering young people with whom I was privileged to work and, through involvement with art, guide toward a less painful and more meaningful existence. It is to them that this book is gratefully dedicated.

Author's Note

The clinical accounts in this book are, in spirit, true. In all instances, however, identities and circumstances have been fictionalized in order to insure the confidentiality of the persons with whom I have worked. The case illustrations are amalgamations of many specific situations. All information regarding patients and clients has been altered and fictionalized in an effort to offer realistic accounts of art therapy in progress while at the same time protecting the privacy of individuals. The artworks presented are recreations of the original works.

CONTENTS

LIST OF ILLUSTRATIONS

Photographers
The photographs of art work, except Figure 2 and Figure 5, are by Ms. Lisa Hinkle, Marywood University. The photograph of the author is by Catherine Moon, M.A., A.T.R. The photograph of the Art Street Studio, Albuquerque, New Mexico is by Amanda Herman. The photograph of the studio at Kids Peace National Hospital is by Cindy Connors.

THE DYNAMICS OF ART AS
THERAPY WITH ADOLESCENTS

Chapter I

ART AS THERAPY WITH ADOLESCENTS

My friend assures me, "It's all or nothing."
I am not worried   I am not overly concerned
My friend implores me, "For one time only,
make an exception."   I am not worried
Wrap her up in a package of lies
Send her off to a coconut island
I am not worried   I am not overly concerned
with the status of my emotions
"Oh," she says, "you're not changing."
But we're always changing

Anna Begins
by Adam Duritz (Counting Crows)

The late afternoon winter sun filtered through the small window panes of the therapeutic arts studio at Harding Psychiatric Hospital in Worthington, Ohio. I was sitting across the table from Tara, a 14-year-old young woman. She had just put the finishing touches on her painting. The image (Figure 1) was of a broken, bleeding heart that was pierced by a silver dagger. For the past several minutes, there had been a heavy silence between us. "Are you going to sign it?" I asked.

She looked up at me through strands of dirty blonde hair, eyes wide, lower lip quivering. "I am afraid to."

Tara had been in the hospital for a couple of weeks. She was leaving later that evening on a flight bound for Salt Lake City. Her mother did not want her anymore and was sending her there to live with an aunt. Her father was in jail for abusing Tara and her younger sister. During her hospitalization, she had completed three or four paintings and many chalk drawings. She had never hesitated to sign her work before.

I quietly said, "You are afraid."

Figure 1. It is how I survive.

A cold February wind rattled the windows; Tara held her arms against her body and shuddered. "When I sign this, everything will be finished here. I don't want to go."

"Tara," I said, "I will always remember you, your paintings and drawings. You have really done well here in the studio."

Tear drops slid silently down her cheeks. She half-turned away from me, reached out her hand and dipped her fingers in chalk dust. She gently smudged her cheek and said, "Art is like breathing to me. It's how I survive." She stood up and took one last long look around the studio. Tara turned to me, opened her mouth as if to speak, but no words came. She picked up her painting and left.

"Art is like breathing to me. It's how I survive."

Over the past twenty-four years in my work as an artist-therapist I have had countless encounters with adolescents (kids) who have been hurt, betrayed, rejected, failed, disappointed, cast out and abused by the world they live in. They came to the community counseling service, or to the hospital, or to the day treatment program, or to the private practice studio, bearing a host of DSM diagnoses: Adjustment reaction, borderline personality, dysthymic disorder, major depression, conduct disorder, schizophrenia, bi-polar disorder, anorexia nervosa, bulimia, post traumatic stress disorder, and attention deficit disorder are just a few of the labels that attended these young persons' entry into art therapy. Despite the distinctive nature of their individual life situations and the uniqueness of their particular struggles, they shared some common aspects. Most of them were not especially interested in, or capable of, engaging in insight-oriented verbal psychotherapy with an adult authority figure, but nearly all of them were willing to make art. This is not to suggest that the first time the adolescent walked into the studio he was immediately compliant or enthusiastic about art making. In fact, the early steps of the art therapy journey were often filled with turmoil and active resistance. However, I must stress that almost every adolescent who came to the studio eventually did make art. The great majority of those who did experienced the creative art making process as a potent and healthy means of self-expression, self-exploration and self-revelation.

It is upon this experiential foundation that my deep belief that art making has a vital role in the successful psychotherapeutic treatment of adolescents has been built. The processes of painting, drawing, sculpting, writing poetry, playing music, dramatizing and dancing engage the adolescent in integrating disparate aspects of experience in the service of creating a new meaningful whole. Artistic endeavors involve the complex procedures of identification, imaginative interpretation, integration of, and reformation of, the elements of existence. Through encounters with external materials and internal image themes, the adolescent renders much more than a painting or a drawing. Through artistic processes, the adolescent offers the world a partial portrait of self: how she sees the world around them; how he feels and thinks about the world within. For adolescents who are in need of psychotherapy, art is not a frill or a filler of time, but rather a dynamic, validating, integrating, expressive and entirely natural and necessary activity.

I do not want to suggest that all mental health difficulties for adolescents can be entirely remedied through an effective creative arts therapy program alone; however, I do believe that the underlying values of art therapy as presented in this text are essential to the development of a different paradigm, an alternative way of thinking about psychological care for disturbed adolescents. This way of thinking harkens back to the efforts of the milieu therapy theorists of the 1950's, 60's and 70's and recognizes that emotional healing for adolescents cannot be reduced to biochemistry, cognitive restructuring or behavioral manipulation. Healing for adolescents must involve perceptual, emotional, imaginal, social, physical and spiritual factors.

The processes that are essential in artistic activity embody these six factors. The making of art is always involved with perception, feeling, imagination, relationship, manipulation of materials and the soul of the artist. The most useful aspect of this kind of engagement is that it is infinitely flexible in relation to one's developmental level. Lowenfeld (1970) comments, "...it can be seen that children create with the aid of whatever knowledge they happen to have at the time. The very act of creating can provide new insights and new knowledge for further action" (p.4).

There is an inherently existential quality that is present when one works artistically with suffering adolescents. In *The Ballad of Reading Gaol*, Oscar Wilde writes, "Nothing in the world is meaningless, suffering least of all." However, many people in the helping professions view their mission as alleviating discomfort. In clinical work with adolescents, a different view is called for. As an existential art therapist, I do not try to make adolescents feel better; I do try to help them understand and to discover the deeper meanings of their feeling bad. It is true that as teenagers discover and express the meaning of their suffering they often feel more at ease, less anxious, less pained, but that is a pleasant side effect rather than the central purpose. I concur with McNiff (1982) who writes, "All healing can be perceived as a creative transformation of one thing into something else. Healing and art are a single process" (p. 122).

Essential to the explorative and creative process of my clinical work with adolescents is the principle belief that struggle and pain are not maladies to be banished from patients' lives, but realities to be embraced by their lives. This regard for suffering is antithetical to current cultural leanings toward pleasure, convenience, self-gratification, and the avoidance of discomfort. To see integrity and value in the pain of another person, or in one's own anguish, presumes that the ultimate concern is not the pursuit of hedonistic pleasure but rather the quest to understand the depths of one's own meaningful existence. The capacity of the artist-therapist to honor the suffering of the adolescent hinges on the art therapist's attitude toward his or her own pain. In commenting on the essential quality of human suffering, Viktor Frankl (1955) said, "Only under the hammer blows of fate, in the white heat of suffering, does life gain shape and form" (p.111). Frankl (1959) elaborated on what he saw as the role of suffering in regards to personal meaning:

> If there is a meaning in life at all, then there must be a meaning in suffering. Without suffering and death human life cannot be complete. The way in which a man accepts his fate and all the suffering it entails, the way in which he takes up his cross, gives him ample opportunity, even under the most difficult circumstances, to add a deeper meaning,to his life (p. 88).

In my clinical work with adolescents I have often been confronted with difficult circumstances and unavoidable, anguish-filled situations. Arnheim (1967) states, "Art is an indispensable tool in dealing with the tasks of life" (p.91). I have seen children artistically struggle with the anguish of their lives with courage and integrity. The arts are a natural language for adolescents who are grappling with the deep concerns of their existence. As Allen (1995) notes, "Art making is a process that when practiced in an involved way, in itself promotes health and wholeness" (p. 163).

Nomenclature

Throughout this book, I will be using several terms in very specific ways. At this point I want to provide some brief definitions of terms that will appear frequently.

The Arts–When I refer to the arts, I will be speaking primarily of painting, sculpture, drawing, music, poetry, dance and drama. I will not be referring to the crafts. This is not to disparage craft or craftsmanship. On the contrary, I have high regard for skillful handling of materials, but I distinguish art from craft. Art, I believe, has to do with the intent to express some essential aspect of human existence. Art involves the use of skill and creative imagination in the creation of objects or experiences that convey a fundamental characteristic of life as it is.

Therapy—The word therapy comes from the Greek root *therapeuticus*, which may best be translated into English as *to attend to*. When one thinks of therapy in this light, there is no particular strategy the therapist must employ. Instead, therapists must be willing to be, to attend. I regard therapy (attending to) as having three central qualities: (1) being with, (2) doing with, and (3) honoring the patient's existence.

Art Therapy—When I speak about art therapy I refer to attending to another through the processes of making art. In my view, attending to, in the art therapy context, is done by (1) being in the company of the patient-artist as he or she makes art, (2) engaging in making art along with the patient-artist, and (3) accepting and honoring the images of the patient-artist. In the art therapy milieu, the process of attending to is accomplished through *metaverbal* engagements with the media, the process, the person, and the image.

Metaverbal—Meta is a prefix that means beyond. Meta-verbal, then, denotes experiences that are beyond words. This term refers to the idea that the critical curative work of art therapy takes place in the interaction between the adolescent-artist, the media, the image, and the process. In this sense, the primary task of the artist-therapist is to set the stage for the work to unfold. The art therapist need not rely on verbal psychotherapy techniques intended to interpret and analyze the imaginal efforts of the patient. The heart of the work with adolescents, whether in the studio or in an expressive art group psychotherapy session, has been done before the patient ever says a word about his or her image. The real substance of the art therapy session is beyond the spoken word. This is not a devaluation of verbalization; it is rather an honoring of action and image.

Artist-as-Therapist Model of Art Therapy—I take a philosophic and pragmatic approach to art therapy that regards the process of making art as the central component of the profession. This is in contrast to other philosophic approaches that regard psychological theory or psychotherapeutic technique as the core of the discipline.

Art Psychotherapy—This approach to art therapy regards the process of making art primarily as a tool used to facilitate verbal expression and insight.

Art as Therapy Model of Art Psychotherapy—This approach, which I will address at some length, examines the notion of art making as a psychotherapeutic process which may or may not involve verbalization and conscious articulation of insight.

The Therapeutic Arts Studio—Allusions to the therapeutic arts studio, or studio art therapy, will refer directly to artistic experiences that take place in a clinical context. Most often, I will be relating events that transpired during my work with adolescents at the Harding Hospital. The studio art therapy model is an approach to this work that encourages adolescents to explore their lives through artistic endeavors. It emphasizes enhancement of artistic skills and the development of artistic techniques. A serendipitous result of this emphasis is that teenagers often discover meanings and experience personal insights through engagement with their metaphoric images, but the interpretation of such insights is left to the individual artists.

Metaphor—In literature a metaphor describes one thing in terms of another. The purpose of this is to shed new light on the character of an object or idea. For the purposes of this book, I will expand the idea of metaphor beyond verbal limitations. I will refer to visual and action metaphors. In this sense, a visual image an adolescent creates is metaphoric of its creator in that it sheds new light on the character of the adolescent by depicting the creator visually in terms of another thing.

Image—When I refer to image I am alluding to two separate but inextricably linked notions: (1) a mental picture of something not actually present, and (2) a tangible, visible, or aural representation. The images adolescents make are the meeting ground of their outer and inner vision. The outer vision explores the world around them; the inner vision explores themselves. Working with the adolescent's images allows them to give form to their external experience and internal meaning. Images become paintings, drawings, sculptures, poems, dances and songs that are the primary communications of adolescent art therapy.

Soul—I will occasionally use the word *soul* in this text. When I do so I will be referring to the definition of soul that is presented in the work of James Hillman (1989), that is, a perspective (or process) that deepens events into experiences (p.15). In the context of adolescent art therapy, this will refer to the process of reflective speculation on art which serves to transform the random into the meaning-filled.

Response Art–By this I mean artistic endeavors by the art therapist that are made in direct response to the artistic processes or products of the adolescent patient-artist. These responsive artistic efforts may serve any one of several functions for the art therapist. They may serve (1) to develop empathy with the adolescent, (2) to clarify feelings, (3) to contain or differentiate affect and (4) to explore the meaning of the art therapist's relationship to the adolescent. In this text, response art refers to the paintings, songs and poems I have created in response to my work with adolescents who are struggling with deep emotional pain.

Chapter II

ADOLESCENT DEVELOPMENT AND ART

The artist-therapist working with adolescents must always be aware of the developmental changes the adolescent is experiencing. He or she must understand the patient's problems and plan effective art experiences that will form the foundation of treatment. Specifically, the therapist must realize that the approximately ten-year span of adolescence is not a single stage of life and behavior. Therefore, behavior that is acceptable at one time during adolescence may be totally inappropriate at another.

Generally, the term adolescence is used to denote the second decade of life and is comprised of three stages: (10 - 13 years) early adolescence, (14 - 17 years) mid-adolescence, and (18 - 20 years) late adolescence. While it is true that within each stage of adolescence there are individual differences, and typically girls will move through the sequence more quickly than boys, each stage does have some characteristics that are considered typical of that stage.

The developmental changes that take place during adolescence are pervasive, and they affect nearly every aspect of the teenager's existence. Beyond infancy, no other phase of life holds so many changes that occur with such rapidity. The beginning of these changes is ushered in with puberty affecting physical appearance, mood, thought processes, behavior and relationships with others. For my purposes in this text, I will offer a brief synopsis of the changes that occur in the adolescent. A wealth of published literature on adolescent development is available to the reader seeking a more thorough review on the topic. Among others, I have found the work of Feldman and Elliott, (1993) *At the Threshold: The Developing Adolescent*, particularly helpful.

PUBERTY

Puberty brings significant changes in the teenager's physical appearance, with the maturing of reproductive organs, increased growth, weight gain, and secondary sex characteristics like body and facial hair for boys and breast development for girls. These changes, which are clearly visible and external, serve to mark to the teenagers themselves and to the outside world their more mature status. Hormonal changes that underlie these physical changes also increase moodiness and stimulate heightened interest in sexuality. Dealing with a multitude of dramatic changes in one's life is a challenge for persons of any age, but it is especially difficult for the adolescent who has fewer experiences upon which to draw, and a less solid sense of psychological identity. Steiner (1996) notes that, "Not surprisingly, there is some evidence that early maturing females—that is, those who start their menses a year or two ahead of their peers—tend to have a higher rate of psychopathology than their 'on time' classmates." In contrast, Steiner suggests that the opposite appears to be true for boys. Early maturation in males tends to lead to positive experiences such as success in competitive sports, being given leadership roles by peers, being seen as attractive by girls, etc.

CHANGES IN THINKING

Extensive changes in how adolescents think allow the teenager to begin to explore abstractions, examine values, rethink ethical and moral issues, question authority and plan for the future. Elkind (1967) suggests that the cognitive changes in adolescence stimulate a form of egocentrism in which the adolescent perceives himself as on stage, always the center of attention. This egocentrism in turn often precipitates a hyper-sensitivity to every nuance of the world (audience) around the adolescent. Since the world in reality is not focused on the adolescent performer, the adolescent constructs a personal story which explains why he or she cannot possibly be understood by others because his or her feelings, thoughts and experiences are utterly unique—no one else in the history of humanity has ever felt the pain or the joy that the adolescent experiences. How dramatic!

WHO I AM

Perhaps the major task of the teenager is to construct an identity, a sense of self as being different from other people and independent of the parents. This sense of "who I am" needs to be meaningful, consistent, and realistic in regards to the individual's talents, abilities and potential. An inevitable part of the process of developing this identity is a period of experimentation with new roles in the peer group and at home. The effort to define one's self often entails definition *via negativa*. Erikson (1963) describes the early adolescent process of appointing well-meaning people such as parents or teachers to serve as their adversaries as they define themselves as over and against these authority figures. During this phase of the adolescent's development, the individual assumes an oppositional stance for the sake of being different. Later, as the adolescent acquires more confidence, there develops an ability to define the self in more sophisticated and refined ways through beliefs, attitudes, likes and dislikes.

CHANGES IN RELATIONSHIPS WITH FRIENDS

Relationships with friends become much more complicated during adolescence than they were in childhood. The teenager, who is driven biologically and psychologically to separate from the parents, is not yet able to function entirely independently. Thus the peer group serves to provide the necessary security for the separation-individuation process. Typically, the peer group changes in composition from the same-sex group of childhood to include opposite-sex members. At the same time, the teenager leaves the predictability and familiarity of the elementary school and its long-established peer groups to attend the larger and more diverse middle school and high school. This expansion of the world stimulates an insecurity which in turn increases conformity to peer values and behaviors. So, the adolescent is simultaneously attempting to carve out a clear sense of self while at the same time trying to blend in with his peers. How confusing!

CHANGES IN RELATIONSHIPS WITH FAMILY

The developmental journey of the adolescent also forces a redefinition of the teenager's relationships with the family. Ultimately, the individual who successfully navigates adolescence will emerge an autonomous adult. However, this significant shift inevitably shakes the identity, not only of the adolescent, but of the parents and other family members as well. Perhaps the most easily observable manifestation of this is the adolescent's increased need for privacy. In addition, in clear contrast to how things used to be, the adolescent expresses a clear desire to spend free time with friends.

For many parents and families, the adolescent's pulling away is a difficult phenomenon. As the adolescent shifts emotional investment and attention from the family unit to the peer group, there is often a notable rise in conflicts centered on activities of daily living. In ideal circumstances, these conflicts ultimately help both the adolescent and the family differentiate and establish emotional independence.

SEXUAL RELATIONSHIPS

It is, of course, during the adolescent "journey" that individuals must learn to deal with the whole range of their sexuality. Sexuality, in a sense, pervades every aspect of daily life. Sexuality is present in explicitly erotic dreams, masturbation, peer relationships and daydreams. Coming to grips with one's sexuality is complicated because it entails moral, societal, physiological and psychological factors that the adult world often does not openly discuss with the adolescent.

SUMMARY

It is typical for adolescent patients to manifest aspects of the normal developmental tasks, although these may be distorted or accentuated in such a way as to resemble emotional dysfunction. Making art is first and foremost a natural way to experience self-exploration, self-expression and self-revelation. Since teenagers are continually growing, changing, bumping into and trying to make sense out of the world around them, their artworks tend to potently express feelings, thoughts, wishes, fears and reactions to themselves and their environment. For adolescents who are in need of psychotherapy, the images generated by such feelings, thoughts and fears are often painfully raw and disturbing. The traumatic experiences that underlie the emotional struggles of adolescents who need psychotherapy cannot be worked through, resolved or healed through talking alone. Successful therapy with adolescents must involve action and engage the senses. Making art in a therapeutic studio setting is one way to ensure that the therapeutic process will have lasting impact upon the life of an adolescent.

Chapter III

THE ADOLESCENT'S METAPHORIC PERSPECTIVE

For artist-therapists who choose to focus their practice on the treatment of adolescents, there is a particularly important function they must serve. One of the most important roles of the art therapist is that of *metaphoretician.* Whether one works in an adolescent residential treatment facility, an outpatient clinic or in a private practice, the artist-therapist must have the capacity to understand the many metaphorical messages the adolescent will send. These metaphoric communications will be transmitted through dramatic and subtle actions, images, words, movements, sounds and silences.

As *metaphoretician* in a residential treatment facility, the artist-therapist will be called upon by members of other treatment disciplines to translate the adolescents' metaphoric messages into theoretical understandings and treatment interventions that are appropriate within the therapeutic milieu. In an outpatient clinic, the artist-therapist will be the professional best equipped to deal with the meaning of the adolescent metaphoric drama as it is enacted in the clinical setting. The adolescent drama is often disruptive and provocative and therefore the artist-therapist's artistic sensibilities are sorely needed by professional colleagues as they struggle to contain their own desire for these kids to "just go somewhere else." In private practice settings, the success or failure of the therapeutic venture depends upon the artist-therapist's capacity to relate to and appreciate the often mysterious and provocative adolescent metaphoric actions.

In order to begin this exploration of the metaphoric perspective of the adolescent, it is necessary to approach such questions as these: What are the recurrent themes that seem to be expressed by adolescents time and again? How are these themes signaled in metaphoric imagery, language and behavior? What are the themes inherent in the metaphors and how do the artist-therapist and other members of a treatment team respond to them? How can the artist-therapist communicate to the adolescent that the metaphoric message has been received? Finally, how can the artist-therapist respond to the metaphoric message artistically and metaphorically?

On the surface, the artistic and metaphoric answers I will describe here may seem similar to efforts to understand what happens in traditional verbal psychotherapeutic interactions. It is evident that an arts-based approach and a verbal approach may share some common attributes; I want to stress that there are significant fundamental differences. Most notably, I will attempt to illustrate understandings of and responses to adolescent metaphors that are not dependent upon verbalization. I do not think that insights, growth, and therapeutic change can, or should, always be put into words. As the old maxim states, "A picture is worth a thousand words." Additionally, the treatment of adolescents poses particular age-related difficulties for artist-therapists. The goal here is to begin to lay the groundwork for the establishment of a positive and therapeutic art studio milieu for adolescents. In order to create a therapeutic art studio milieu, we must make every effort to understand the suffering adolescent patient's view of the world. Further, we must apply our understanding to the realities of the adolescent's need to resist our efforts. And, we must develop artistic strategies for responding to the metaphoric themes the adolescent enacts.

THE HARD WORK OF TREATING ADOLESCENTS

I have often heard art therapy colleagues exclaim things like, "I'll work with anybody except adolescents!" or "Keep those kids away from me!" An important characteristic of adolescent clients, both as individuals or as a group, is that they present adult therapists and caregivers with powerful difficulties. As much as I love to work with them, I would be the first to admit that it is not easy work. Adolescents do not sit passively, they do not behave predictably, they are seldom grateful, they are never satisfied. In the therapeutic arts studio, they can often be mean, demanding, moody, destructive, self absorbed, hostile, provocative, manipulative, seductive and inconsistent. Rinsley

(1980) notes, "The literature devoted to the psychotherapy of adolescent patients reveals a variety of treatment modes and modifications of technique that reflect the peculiar therapeutic problems encountered" (p.5). Anna Freud (1958) goes so far as to describe all adolescents as suffering from a sort of "normal psychosis." While I do not subscribe to Freud's depiction, it is clear that adolescent patients tend to provoke strong but mixed reactions in adult artist-therapists, and unless these are understood and worked with openly, the therapeutic endeavor will suffer.

Chapter IV

THE ARTIST AS THERAPIST WITH ADOLESCENTS

In the professional art therapy community, there is a philosophic debate that has existed throughout the history of the discipline (Wadeson, Landgarten, McNiff, Free, & Levy, 1976). The crux of this debate is often described in terms of competition: *art as therapy versus art psychotherapy*. Lusebrink (1990) writes, "At one end of the art therapy spectrum is the use of visual media with focus on the product and artistic aspects. At the other end is emphasis on process, verbal free association to the images rendered and insight" (p.10). In the preface to *Art Psychotherapy*, Wadeson(1980) states, "The field [art therapy] is a broad one with much variety among the approaches of different practitioners. Some place emphasis on the art, some on the therapy . . . Some art therapists consider themselves psychotherapists using art expression as a therapeutic modality" (p.xi).

Authors whom I would regard as proponents of the "art as therapy" position (Allen, 1992; Kramer, 1971; Haeseler, 1989; Jones, 1983; Lachman-Chapin, 1983; Levine, 1993; McNiff, 1989, 1993; Moon, 1995; Watkins, 1980; and Wolf, 1990) suggest that the creative and expressive quality of art making is, in and of itself, therapeutic. They contend that art therapists should regard themselves primarily as artists in the therapeutic context. For them, the process of making art is the central experience. Deborah Gadiel as quoted in Allen (1992) exemplifies this postion. "I see my identity as that of an artist. I am most in sync when I am making art. This drive to do art work, this enthusiasm for the artistic journey is the most powerful tool I have to share with the client" (p.26).

The idea of art as therapy is perhaps most closely associated with the literature of Kramer (1958, 1971). Kramer asserts that the creative process itself is therapeutic. According to Kramer, the art therapist establishes the conditions for nurturance and support of the creative process by maintaining the studio space, and by offering technical advice and emotional support. In this approach, the art therapist serves as an artistic role model and teacher. Verbalization and insight on the part of the client is not emphasized.

In the art psychotherapy approach, the emphasis is less on the artistic aspects of the work, and more on the process of expression and the patient's verbalizations about the visual product. The development of insight is the prime objective in this approach, and thus the artwork is regarded as a means to an end, that end being verbal expression. Proponents of this position seem to imply that simply making art is not enough. They contend that art therapists should regard themselves primarily as psychotherapists who use art processes as a means of stimulating therapeutic dialogue.

As the art therapy profession has evolved in the United States over the past three decades, influential spokespersons have taken one or the other of these polar positions. The debate has continued (Rosenburg, Ault, Free, Gilbert, Joseph, Landgarten, McNiff, 1983) throughout the life of the American Art Therapy Association.

The "art psychotherapy–art as therapy continuum" is of course an artifact of the Western scientific tradition which rests upon the binary assumption that all things (art therapy included) must be either this or that. While I have long participated in the debate and wrestled with just where I fell on the continuum, I now find these distinctions cumbersome and not particularly helpful. I would like to replace the old either-or conception with a *both-and* approach. Feder and Feder (1984) note, "...despite increasing evidence that the old dichotomies are based on simple-minded views of the world, these either-or distinctions still dominate much of our commonsense thinking" (p. 58). The gulf between emotion and cognition has become quite apparent in our culture, and it is clear that rationality and reason have the upper hand in terms of being valued. The separation of feeling and thought underlies much of the theory and practice of psychotherapies. Feder and Feder assert, "It is conceded that emotional problems will affect and influence an individual's thinking, but the resolution of emotional problems usually involves a re-cognition of a problem–which must almost always be verbalized" (p. 59).

To some degree, this book is an effort to add my thoughts, voice and images to what I describe as the *artist as therapist* model of *art psy-*

chotherapy service as it relates to adolescents. I believe that the truly unique gift art therapy has to offer to the adolescent clinical milieu, whether it be in a psychiatric hospital, day treatment program, counseling center, physical rehabilitative hospital, public school or addictions recovery center, is the art making process. Robbins (1988) writes, "The language of the artist and our psychoaesthetic perspective are our unique contribution to the treatment process" (p. 100). Art therapy with adolescents is a *metaverbal* treatment modality. The implication of this description is that art therapy is beyond words. This does not mean that words have no place in the therapeutic arts studio, but it does accept the probability that words will always be insufficient to describe what is occurring in the work.

In order to work effectively and authentically with adolescents, in my opinion, it is imperative that an art therapist first be an artist. Art is the anchor, the heart, the taproot of the work with teenagers. Artist-therapists who want to work with suffering adolescents should have a profound belief in the power and the goodness of art making. Allen (1992) notes, "The most crucial factor in the life or death of the field of art therapy is not certification, not licensure, but whether sufficient numbers of individual art therapists maintain an ongoing connection to their own art" (p.28). I know art therapy colleagues who are working with adolescents and who have had very difficult periods in their professional lives. They are often those who for one reason or another are inactive artistically. In the absence of ongoing personal work in one's own art studio, an art therapist's work with adolescents may lack depth, passion and authentic life. The art therapist who finds no joy in his/her effort will be unable to provide a healing milieu to the adolescent patient. The only way back into authenticity is through the door to one's own art studio.

The artist-as-therapist model of art psychotherapy with adolescents is an approach to clinical work that emphasizes the goodness of art making for both the patient and the art therapist. The inherent goodness of art making is the foundation upon which the therapeutic discipline is built. As noted earlier, this emphasis on the art process as being the art psychotherapy is in sharp contrast to a more verbally oriented and psychologically based approach in which art making is regarded merely as a tool to stimulate verbal therapeutic interaction.

THE ROLE OF RESPONSIVE ART MAKING

One of the core components of the *art as therapy model of art psychotherapy* with adolescents is responsive art making. Responsive art making is a process that involves the artist-therapist in creating art works as a form of therapeutic intervention in response to the images of adolescent patients. This process is extremely helpful to art therapists in three ways: (1) as an aid in establishing empathic relationships with adolescents; (2) as an expressive outlet for the art therapist's powerful feelings that are often stirred up in the clinical context; and (3) as the starting place for imaginative interpretive dialogue with adolescent patients.

Several authors have focused attention on the process of art therapists making art in the therapy setting, either during or post-session (Cohn, 1984; Haessler, 1989; Kielo, 1991; Lachman-Chapin, 1987; Robbins, 1988; Wolf, 1990). Kielo (1991) summarized the themes that seem to emerge repeatedly in her studies. Kielo's research suggests that there are five basic uses for responsive art making:

1. Art used to develop empathy through replication of a client's imagery;
2. Art used to clarify feelings;
3. Art used to explore the preconscious and unconscious;
4. Art used to help differentiate affect;
5. Art used to explore the relationship.

The process of responsive art making that I depict in this text differs from that described by Kielo and others in two ways. It is art that is created in the studio in the presence of the patient as opposed to in post-session reflection, and it is more extensive than the quick sketch approaches described by Kielo and others. However, my approach is a process of art making that clarifies feelings, explores levels of consciousness, and deepens relationships.

One of the earliest examples of an artist-therapist making art in response to the images of patients is found in the person of my mentor, Don Jones. While a conscientious objector during World War II, Don was assigned to alternative service as a psychiatric aid at Marlboro State Hospital in New Jersey. Naive, untrained, and thoroughly out of his element, this young artist was fascinated by the spontaneous images created by the disturbed patients in his care. The patients made images with pencil, charcoal, blood and feces–anything that would make a mark–to capture the terror, turmoil and angst of life in the back wards.

During his years of service there, Don was exposed to many horrific experiences. He was surrounded by psychotic, chronically depressed and institutionalized insane people. In an effort to handle his feelings about his work at Marlboro, Don began to paint scenes from the hospital. It was a series of such paintings that caught the attention of Dr. Karl Menninger, who eventually offered Don a position as an arts specialist at the Menninger Clinic in Topeka, Kansas. As Don recounts stories of this phase of his life he says, "My paintings really kept me alive back then" (Figure 2). In this instance responsive art was in fact "survival art."

> My own paintings, drawings, and sculpture were always done continuously during my professional life and since retiring and doing consulting. Also I painted and sculpted with my clients and patients in all art therapy sessions, and they influenced my own art. Creating art has been as essential as eating and sleeping.
>
> (Feen Calligan and Sands-Goldstein, 1996, p. 50)

Figure 2. Inspiration won't stay on the canvas–by Don Jones.
Photograph by Don Jones.

As my mentor and clinical supervisor, Don provided me with a role model of an artist-therapist. At every opportunity during my art therapy training, Don emphasized that although he was educated in psychotherapy and psychodynamic theory, he was first and foremost an artist.

The process of responsive art making involves the artist-therapist in a form of creative therapeutic intervention in response to the images of adolescent patients. Again, this process is extremely helpful to art therapists in three ways: (1) as an aid in establishing empathic relationships with adolescents; (2) as an expressive outlet for the art therapist's powerful feelings that are often stirred up in the clinical context; and (3) as the starting place for imaginative interpretive dialogue with adolescent patients.

The following are examples of how the responsive art-making process works in adolescent art therapy.

1. Responsive Art Helps To Establish Empathic Relationships

Debbie's Room

Debbie shuffled into the studio hesitantly. She was accompanied by one of the attendants from the adolescent unit. She did not say anything about being I-A'd (individually accompanied due to her attempts at suicide), but I could sense a deep feeling of resentment coming from her. It was a cold November day and as she took off her coat, I noticed that her left wrist was wrapped in gauze and there were small bloodstains seeping through the sterile bandages.

"Welcome to the studio, Debbie. My name is Bruce. I am an artist. What we do here is make art about the feelings inside us. Feel free to take a look around at the work other folks are doing. I'll touch base with you in a few minutes and we'll get you started making something."

She did not respond, but her eyes seemed to sweep the room quickly. I was placing a new canvas on my easel when Debbie approached.

"Well, Debbie, do you have any idea about what you'd like to do?"

"No," she said. "Maybe I'll just watch."

I responded, "I'm not sure watching is going to help you very much. How about doing some drawing?"

"No." She sat in a chair not too far from my easel.

"All right," I said. "But you know it really isn't such a good idea to be out here in the studio and not doing anything."

"So send me back to the unit. I don't care." She sat on a stool and tilted her head toward the floor and closed her eyes.

At that point, I could have done one of several things. I could have asked the staff member who was I-A-ing her to take her back to the unit. I could have directly confronted her about her resistive behavior. I could have tried to cajole her into engagement. But, I did none of these things. Instead, I asked her if it would be all right if I did a painting of her. "Debbie, that pose you are in right now is perfect for this painting. Do you think you can stay that way for awhile?"

"Whatever." She replied.

"I am warning you, I can be a slow painter sometimes. This could take several sessions."

She did not respond.

And so, over the next several sessions of adolescent art studio, I painted a portrait of Debbie, complete with her blood stained bandage (Figure 3). I was careful not to talk too much. Mostly I painted, but from time to time she would look up and ask a question, or make a comment about the painting. I was always sure to respond to her overtures in a warm and accepting way. My sense of Debbie was that she was a very sad and hurt girl. I decided I would try to capture those feelings in the painting, in an effort to empathize and commiserate with her. Rather than place her in the arts studio, I decided to paint the background as an empty room. During the third or fourth session, I asked her, "Debbie, what is your favorite color?"

Figure 3. Portrait of Debbie.

"Purple. Why?"

"Well then, I think I'll make the walls of this room be a sort of yellowish white.

That would be about the opposite of purple, I guess."

She looked at me. "I don't get it."

"Well, I assume that since purple is your favorite color, you have good feelings about it or it makes you feel good. Right?"

"I suppose. So why do the opposite."

"Debbie, I am trying to express hard feelings, not happy ones."

Later during that session, Debbie asked, "How did you know I feel so shitty all the time?"

"I'm not sure I really knew, Debbie, until I started working on this painting. You know, it just made me stop and really be with you. This is what I see."

"Yeah, me too." She sighed.

As my portrait of Debbie was nearing completion, she entered the studio one afternoon and announced, "I think I'd like to paint."

I asked, "Do you want to build a canvas or would you rather start by painting on a Masonite board?"

"I want to do it the way you do, Bruce."

2. Responsive Art as an Expressive Outlet for the Art Therapist

One day I was sitting across the table from Shawn, a small, twelve-year-old,boy who had been admitted to the child and adolescent unit earlier in the week. He,was drawing a picture of a "bad memory" from his life. The image was of a little,child's face looking out of a large picture window as a car was pulling away from the house. As I watched, Shawn's eyes began to fill with tears. He was trying to be brave and so he wiped them away with the sleeve of his shirt.

He noticed me looking at him, and without any prompting at all from me he told me the story of how his "mommy and daddy" had dropped him off at a baby-sitter one morning and never came back. Shawn said, "I was six, it was winter, and a semi-truck slipped on the ice and ran over the car. I don't get to see them ever again."

Shawn crumpled up the drawing and threw it into the wastebasket. He then started a new drawing. I asked him if he wanted to say anything more about his mom and dad. "What else is there to say," he replied.

My own father died when I was an infant and Shawn's drawing and story brought back the memory of my own feelings of loss. The stark simplicity of Shawn's tale moved me deeply. Coincidentally, that evening my family and I happened to watch the movie, "Field of Dreams" on television. One of the primary elements of W.P. Kinsella's novel, *Shoeless Joe Jackson*, that the movie is based on, is the loss, and eventual reconciliation, of a relationship between a father and his son. I confess that by the end of the movie I had tears flowing down my cheeks. In my imagination's eye, I could see my father playing the game of catch with me that we never had an opportunity to play. I could see Shawn as a little boy looking out the window at his parents for the last time. I knew I had to do something with these feelings. The idea for a painting presented itself and I quickly went about the process of building a canvas. (Figure 4)

Figure 4. Response to Shawn–Baseball.

For me, this painting contains the wistful sadness of my life without my father. It was a hard painting for me to make, and yet it was a very necessary one. Putting the ghost-like image of my father standing in the outfield of a baseball stadium allowed me to express my longing for him. It gave me a chance to acknowledge the confusion and anger that his absence from my life had inspired. And, it afforded me an opportunity to depict graphically the love I have for a man whom I barely knew. This painting also helped me to contain those feelings and to be able to see clearly that my story was not the same as Shawn's. Thus I was able to achieve the objective distance from Shawn's issues I needed in order to be therapeutically effective with him. I could not have treated Shawn ethically if I could not separate my feelings from his. To be sure, the theme of parental loss was an important one that we shared, and it is true that I was able to be particularly in tune with his feelings about this. But it is also important that I was able to differentiate his feelings and experiences from my own.

Art therapists working with adolescents who are suffering from emotional and mental disturbances will come into intimate contact with kids who have been physically, emotionally or sexually abused. They will hear some incredibly painful and horrific stories during their careers. They will see countless images of shattered hearts, bleeding wrists, grim reapers, barren landscapes, defiled beds, invaded bodies and broken promises. The weight of these images and their accompanying stories can be overwhelming at times. Seeing and hearing the effects of trauma, day in and dayout, can become vicariously traumatic itself. Art therapists cannot avoid being moved by their patients. They cannot shield themselves from their own powerful feelings. Yet, they cannot afford to be consistently overwhelmed and traumatized by their patients either. The most effective way for art therapists to protect themselves from vicarious traumatization is through making their own art. Making art provides a healthy, practical and authentic mechanism for art therapists to handle the intense feelings that accompany clinical work.

The following image and poem, "A Razor In His Heart," is another example of responsive art making as an expressive outlet for the feelings that have been aroused in me as I have worked with adolescent patients. This was presented as a performance art work at the 27th Annual Conference of the American Art Therapy Association in 1996. The main character of the poem, Antoine, is a fictionalized amalgam of many hurting adolescent people I have known. The poem is a chronicle of several encounters that take place on an adolescent psychiatric unit, and in a private practice.

A Razor in His Heart is a responsive art work and should not be construed as a factual case study. I offer it here as an extended illustration of how I use my feelings about clinical work as the source of creative inspiration, and how I use my art as a way to handle my feelings (Figure 5).

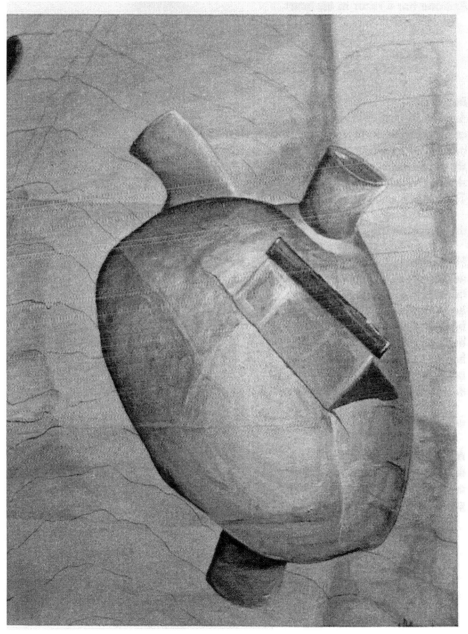

Figure 5. A razor in his heart.
From the collection of Ellen Harovitz, A.T.R.

Antoine Has a Razor in His Heart

Antoine has a razor in his heart
everyone can see it cuts him apart
stand close to him
you can feel the wind blow, 'cause
Antione has a razor in his heart

> He says, My real momma was a
> African Queen
> My daddy mus' been some kind'a fine man

But I know
Antoine's mother was addicted to
crack cocaine on the day she gave birth to this
boy, was just fourteen years young herself
she never said who the father was
she never said who the father was
The record says they suspect...

that Antoine has a razor in his heart

He comes to the asylum in the
winter of his eleventh year
he is failing in school
he is fighting at home
he is always angry
he is running away
he bangs his head
he punches his face with his small
dark hands till his face bleeds and his hands bleed

yes, Antoine has a razor in his heart

And on the third day
the fourteen year old African Queen
cocaine addict abandoned him
gave him away
> Antoine says, my mom and dad
> has blonde hair
> an' blue eyes
> they say they picked me out
> 'cause they could'n have no
> kids a' their own
> they picked me out

jus'like when we went to the
pound to pick out my dog
I don' think they pick very good
I don' look nothin' like them
They got fine blonde hair
They got clear blue eyes
They got skin that turns red in July
skin that turns white in November

I don' understand
They say they could'n have
kids but then my mom got big
and my sister Carla was born
an then she did it again
an my brother Justin was
born, I remember
Carla an' Justin, they got
skin looks like
the palm a'my hand

Mom says they picked me out
like when we went to the pound
to pick out my dog
there mus've been some kinda
mistake
there mus've been some kinda
mistake
there mus've been some kinda
mistake

Antoine has a razor in his heart
has a razor in his heart
I can see that it cuts him apart
I feel the wind blow

Antoine's a wild boy,
a terror everybody says so
I read his chart
I know his past
discarded by his mother,
left on the floor in the bathroom
of a bar

this little boy
hits, spits, shits

teeth clenched he bites
hands clenched he fights
eyes closed recites
     they picked me out
     jus' like when we went to
     the pound
     to pick out my dog
     there mus've been some kinda
     mistake
     there mus've been some kinda
     mistake

Fine blonde-haired
clear blue-eyed mother says
he's a monster
Fine blonde-haired
clear blue-eyed father doesn't say
anything at all

This little boy
he scares everyone
he scares everyone
and though the fine blonde
clear blue parents
say they love
they also say, we may have
to give him back
we may have to give him back
to the county children's
service because

Antoine has a razor in his heart

Mother says
he's made our lives
miserable for the last two years
he is out of control at school
suspended all the time
he set fire to my drapes
thousands of dollars of damage

he ran away
he won't talk
for days at a time,

other times he won't shut up
He's wild, a terror

Antoine has a razor in his heart
Everone can see that it cuts him apart
stand close to him
you can hear the wind blow

The fall of 1988
Antoine in the hospital
This little boy
He swaggers into the studio
he walks the walk, he talks the talk
I like him right away
his images and his rage

On day one
I tell him—make whatever you want
Antoine looks at me
and without speaking he asks,
        are you serious man

I assure him
make whatever you want
use whatever you want
draw or paint whatever you want
He grabs all of the tempera paints
arranges them on a table
        He asked, "Can I paint on that black paper?"

Jackson Pollack and Pig Pen would have been proud
of Antoine that morning
When he finished, the
studio was a disaster
Paint was everywhere
        He says, this is, the blob man
        "This what I see when I close my eyes at night."

Blob man is
chaotic,
is confusing
is overwhelming
on the black background he
swirled rivers of red,
purple, brown and blue

he poured streams of yellow and orange
he dripped beads of white and gray

I sighed, "It must be hard to sleep with
all that going on"

> Yeah, sometimes I hardly sleep at all in the night,
> don't tell my mom,
> she'd be mad if she knew

> Then he spit onto his painting
> So can I leave now

Yes Antoine, you can go
if that's what you want to do
but I wouldn't mind it
if you wanted to help me clean up
he picked up a wet sponge
began to work on the paint splatters he'd made
Nothing more was said

Antoine had a razor in his heart.

There were other tests
of patience and determination
Antoine
suspicious of adults
Antoine
no desire to be hurt again
Antoine
in the hospital for eight or nine months
discharged with a plan that no one believed

He will come to see me once in a while
Antoine sitting at a table
he's been working on a painting
trying to make a dark room
He wants two doors
each standing open revealing long hallways
a silhouette huddled on the floor
He slams his brush against the canvas

> This looks like shit
> I turned from my easel
> lay down my brush

went to his side

Hmmm. I see what you mean, Antoine

He snaps the paint brush in half

Antoine, I think it is the person.
You only used black
Everything else has colors
the black looks out of place
He throws the pieces of his brush
against the wall

I don't mean just that
the whole thing looks like...

It would probably work better
if you add some color
maybe you could try to make the
pants the color of old blue jeans
Maybe you could have the shirt
be the color of your Lakers shirt

I pick up his painting
put it on my easel
step away a few feet
then I call him to my side
Yes, I think that will work Antoine

The hallways give it an eerie and lonely feeling
Let me know if you need any help
with the purple for the shirt

I can't do this he groaned

I went back to my painting
I have faith in you Antoine
I'll help you when you need it

Later he asked for help mixing
the yellow that he wanted for the trim
on the Laker's shirt

he didn't need my assistance at all
he just wanted my support
As he was leaving -

Momma says I won't be comin' back here no more
I turn to him
She says this is a waste of her good money
I don't know what to say

Antoine walks away
He has a razor in his heart
everybody can see that it cuts him apart
stand close to him you can feel the wind blow

Time passes days, weeks, months...a year or two
I do not see him
his face fades
hundreds more walk by in
the line of the longing
Time passes

days, weeks, months...a year or two
I do not see him
his face fades
hundreds more walk by in
the line of the longing

* * *

September 19th, 1974
I make my way onto the hospital grounds
I make my way into the hospital life.
I am twenty-three years old
my head full of hair
my head full of ideas
I know that I will not be here long
I will not be here long
I do not expect to be here long
There are people walking
everywhere I turn...people walking
I am lost I do not know my way

A man walks by
fingers browned by cigarette smoke
I ask, can you tell me where the
art therapy office is
yes sir...he walks on
can you tell me how to find
the art therapy building
yes sir...a cloud of smoke
yes sir

An old woman shuffles by
back bent, head turned left and down
eyes haunted...empty...she does not speak
A tall man with a beard and an ID badge
hands clasped behind his back
pipe clenched between his teeth

I ask can you tell me
where the art therapy office is

    hmmm....could you say somemore

Can you tell me
where the art therapy office is

    Tall, beard, badge, pipe, hands says
    It would be better if you
    could find your own way

    I am K.
    This must be the Castle
    This castle is made of oak trees, hickory trees
    immaculate lawns, white walls shining in the sun
    early fall flowers and voices
    there are people walking
    everywhere I turn...I will not be here long

* * *

    In those days the average length of stay
    In those days the average length of stay
    was a little more than one year
    was a little more than one year
    In those days
    long before HMO - PPO - CFO - CEO
    long before PruCare - NetCare - Managed Care -
    Who Care - No Care
    We Cared

    In those days long before
    August, 1992

    Antoine has a razor in his heart
    everyone can see that it cuts him apart
    stand close to him

you can feel the wind blow
Antoine is hangin' out
killin' time foolin' around in the
Upper Carlton Library

messin' around
killin' time
hangin' out
he pulls an album from the shelf he lays it on the turntable
puts the head phones on and hears
the Last Poets scream

"and you'll die next because
the white man's got a God complex"
        he listens
        he looks around
        wonders

        can anybody else hear
        wonders
        has anybody else in
        Upper Carlton ever taken this
        album off the shelf
        he listens...

Dexedrene, Amphetamine, LSD and Grass
All this shit will kill you fast...
and you'll die next
cause, the white man's got a God complex

        The rage,
        spoken so clearly
        shouted so loudly
        the rage
        he listens
        and for the first time in a long time
        he feels calm inside
        still
        peace

        someone else knows that

Antoine has a razor in his heart

That night Antoine doesn't say much at dinner
Fair, blue, blonde, father is away on business again

Fair, blue, blonde, mother is overwhelmed
all the places she must take Carla and Justin
overwhelmed
by volunteer work
and church committee
and house work
she does not notice...Antoine
doesn't say much

Antoine walks out the door
two small stamps resting
neatly in the pocket of his shirt
he will lick them tonight
he will lick them tonight

At one thirty five in the morning
a hunter green cadillac
rolls down Lane Avenue
The driver slams on his brakes
swerves but still feels a
dull thump as rear tire
compresses Antoine's left leg
he does not scream
he does not feel anything
because Antoine is not there

* * *

I see him
his wooden crutches move
in rhythmic reaches
stretching out in front of him
longing for more
pulling the rest along
I open the door and
when he is a few crutch strides away I say
welcome to the studio

Antoine struggles on the steps almost falls
I dare not move
I hold my position
I hold the door
Antoine, I'm glad to see you again
Antoine I'm sorry to see you again
Antione, I'm glad that you are not dead

He has a razor in his heart
I can see that it cuts him apart
as he hobbles by me
I can feel the wind blow,
he does not speak

As you remember
we make art here
you can do anything you want
as long as it is about your feelings
He stands, shoulders slumped
head down, arm pits pressed
against the crutch pads
don't give me that shit

Strike one - Antoine
what?
Antoine, we make art here
you can express anything
but I do ask that you not swear
swearing makes for a hostile environment
you don't need that here
          don't give me that shit

Strike two
          what's with the strikes
It's like baseball, Antoine
three strikes you're out
of course I know that you want to stay here so...

he stares at me
glares at me
curls his lip...
          bullshit

Stee-rike three...you are out, Antoine
We'll try again tomorrow
we'll have a better day tomorrow
welcome to the studio

                    * * *

I close the door behind us
So, Antione, what do you want to make
he lowers himself into the chair
puts his crutches on the floor
          nothin

Nothing?
      nothin!
What color do you want your nothin' to be
      are you damn deaf
Strike one, what color will your nothin' be?

I bring him canvas
I bring him paint
I bring him water
I bring him brushes
What color is nothin?

      You know, I could smash
      your face
      with one of these crutches
Please don't threaten me Antoine
it makes the studio unsafe for everybody
what color will your nothing be?

      Don't you ever give up man
      don't you understand
      let me make myself clear
      I don't want to be here
      white man gotta god complex

Antione, I was born in the morning
but I was not born this morning
you don't want to be here,
and I don't care
because the truth is
you don't want to be anywhere
now turn your face
and listen to me
I want to know
what color will your nothing be

Antione spits
      half white
      half black
      just like me

Antoine has a razor in his heart
everyone can see that it cuts him apart
you stand close to him
you can feel the wind blow

I had a dream
in the dream I was driving
through the south
I stopped at a gas station
outside of Athens, Georgia
They had a black bear in a cage
the cage was about ten feet long the black bear
swayed and paced swayed and paced
swayed and paced
I watched him for awhile
wondering if he would stop
be still
he did not, he was not
perhaps the swaying and the pacing
provided some desperate illusion
that he was free

      time passes
      days, weeks, months...a year
      I do not see Antoine
      his face fades
      hundreds more walk by
      in the line of the longing

      December 1993
      The weather outside is frightful
      but the fire is so delightful
      and since we've no place to go
      let it snow, let it snow, let it snow

      I am passing through the sports page
      at first I don't notice
      passing through
      don't notice

      the picture...the picture...the picture
      Caption reads, GOLDEN EAGLE SCORES 35
      then I see Antoine
      I see Antoine flying through the air
      orange ball held tight in one hand
      arched high above the rim
      I see Antoine...I know it's him

      When we finally kiss goodnight
      I hate going out in the storm

In those days the average length of stay
was a little more than one year
In these days the average length of stay is
a little more than six days
        Long before HMOs PPOs Net Care, PruCAre
        long after CEOs CFOs
        Who cares

that Antoine had a razor in his heart

April 1995
Phone rings
Art therapy services
this is Bruce
Art therapy services
this is Bruce
silence

somebody hangs up
the phone rings
Art therapy services
this is Bruce
silence

then - Bruce, this is Antoine
do you remember me
I need to see you
can I come to see you

next day
4:00 on the next day
I hear footsteps on the metal stairs that
lead to my office door
I hear the door open
Hello Antoine,
it's good to see you again
What's it been two years or so
yes I think it was two years ago

Antoine's hands jammed deep
into the pockets of his black leather coat
his dark eyes are
his dark eyes are red around the rim
What can I do for you Antoine
What brings you to my door

We sit for awhile in the unspoken place
he stares at the floor
I watch dust float through the late afternoon sunlight

Then his right hand moves
and pulls out of his coat
a folded piece of paper
he pulls it from his coat
and he hands it slowly to me
he says,

> I want you to see
> and there, detailed in
> black and white
> an image of a heart
> a razor blade protruding
> a razor blade slicing
> a razor blade fileting
> an image of a heart
> captured here in art
>
> and he said
> and he said
> My mom has cancer
> she's gonna die
> Carla's off at boarding school
> Justin's gone there too
> Daddy's never home anymore and I
> don't know what...
>
> I drew this picture the other day
> and then Bruce I thought of you
>
> they picked me out
> like when we got our dog
> they picked me out
> like when we got our dog
> there must've been some kinda
> mistake
> I don' look nothin' like them

and I said,
Welcome to the studio, Antione
Welcome to the studio
His hands shake

His head is down
I see wet splatters
stain his heart
we do not speak
and at the end of
the hour he stands
hands me the stained
image of his heart
and walks

time passes
days, weeks, months,
I hear about Antoine's mother
I send a card, but
I do not see Antoine

the world changes
I wrestle with my life
May, 1996
I decide to leave the hospital
I decide to leave Ohio
I decide to leave
The summer is spent packing
saying good bye
letting go
excited
scared
confidently full of doubt

My office
filled with 22 years of stuff I am sifting through my life
I throw some things away
I look at photographs
I place some things in boxes
because they must accompany me
I place some things in boxes
because I cannot throw them away
I place some things in boxes
because I cannot think of anything else to do with them

Late afternoon sun filters
through my office window that overlooks the ravine
I wonder whose office this will become
how could it be someone else's
how could it be

In the bottom of a drawer
folded haphazardly
Antoine's drawing rises to the surface
It asks me
what you gonna do with me
what you gonna do
I hold it in my dusty hands
I am tired of all this packing
I am tired of all this saying goodbye
I am tired of all the tears

I place the drawing on my desk top
I promise to think about it tomorrow
but I lose track
It is Late August

Now here
I sit in this
new place
I am the new face
no one knows me
I know no one
as I open boxes
cram books on shelves
fill file drawers
re-settle my life
in this strange
mountainous place

And then
there it is
tucked between
a book and box of tissue
dirty, folded, stained
I did not want to bring it here
I did not mean to bring it here
I did not decide to bring it here
I pick it up gently
I hold it
I can see the face of that little boy
I can see the face of that flying basketball player
I can see the face of that crippled,
enraged adolescent
I can see the face of that young man

Black...white...
white...black
I remember that
Antoine had a razor in his heart
you could see that it cut him apart
I stood close to him
I felt the wind blow, 'cause
Antoine had a razor in his heart

So into this nice new office of mine
with its freshly painted walls
its new computer
its spotless carpet
I bring my battered easel
I bring an empty canvas
and I paint and I wonder where Antoine is today
and I wish that I could stand close to him
and I hope that I would feel no wind
blow through his wounded heart
and I pray that Antoine's razor was
stolen by art

The power and burden of relationships with adolescent patients, their images and their accompanying stories can be overwhelming at times. I cannot avoid being moved by my patients. I cannot buffer mysef from my own feelings. But, I also cannot afford to be overwhelmed and traumatized by my patients either. I have found that the most effective way for me to protect myself from vicarious traumatization is through making my own art.

3. Responsive Art as Imaginative Interpretive Dialogue

The process of the art therapist making art in response to a particular adolescent patient, or an adolescent's artwork, is a potent way for the art therapist to engage in imaginal dialogue with the patient-artist. I call this an imaginative interpretive dialogue because the artist-therapist always projects her own feelings and thoughts into the artwork she creates in response to the patient-artist. Typically, the patient-artist is inspired to make another image in response to the therapist's response. This, in my view, is a powerful and authentic method of interpretive interaction that engages both parties in a process of deepening their relationship to one another.

Dee's Blue Rock

Dee was passive and bored during her first few sessions in the art studio. She seemed to be just going through the motions in her early attempts at watercolor paintings and craypas drawings. At that time I was working on a painting of a street scene. One of the buildings in the painting had a large, open garage door. The inside of the building was dark (Figure 6).

Figure 6. Street with haunts.

My first encounter of any consequence with Dee came when she looked up from where she'd been doodling and asked, "What is going on in there?"

I stepped away from the easel and replied, "I don't really know...it's sort of mysterious though, and a little bit frightening. I'm not sure I like it."

This seemed to interest her. She asked, "So if you don't like it, why are you wasting your time painting it?"

"That's hard to explain, Dee. You see, for me, images just come."

"Huh?"

"They just come," I said. "I get a picture in my head and it's like it won't go away unless I paint it away."

"But you said you don't like this one." She said.

"It doesn't matter if I like it or not," I replied. "It's not about liking. It's about working with it."

The next day Dee informed me that she had decided she should paint. I asked her if she wanted to build a canvas or work on a Masonite board.

"I really want to start! Which one is fastest?" There was a pressure-durgency to her voice.

"There are some Masonite boards that have already been gessoed. They are ready to paint on right now," I said.

"Give me some Masonite then," she replied.

Dee got right to work. She mixed a dark midnight blue and covered the whole board with the deep, rich color. She then used a lighter, but still intense, blue to paint what appeared to be a rock. A long silver sword penetrated the right side of the rock. Then she added dark, red drops of blood oozing from the crack in the rock. She painted all of this in about forty-five minutes.

The next day, when she returned to the studio, she put her painting on an easel next to mine, stepped back a few feet and grimaced, "Crap, this isn't the way I want it to be."

"Dee," I said, "it's a beautiful piece. What is wrong about it?"

"I don't know. When I step back, it all just seems so flat. I mean, I can see the rock and the sword ok, but the blood seems to disappear in the dark blue."

I said, "I see what you mean. Can I make a suggestion?"

She nodded affirmatively.

"I think the drops of blood need some more work. You might try mixing your red again, then add some white to it. If you highlight the right side of each blood drop, and softly blend the pink gradually into the dark red it will make the drops really stand out against the background."

She grimaced again. "I can't do that. I'll just keep it the way it is."

"Dee, trust me," I said. "I'm an expert at this. Try it, if you don't like it you can always paint over it again. But don't quit without even trying."

* * *

Later that week I talked about this encounter in a group supervision session with colleagues and graduate art therapy students. One of the students in the group told me that he was appalled by what he thought was my judgmental reaction to Dee's image. He angrily suggested that I should have been accepting and supportive of whatever Dee did and that by my offering her technical advice, I was acting more like an art teacher than an art therapist. I responded that there was a deeper level of communication going on that he was not hearing. The entire discussion, I thought, was a metaphoric interchange, an interpretive dialogue, related to Dee's self-image and the feelings that had led her into treatment in the first place. I added that I thought art therapists were obligated to help our clients become more skillful artists. As my friend David Henley (1986) writes, "The art therapist must be prepared to function both as an artist and teacher, as well as a therapist." I said, "Think of it this way. You do not talk in the same way today that you did when you were a child. You have learned how to express your ideas more eloquently. Your vocabulary has expanded and you've learned how to construct your thoughts in a sophisticated way. The same thing is true in art. Of course, Dee's work was acceptable, but she can make it even more effective by learning new techniques...expanding her artistic vocabulary."

The point that I am making here is a subtle, but very significant one. By involving the patient in art making, and relating to the patient through art tasks, art therapists are engaging in a process of imaginal interpretive dialogue that alwayshas potent metaphoric meanings for the patient. These may, at some point, be put into words by the patient, or they may remain forever unspoken. Regardless of whether or not the patient is able to verbalize the meaning of the encounter, the meaning is there. Franklin (1992) comments on this phenomenon, "To work with art materials is to transform their physical and symbolic potential. Thus, art may be considered a simultaneous process of reformulating the self through the active formation of an object" (p. 79).

* * *

The next day, Dee highlighted the drops of blood. They seemed to come alive on the Masonite board. She asked, "Could I do that to the rock and the sword?"

"Of course," I said, "the concept is simple. The light on the blood is coming from the right side, so just add touches of light to the right side of the rock and the edge of the sword" (Figure 7).

Figure 7. Dee's rock.

As I worked on my street scene and Dee painted her rock, we seldom talked directly about what these images meant to us. She would make a comment about the powerful force that would be needed to embed a sword into a rock. I would respond by trying to make the sound of metal penetrating granite. She would ask about the things I had painted sitting on the table in the foreground. I would respond by asking her to imagine what the titles of the books should be. I would wonder if the surface of her rock was cold to the touch, and she would assure me that it was warm but very rough. We used our images and imaginative responses to them in our efforts to get to know one another. Dee never talked directly about what this painting meant to her. But she held it proudly as she carried it out of the studio. It was as if she was carrying something precious, protecting it...caring for it. In fact, I believe, that is exactly what she was doing. Henley (1987) suggests that the artwork of an individual such as Dee stands as a statement of wholeness, of who she is, "without bowing to a clinical analysis and dissection that eventually reduces one to a group of symptoms" (p.65).

Chapter V

THE PROBLEM OF INTERPRETATION IN ADOLESCENT ART THERAPY

In this chapter, I will discuss some of the problems associated with labeling and interpretation of adolescent artwork and I will propose a method for interpretivedialogue that is based on the *art as therapy approach to art psychotherapy*.

I have written about what I describe as *imagicide* (Moon, 1990, 1995). Imagicide is the killing off of the image through destructive psychological labeling and interpretation of artworks. Imagicide is attributable to the core problem of an artist-therapist "authority" who analyzes and explains what an image or a piece of art "really means" without regard for the artist who created it or the image itself. The destructive impact of this is compounded by assessment systems and manuals designed to aid in the interpretation of patient artworks. Just as the original creation of an image is a projective interpretation of life on the part of the artist, so too any subsequent attempt to interpret the image is a similar projection on the part of the interpreter. The effort to place a label or static interpretation on the image is *imagicidal.*

Art therapists working with adolescent populations inevitably must face the problem of artistic interpretation in their practice. Linesch (1988) states, "...the value of an interpretive art therapy approach is particularly controversial" (p. 54). There are those in the art therapy profession who argue that the very survival of the discipline hinges upon the capacity to expertly analyze and interpret imagery for the purpose of diagnostic inquiry (Cohen, Mills, & Kijak, 1994, pp. 105-110). Other art therapists also regard interpretation as central to their work. They identify one of their professional tasks as the translation of the metaphoric images of their patients into cognitive psychological constructs, for the purposes of interdisciplinary communication. In my view, this is problematic, particularly in relation to adolescent patients who typically are not able or willing to verbally validate or refute the accuracy of an interpretation by an adult authority figure. The absence of adolescent's validation or refutation of an interpretation leads directly to abuse of both the images and the kids who make them. There is nothing an art therapist can do that will more swiftly and surely destroy the therapeutic relationship with an adolescent patient than to psychologically label or interpret his or her work in fixed way. McNiff (1989) writes, "The intentional interpretation of art is widely misunderstood and limited in both psychology and art history. Both disciplines attach excessive emphasis on labeling and the classification of images according to a particular frame of reference" (p. 55). Artist-therapists working in this way attempt to establish themselves as *authorities* who can detect the hidden or unspoken meaning of the adolescent's art products, with or without their patients' cooperation, participation or permission. I view such interpretation of an adolescent's work as being disrespectful and potentially harmful to patients and their images because, as Champernowne (1971) suggests, translation from one language (art) to another (words) "is bound to bring loss or error" (p. 142). Adolescents who need psychotherapy of any kind have already experienced enough loss and error at the hands of the adult world.

Based on my experiences in over two decades of working with thousands of emotionally disturbed adolescents, I am convinced that there are no more sure ways for an art therapist to damage the therapeutic alliance and ruin a relationship with an adolescent patient than by affixing pathological labels to the adolescent's artwork, giving premature interpretations of the patient's art, or making "expert" interpretations outside of the context of a direct encounter with the patient.

I do not want to suggest that art therapists working with adolescents should never interpret and project themselves into the images of their patients, but the artwork must be seen for what it is and this means that there will be many interpretations that are equally valid. There is no *one* way to interpret the artwork of an adolescent. As McNiff (1989) says, "The artwork is a fountainhead of interpretations. One interpretation follows another" (p. 56). Henley (1997) notes, "As a trained art therapist I found myself analyzing all the time, yet it was what I did with these interpretations that defined my role as a teacher and therapist. These interpretations were used to guide and inform my interventions. It was the art process that functioned as a vehicle and, in turn, lent structure and guidance to the themes and accompanying images which were worked through." Let me say this again very bluntly; unless the art therapist is extremely skillful and is working from a perspective that generates and honors multiple interpretations, ***psychological labeling and interpretation of an adolescent's art = the end of the therapeutic relationship***. If an artist-therapist wants to be rid of a troublesome adolescent patient, all she needs to do is begin to pretentiously tell the adolescent what his or her picture really means.

One clinical example of an art therapy student who severely damaged her relationship with an adolescent was told to me by a colleague. My colleague was visiting a private psychiatric hospital in order to supervise one of her students who was doing practicum field work there. During the one-to-one art therapy session, the patient, a 14-year-old girl, made a drawing of a human figure. She drew an exaggerated tongue protruding from the mouth of the figure. In responding to the girl's drawing the art therapy student said something about an article that she had read in which the author suggested that protruding tongues may indicate sexual abuse. [Dracknik, C. (1994). *The tongue as a graphic symbol of sexual abuse.*] The patient stormed out of the room, vowing to never return.

In this example, the art therapy student made several errors. First, her comment had the effect of fixing a pathological label to the girl's artwork, i.e., that it might indicate sexual abuse. By doing so, all other possible meanings were closed off and the result was imagicide. The image had many potential interpretations, the possible indication of sexual abuse was only one of these. Second, the student's comment is an example of a premature interpretation of the patient's art. There was no need for this kind of intervention. It would have been much more advisable for the student to ask the girl to make a face like the one in her drawing, or to make a sound that would fit the drawing, or to tell a story about a person who sticks out their tongue...or...or. Third, my colleague said that it seemed that her student was trying to "come off as an authority" for the benefit of her supervisor. By making the "expert" interpretation without having established a solid relationship with the patient (it was only their third session), the student severely injured the fragile alliance she had with the girl.

RESPONSIVE ART MAKING AS INTERPRETATION

I would like to offer art therapists who are working with adolescents a model of how to generate and work with multiple interpretations of their patient's art by demonstrating the premise that one way to engage with the art of teenagers in an authentic manner and to avoid the negative aspects of labeling is by making art in response. The process of responsive art making brings the art therapist into a deeper understanding of the life of the adolescent by intensifying empathy and providing another way of knowing the person. The process also serves as a basis for dialogue with the patient-artist. Responsive art making is a form of interpretive dialogue with adolescents that is anchored in a reverence for the mystery, the unverifiable qualities, of human existence and images. Robbins (1982) states that, "As a therapeutic artist I carry the conviction that knowledge invariably transcends the limits of words" (p. 8). Along these same lines, Don Jones (in Feen-Calligan and Sands-Goldstein, 1996) states:

> In the beginning, art was made to overcome chaos. Prehistory andpre-verbal humans created art forms. Imagery, visualization, symbol, metaphor, movement and sound are the universal elements of humanity's 'soul' language. . . (p. 51)

It has been my experience that when I make art in an effort to respond to my patients' image, they, in turn, are motivated to make art in response to my work, which inspires me to make again. Each artistic responsive act is essentially an interpretation of the image that preceded it. By creating mutual artistic interpretations, an atmosphere of openness to many possibilities is fostered and an imaginal interpretive dialogue takes place that feeds upon itself. One image begets another, begets another, and another, and through this process a relationship is built between the adolescent and me.

An example of a relationship that was established through the imaginal interpretive dialogue process of responsive art making is found in my work with Bobbi, an eighteen-year-old woman I saw in weekly art therapy sessions for nearly two years. Bobbi's psychiatrist originally asked me to consult with her because Bobbi was "so resistive" to therapy. Bobbi was, by all accounts, quite successful in her efforts to defeat treaters. She was a senior at a large suburban high school, the youngest of five children, all of whom had behavioral problems when they were adolescents.

Bobbi's early images were very tight and constricted drawings that she did with a hard lead pencil. Although she was able to use the pencil skillfully she seemed to take little or no pleasure from her efforts and the finished products seemed empty and devoid of feeling content. She usually ended her sessions by wadding up her drawings and throwing them away.

During one session, I noticed that Bobbi's face brightened up a little as she talked about her car, a 1965 VW Beetle. Most of the time she was a rather rigid, guarded and up-tight sort of kid, but whenever she happened to mention her car there was a trace of a smile. I shared with her that I had owned several Beetles myself, "but the '68 Mustang I had when I was in college still stands out as my favorite car." I said, "I've had probably fifteen other cars since then, but that one is still special." Bobbi grinned.

It was my sense that the pencil drawing process was not helping Bobbi because she usually chose to discard the products of her work. One possible interpretation of this (which I kept to myself) was that it might suggest her wish to throw away parts, or all, of her life. So I decided to shift our work to painting.

I worked alongside Bobbi, every step of the way, as we built stretcher frames, stretched canvas, and gessoed. I hoped that by involving her in a process that demanded investment of time, energy, and a little sweat, Bobbi would be able to invest more care and commitment in her work. I also hoped that my doing each task along with her would serve to strengthen our relationship.

When our canvases were ready, Bobbi wanted to know what we were going to paint. I suggested that we begin by thinking about a place and a thing that were significant in our lives. After giving this some thought, Bobbi said that for her place she had thought of a field that her uncle used to own. "It was just a field that he would plant corn in, or wheat. I used to go there when I was younger, to be alone. It was always quiet and peaceful there." For the thing, she said, "it's gotta be my car" (Figure 8).

In response to Bobbi's verbal descriptions of her significant place and things, I decided that I would do a painting of a street in my hometown, and that for my thing, I would do a painting of my Mustang, too.

Figure 8. Bobbi's Beetle.

I believe that it is very helpful for first time painters to cover the entire canvas as quickly as possible with a background color in order to get rid of the stark white gesso. I asked Bobbi to think of what color the sky should look like at the farthest away point on the horizon above her field.

"Sort of bluish gray, cloudy" she said. "Like it is almost dusk" (Figure 8).

I helped her mix the color she wanted and then told her to cover the entire canvas. I envisioned my street scene to be sort of dark, so I covered my canvas with burnt umber (Figure 9). As we worked, Bobbi told me the story of the day her dad had taken her to buy her Beetle. It was a warm memory for her.

During one particular session, as we worked on our paintings, she said, "You know, that store reminds me of my old boyfriend."

Figure 9. In 1968.

I responded, "How so?"

Bobbi replied, "I don't know. I guess it's the tuxedos. Reminds me of the Prom. How sad!"

"Why sad?" I asked.

Bobbi didn't say anything but tears welled up in her eyes.

After a few minutes, I said, "Hmmm, you know I was thinking about painting over those tuxedos. I thought maybe they look out of place."

Bobbi reacted immediately, "No, no I think they should stay there."

"But they make you sad." I said.

"It is ok." She said. "You can't always avoid sad things."

I made no effort to verbally link or interpret her associations to my image and her statement about her boyfriend, whom I knew had broken up with her, to her prior behavior of throwing away of her artworks.

I looked at her evolving image of her car sitting in the middle of a farm field. I asked, "Bobbi, I wonder what you will call your painting?"

She sighed and quoted an old Paul Simon (1983) song, "If some of my friends had been more like my cars, I probably wouldn't have traveled so far."

Through the process of creating our paintings together, Bobbi and I engaged in an artistic and interpretive dialogue that was both therapeutic and humane. Many other paintings and drawings followed our automobile images. She did not throw them away. Sometimes her work inspired me, while at other times my images stimulated her ideas. I have no way of calculating how many possible interpretations our responsive process may have generated. Hundreds, thousands I suppose. The possibilities really were endless. Through the process of imaginal interpretive dialogue, Bobbi and I developed a strong and meaningful relationship. I do not believe that such work could have been done in verbal therapy. In my clinical work, I am always aware that it is the patient's interpretations of images that is most important.

In the preface to *Fundamentals of Art Therapy*, McNiff (1989) quotes the poet Jean Paul Richter: "The essence of poetic presentation, like all life, can be represented only by a second poetic presentation" (p. vi). Reflecting upon this, McNiff writes, "He [Richter] felt that aesthetic experience is to be described in images that mirror kindred life" (McNiff, 1988, p. vi).

The process of creating "a second poetic presentation" via responsive art making has profound implications when applied to the problem of interpretation of a patient's artwork in the context of adolescent art therapy. I have, on occasion, witnessed colleagues and students mistakenly make interpretations of an adolescent's image, and I have always experienced this as being abusive to both the person and their artwork. In my view, the whole phenomenon of labeling and psychological interpretation of images, in any form other than imaginative engagement, ultimately impedes the establishment of a genuine therapeutic relationship with the adolescent who made the art.

In contrast, whenever art therapists make art in direct response to patients or their images, they open up the possibility for deepening of relationships. This deepening of relationship leads to richer, more imaginative interactions with the patient-artist. Ultimately such inter-actions make for profound therapeutic relationships. Commenting on this form of relating, Allen (1995) says, "Making art together breaks down barriers and boundaries between people, creating compassion and empathy" (p.163).

THE PROBLEM OF INTERPRETATION IN ADOLESCENT ART THERAPY ASSESSMENT

I have struggled with the problem of interpretation, especially in relation to art assessment procedures with adolescents. There are many art assessment tools now documented in the literature of the art therapy profession. Prominent among these are: The Diagnostic Drawing Series, The Silver Drawing Test of Cognitive and Creative Skills, The Levick Emotional and Cognitive Art Therapy Assessment, The House-Tree-Person Test, The Kinetic Family Drawing Test, The Draw a Person Test, The Ulman Assessment, and others. In 1988, my colleague, Debra DeBrular, and I were asked to develop an art assess-ment procedure for a short-term, crisis intervention, child and adoles-cent unit. In essence, we were asked to create a framework for inter-preting patients' artwork. Although we had misgivings about doing so, we developed a projective art assessment process that resulted in a narrative report of the artist-patient that became very popular with the adolescent treatment teams at the hospital. In the years between 1988 and 1996, the Projective Art Assessment became one of the standard evaluative measures given to nearly every child or adolescent patient who entered the hospital. In 1993, my colleague resigned from her position, leaving me as the primary projective art assessor. Despite the popularity of the narrative reports I wrote, I became uncomfortable with the endeavor. I worried that I was killing the artist-patient's image. I worried that I was pathologizing images by attempting to label and analyze them. I wondered, what had I done? The adminis-tration of the hospital appreciated the art assessment narratives because they were paid for by third-party payers. The medical direc-tor of the child and adolescent unit loved to read my reports. He said, "It's like reading poetry." The social workers said that patients' families often wanted to meet me because I seemed to understand their angry, isolated, hurt teenager so well. The nurses on the unit said that they read them to remind themselves that the adolescent patients were not really monsters. Everyone seemed to love my art assessments except me.

I felt as if I was betraying the images that were made. I felt as if I was betraying the artist-patient who made them. When I sat in my office, surrounded by images, wondering what a particular painting meant, I was essentially asking it to translate itself into an idea or concept that I could be comfortable with. I did not like these feelings. I felt that my interpretations too quickly put on the pretense of fact, disregarding that they were themselves the products of my imagination.

A patient once said to me, "I never use purple and orange side by side in my paintings because I read somewhere that people who use purple and orange together are schizophrenics. In fact, it worries me that sometimes I think about using orange and violet. I never do, but do you think I might be crazy for having those thoughts?"

I wrestled with my feeling that I was betraying the images and the artists who made them every time I wrote a narrative report. But I also wrestled with my sense that maybe it was important that I was writing a report that the medical director of the unit referred to as "poetry." I wondered if it was ultimately helpful to the adolescent when his or her parents could read my narrative and understand their child in a deeper way. I wrestled with my concern that nurses needed to see their adolescent patients as human beings rather than monsters. I wondered if these benefits outweighed my concerns about image abuse. I asked myself, what right did I have to do this, and what right did I have to not do it?

One morning, in March of 1996, I was administering an art assessment to a sixteen-year-old young woman. She had made a painting about her recent suicide attempt. The painting had a dark brown background and she had made red slashing lines across the page. She looked up at me and said, "I hate everything."

I responded, "That must be hard."

She replied, "I don't care." She didn't say anything else during the assessment session, but I was deeply touched by the matter-of-fact despair her few comments seemed to convey. For some reason, as I wrote the narrative description of her work that afternoon, I could not shake the feeling of sad emptiness that I'd had during the assessment session.

Later that evening I was plunking around on my guitar and her two sentences came back to me. I began to play around with a tune and a verse.

"She cuts her arms now and she takes pills
she says suicide would cure her ills
she's always bored, she says life ain't fair
she hates everything and she don't care
she just don't care."

As I worked on the melody, guitar accompaniment and additional verses my feelings of heavy emptiness dissipated. I felt as if I could imagine how she felt about the world. I felt an odd sense of connectedness to Sara as I sang through the song.

Her name is Sara,
she's sweet sixteen
but she ain't sweet
if you know what I mean
        she's tried everything
        at least once or twice
        her momma always wanted
        her to be nice
but she don't care, she just don't care

She started drinking
when she was twelve
Father Kelly says
she's goin' to hell
        and she got pregnant
        in her thirteenth year
        had an abortion
        never shed a tear
'cause she didn't care

you could say she likes the wild life
yeah you could say she likes the wild life
but she don't care

On her fifteenth birthday
she hit the road
where she was for six months
nobody knows
        she got arrested
        out in Idaho

suspended sentence
    judge sent her home
but she don't care

She cuts her arms now
and she takes pills
she says suicide
would cure her ills
        she's always bored
        she says life ain't fair
        she hates everything
        and she don't care
        she just don't care

In the making of the song I was able to establish a fleeting connection with this girl. I was all too aware that she would probably be discharged within a day or two and that in all likelihood I would not see her again. Still, there was something important in the connection. As I played the song, it did not matter that I had already written dozens of art assessment narratives that year. For a brief period, it did not matter that so many patients came into and left the hospital so quickly that I often imagined a revolving door being installed in the admissions office. Momentarily, it did not matter that I was always being pressured to do more assessments more quickly. For three or four minutes, as I replayed the song, I was not objectively analyzing her. I was not making treatment recommendations. I was not providing a clinical depiction of her traumatic recent past. I was honoring her suffering and my own. I was relating to her.

In retrospect, I believe that this was a significant event in my life. It began a process of clarifying my thinking about the problem of interpretation. It reintroduced me to the potency of responsive art making and it spurred me to take action, to make art, and to reflect on how I think art therapy with adolescents should be.

In their summarization of the problematic nature of interpretation, Franklin and Politsky (1992) assert that art therapists work to observe the production of artwork unfold from inception to completion. Once this is finished, a clinical impression is formed about the work that hopefully is faithful and accurate to both the client and his or her artwork. Allowing clients to tell the art therapist about the work in as much detail as possible helps to arrive at accurate conclusions that include the client's perspective. They also note that there are potent pressures to contribute diagnostic information so that treatment can progress. Thus, art therapists are placed in the awkward position of having to translate to colleagues from other treatment disciplines the multiple potential meanings contained within the single image.

The pressures alluded to above are intense. During the 1990s, the average length-of-stay for hospitalized patients and the average number of reimbursed visits for outpatients has decreased considerably due to financial pressures applied by managed health care and insurance companies. As a result, art therapists are often expected to assess, treat, and terminate adolescent patients quickly. In response to these economic limitations, institutions continue to scale down their staffs, resulting in a constant push for therapists of all disciplines to "prove your worth, or be gone." Often proving one's worth as an art therapist means presenting yourself as an expert authority on the meaning of patients' images, and doing it quickly.

The problem with most forms of interpretation is that they attempt to force the adolescent's image into a cognitive explanation, to translate it from visual to verbal form. This stems directly from the fact that in our culture, and in psychotherapy, primary value is placed on self-assertion and being able to "talk things out." In my experience though, most adolescent psychiatric patients cannot tolerate or are not capable of the direct, verbal expression of feelings. Reasons for this intolerance are many: fear of disclosure, fear of relationship with the art therapist, developmental unreadiness, reluctance to make words their language of choice for emotional material, etc. Regardless of the reason, many, perhaps most, of the teenagers I engage with have trouble talking directly about their feelings. Attempts at interpreting their images for them usually lead to frustration, denial, or angry silence. This is clearly not helpful. Through making art, however, I am able to establish a metaverbal dialogue. The patient makes a picture, and I make a picture in response. If I respond, as Ellen Levine (1995) describes, "with sensitivity, imagination and aliveness," then the adolescent patient usually feels understood and validated. In commenting on this sort of work with her patients, Haeseler (1989) writes, "I focus my attention on my own artwork, and if that artwork is about or in response to them, the client and I can make deep connections with the necessary distance and boundaries in place" (p.71).

In summary, I find myself in agreement with Cohen, Mills and Kijak (1994) who suggest that every art therapist must make a choice regarding how [and if] they will involve themselves in interpretive work with patients. I assert that one must approach the task with a combination of openness, enthusiasm, honesty, flexibility and genuine interest in promoting an imaginal dialogue that leads to multiple inter-pretations rather than fixed meanings.

Chapter VI

RELATING TO ADOLESCENTS' IMAGES

I have sometimes heard professionals from other therapy disciplines express discomfort about the processes of artistic expression. One psychologist I knew was especially concerned that art therapists encouraged adolescents to draw "inappropriate pictures." He believed that making images of painful or disturbing emotional material invites psychosis. We debated on several occasions about which is more damaging to kids, artistic expression or suppression.

My colleague regarded the images produced by hospitalized adolescents as pathological. This, of course, meant he believed that artworks could bring on or alter disease. In contrast, I think that artistic endeavors are an expression of pathos, which means they are a creative endeavor that evokes compassion. Honest expression of feelings is seldom harmful to people, but I know that keeping secrets and constricting the expression of feelings most definitely is destructive.

This a critical philosophic question for art therapists. Are adolescents' images pathological expressions of illness or evocative expressions of compassion? This question lies at the heart of the essential dilemma regarding the role of imagery and interpretation of imagery that pervades the art therapy discipline. How art therapists answer this question profoundly affects every aspect of professional identity and practice.

In a paper presented to the annual meeting of the New England Association of Art Therapists, Watkins (1980) described six approaches to the image in art therapy. Her work has been very helpful as I have thought through my own views regarding imagery. In Moon (1994), I discussed four styles regarding imagery that I have seen enacted by art therapists. For my purposes here I suggest that there are three basic styles of relating to and regarding the images that adolescents make. The first style views imaginal graphic products as overt expressions of unconscious conflicted material. This model has grown out of Freudian analysis and asserts that particular meanings can be ascribed to symbolic images. In this model, images are regarded as minions of the id and are representations of strong sexual and aggressive drives. When art therapists operate from this style of relating to the imagery of patients, it is likely that their interpretations of images may focus on a disease orientation, or on the dysfunctional aspects of the individual. From this perspective, images are visual representations of the sick or pathological. Such interpretations can lead to equations regarding the meaning of an image. (For instance, cylinders always equal phallic symbols, doorways always equal vaginal openings, and so on.) In a keynote presentation to the Buckeye Art Therapy Association annual symposium in 1988, Dr. Shaun McNiff commented on the tendency to create formulas for interpretation. He said, "The snake in your dream is not always a penis. You have to be careful calling it that because you might offend the snake and he won't come back again."

A second style of relating to imagery, which I refer to as "diagnostic-psycho-stereotypical," stems from another pathological understanding of art products. "Diagnostic-psycho-stereotypifying" suggests that persons with certain types of psychiatric disorders tend to create art that is similar enough as to allow classification. There are notable contemporary authors who have advocated for classification of images, but this approach has historic roots as well. Lusebrink (1990) cites the early work of Volmat (1956) as an exemple of such classification. Wadeson (1980) gives a clear example of artistic categorization by proposing five basic pathological characteristics of schizophrenic art. Logically, for those who regard images in this way, it is reasonable to deduce a psychiatric diagnosis based on observation of a patient's images. For instance, if an art therapist from the psycho-diagnostic-stereotypical school of thought observed an artwork that embodied the characteristics of schizophrenic art described by Wadeson, it would follow that the art therapist might assume the creator of the image was ill with schizophrenia. The process of diagnosis is designed to conceptualize illness. If one approaches imagery from a diagnostician's perspective, there is an implicit understanding that images are manifestations of disease.

The third style of relating to imagery is at the other philosophic pole from these *pathological* positions. This view suggests that images are benevolent forces. McNiff (1993b), a prominent spokesman for this perspective, suggests that images do not come to hurt you. This viewpoint holds that images are a benevolent force in the life of the individual. In my work with adolescent patients, I have often encountered this benevolent phenomenon. Rather than view adolescent patients' images as symbols of repressed, conflicted material, or as indicators of dysfunction, I approach them as friendly messengers who have come to tell stories about themselves and their creator.

I believe images have a life of their own. They are creations, of course, and in a sense are reflections of their creator, but they are more. As evidence of this, I have often asked groups of adolescent patients to create a story in response to a particular image. Each patient tells a very different story, and each of their stories is significantly different from the story that is told about the image by its creator. I am sure that if the image could tell its own story it would be quite different from that of my patients and the creator. Commenting on this point in a personal communication, Pat Allen said, "Bruce, in my experience, when I ask the image what it's about, I get very clear and definitive answers."

From this point of view, one may think of images as metaphoric mentors capable of teaching. As I work in the therapeutic studio with adolescents I remind myself that I am dealing with the living, breathing artist, and the living image. Both the artist and the image command deep respect from me. From this standpoint, it is impossible for me to establish a formula for interpretation or an equation for analysis. The reality is that *this* does not always mean *that.* Images are not tumors to remove, measure and label. The world of adolescent art therapy embraces the mystery of ambiguous places where nothing is absolute. This is tremendously valuable to the adolescent.

> ...art and imagination are often taken as the "frosting" to life
> rather than as the solid food. . . What if imagination and art are
> not frosting at all, but the fountainhead of human experience?
> (May, 1975, p.124).

In order to be clear about the theoretical orientation I use when I am relating to the images of adolescent patients, it may be helpful to review briefly some of the prominent historic theories related to art making and health. It is not my intent here to present the entirety of these contributions, but rather to focus my review on concepts of the role art making plays in a healthy personality . As I have said, I believe art making and creative expression are inherently healthy acts, therefore I will relate my work to ideas of health rather than pathology. As May (1975) states, "The creative process must be explored not as the product of sickness, but as representing the highest degree of emotional health, as the expression of the normal people in the act of actualizing themselves" (p.40).

A PSYCHOANALYTIC VIEW OF ART AND HEALTH

Sigmund Freud (1949), the founder of the discipline of psychoanalysis, stated that health consisted of the ability to love and to do productive work. Healthy personality in psychoanalytic terms is an outcome of harmony among id, ego and superego, the three substructures of the personality. *Id* refers to instincts. *Ego* refers to the acting, controlling and learning functions of personality. *Superego* refers to the moral ideas people require as they develop. Psychoanalysts assert that if a person's upbringing has been adequate, the ego is strong enough to resolve conflicts among needs, impulses and morals.

Under this framework, creative and artistic work is generally regarded as a neurotic compensatory activity, or a sublimated expression of id. From this perspective, images tend to have a pathological origin.

I do not agree with the psychoanalytic perspective in regards to healthy personality and art making. I mention it here for historical reasons, and also because it has had such a profound effect on the entire field of psychology, which has, in turn, had tremendous impact on art therapy. However, this is clearly not the sort of psychological foundation upon which I base my artistic and therapeutic work with adolescents.

AN ADLERIAN VIEW OF HEALTH AND ART

Alfred Adler was an early follower of Freud's work. However, he soon found himself in disagreement with Freud about the role of sex in the development of a healthy personality. Ansbacher (1956) describes Adler's assertion that social interest, or a feeling of connectedness with one's fellow human beings, is the most important goal of personal growth and health. Thus, Adler introduced an explicitly interpersonal dimension to theories of health personality. By doing so he presents a wholesome correction to the pathology-oriented psychoanalytic theories.

It is this author's sense that art therapists working out of an Adlerian theoretical model would regard artistic activity as an expression of health and commitment to communicate to others, rather than as an expression of illness.

OTTO RANK'S VIEW OF CREATIVITY

Otto Rank was another of the early followers of Freud who found himself in disagreement with Freud. Rank (1932) asserts that a healthy personality has to do with the capacity to exercise will and creativity. He held the creative artist as the ultimate expression of human growth. Rank regards the artist as one who has the courage to be an individual. Healthy personality, Rank suggests, implies the courage to express and embrace one's differences from others, and the courage to be creative in a variety of situations.

From Rank's perspective the process of art making is an expression of health. I very much appreciate his view of the human being as artist and I echo the idea that psychological health is nurtured and maintained through ongoing creative work, especially with adolescents.

JUNG AND THE SHADOW

Carl Jung is yet another of the early followers of Freud. At one time, he was a student of Freud; he also eventually parted with Freudian theory. Jung viewed human beings as having an overt, or conscious, side of the personality, and a covert, dark side, which is generally unconscious and invisible. He developed a very complex theory of personality which gave rise to the archetypal psychology which will be discussed later in this section.

Jolande (1953) provides a useful introduction to Jung in which he describes Jung's model of health and personal growth as being a gradual unfolding and expression of the shadow side, and the capacity to integrate these unconscious attributes in a meaningful manner. The imagination is regarded as the place to explore and express the shadow. Many art therapists identify themselves very closely with the Jungian approach. In a simplistic way, adolescents are often intrigued by the concept of the shadow side of their being. However, in relation to therapeutic work with adolescents, I have found the Jungian model to be rather complex and difficult to apply due to its depth and reliance upon abstract concepts.

THE PERSPECTIVE OF GESTALT THERAPY

Fritz Perls developed a therapeutic approach based on his theory of health and neurosis that he called Gestalt therapy. He asserts that personal growth is best seen in one's capacity to emancipate oneself from dependent relationships and in one's ability to be directly aware of perceptions and feelings.

Similar to Freud and Jung, Perls paid much attention to the dream images of his patients. His method of therapy involved asking patients to act out all parts of the dream during the therapy session. The central idea was that every aspect of the dream represented some dimension of a person's experience. Hence, Perls' emphasis on all images of the dream is quite similar to the emphasis that most art therapists place on attending to all details of a painting or other visual image. My work with adolescents as an art therapist is deeply indebted to Perls' emphasis on engaging the patient in an interpretive dialogue related to the imagery of the dream.

TRANSACTIONAL ANALYSIS AND HEALTH

Eric Berne (1969) developed an approach to psychotherapy he called transactional analysis. The essence of his view of health is that it consists of the capacity to affirm one's personal worth, honestly ask for what one needs, and to deal directly and openly with others.

From this perspective, art making serves the individual by providing an opportunity to validate one's self-worth and to develop and demonstrate honest self-expressive capabilities.

AN EXISTENTIAL VIEW OF HEALTH

Existential psychology authors Frankl and Yalom present the central idea that human beings are capable of choosing their behavior and can thus create their own essence. One discovers or creates the meaning of one's life by dealing with the ultimate concerns of existence. This is the concept at the core of existential psychotherapy.

In Moon (1995), the assertion is made that art has been existential in its nature throughout all history. The images adolescents make in the therapeutic arts studio are almost always an effort to express the meanings of their lives as they contend with loneliness, freedom and the inevitability of suffering.

A difficulty I have encountered in exploring the relationship of adolescent art therapy, as I practice it, to psychological theorists is that psychology has tended to be reductionistic. Regarding this tendency, Simon (1986) writes, "The traditional analyst often sees all higher human functions as derivative of sexuality. The behaviorist's paradigm of classical and operant conditioning is thought to permeate all human functioning. Association theory is often used to explain learning while reduction theory will explain motivation" (p. 103). Simon regards this as a significant shortcoming of psychology.

Commenting on this view of psychology, Sheldon Kopp (1976) wrote, "It has denied the immediacy of each man's [sic] experience, his encounter with metaphor, and reduced beyond recognition the concerns that make man [sic] most human. Modern psychology has lost the vision of life and growth to a preoccupation with psychopathology and conditioned responses" (p. 24). The psychology from which my thoughts on adolescent art therapy have come, and upon which my clinical work as an artist-therapist is based, is a psychology that is inextricably attached to metaphor, image and humanness. It is a psychology that shares many attributes with archetypal psychology.

A basic premise of archetypal psychology is that psyche and soul are synonymous, and that the language of psyche is image (Hillman, 1975,

1988, 1989; Jung 1958). It follows then that the process of engaging with one's images, working with them, crafting them into paintings, is by definition a psychological and soulful process. In the preface to (in Moon, 1996) *Art and Soul: Reflections on an Artistic Psychology,* art therapist Lynn Kapitan writes, "Where is the soul? Not a material object, the artist's soul is rather a viewpoint that is an enlivened way of seeing the world ensouled in imagery...The task at hand is to give form to the essential story of our particular life or time found in the images we create" (p. xii). I think of my work in the therapeutic arts studio with adolescents as an example of wrestling with this *task at hand.* When adolescents engage in art making, they are living out Rollo May's notion that creating art is "the most distinguishing characteristic of the human being" (p.7).

My work with disturbed adolescents has grown from its close association with existential psychology, depth psychology, imaginal and archetypal psychology. The psychology of image I envision proceeds from the nature of the imaginal. It is grounded in the phenomenology of images. "A phenomenology of the imaginal is dependent on the endless discovery of ways of imagining—each yielding both a new vantage point to other images as well as a new experience of oneself "(Watkins, 1976, p.151).

In his small text, *Archetypal Psychology: A Brief Account,* Hillman (1988) says, "The datum with which archetypal psychology begins is the image. . .image is psyche, [this is] a maxim which archetypal psychology has elaborated to mean that the soul is constituted of images. . ."(p. 6). My sense of the interrelationship of art and art therapy with depth, existential and archetypal psychology has evolved out of my work as an artist-therapist with adolescents in a psychiatric hospital setting over the past two decades. Daily, I was witness to the ways the arts deepened the lives of the patients I worked with. My work in the hospital was directed towards engaging in an artistic-therapeutic relationship with the most complex, mysterious, painful and personal aspects of human existence. This was work that had to be done, for as Peck (1978) asserts, "it is the attempt to avoid legitimate suffering that lies at the root of all emotional illness"(p.133). In commenting on the nature of artistic-therapeutic relationships, McNiff (1989) writes, "Although our artistic methods are different from those of the early psychoanalysts, we work with the same terrain. Depth psychology is soul psychology" (p. 3).

When I write of depth in this context, I refer to the process of inward, immersive self-reflection. I associate depth inquiry of this kind with darkness, anguish, struggle, descent and what the existential psychologists describe as "the ultimate concerns of existence" (Frankl, 1959; Yalom, 1980). Archetypal psychologists would call this sort of inquiry an exploration of the soul (Berry, 1982; Corbin, 1979; Hillman, 1989; Lopez-Padroza, 1977; Moore, 1992; Watkins, 1976). Moustakas, a humanistic depth psychologist, would describe this form of inquiry as a heuristic process (Moustakas, 1994).

Since the origins of the words "psyche" and "soul" are synonymous, in a classic sense, *psych-ology*, may be thought of as the study of soul. It is from this perspective that Hillman called for a revisioning of psychology. Hillman states that his work is about soul making. Archetypal psychology then is an attempt at articulating a psychology of soul, an effort in revisioning psychology from the point of view of soul. Archetypal psychology "is therefore old-fashioned and radically novel because it harks back to the classical notions of soul and yet advances ideas that current psychology has not even begun to consider" (Hillman, 1975, p.ix).

Archetypal art therapist Howard McConeghey writes, "art transforms the world which appears to the eye into a world that takes on reality in the human mind. It recreates the outside world in a metaphor of colored forms, whose symbolic character can at the same time make visible the real response of the artist" (McConeghey, 1986, pp. 111-114). As I work with the images that arise during the process of treating emotionally disturbed adolescents, I attempt simply to accept whatever presents itself. I discipline myself to attend to whatever appears in the patient's imagery. Whether it is a thing, a feeling, an event, a relationship or a situation, I trust that its appearance will offer a basis for transformation and understanding. Moustakas (1994) states, "Letting what is seen be encourages the person to explore its nature and meaning. Letting it be provides an opening to learn from it, to learn from it while questioning it"(p.13).

At the foundation of adolescent art therapy is the relationship between art making and existential psychology. As an essential part of the process, we engage with the patients' artwork through responsive art making.

I confess, there was a time when my professional identity was based on my capacity to know the meaning of my patient's work, whether they knew it or not. Now I stand before their images (and my own) in an attitude of wonder.

Chapter VII

MORE THAN WORDS CAN SAY

Artistic activity always draws upon the three-fold relationship among the artist, the media, and the world around him or her. As Lowenfeld points out, "Painting, drawing, or constructing is a constant process of assimilation and projection: taking in through the senses a vast amount of information, mixing it up with the psychological self and putting into a new form the elements that seem to suit the aesthetic needs of the artist at the time" (p.4).

The traumatic experiences that so often are at the root of emotional dysfunction for an adolescent are almost always sensual. Something happened: cruel words were screamed; faces were slapped; genitals were inappropriately touched; bodies were intruded upon; deprivations were endured; rejections were felt. The painful things that lead up to an adolescent seeking or requiring therapy are visual, auditory, olfactory, sensual experiences. It is a fallacy to presume that such painful experiences can be worked through, resolved or healed through talking alone. The success of therapeutic endeavors with adolescents hinges upon their capacity to involve the senses. Therapeutic methodologies that rely solely on verbalization, or on biological intervention, inevitably fail to have lasting impact upon the lives of adolescents.

The research of Pfeiffer and Jones (1981) demonstrates that people learn more efficiently, retain information longer, and perceive meaning more completely when experiential modalities are engaged. Unfortunately, many therapies use methods with adolescents that neglect the value of experiential learning, relying instead on verbal interaction. Pfeiffer and Jones suggest that verbal interaction is the least effective way to convey information, and particularly that the meaning of the information may be lost (p.2).

The processes of art making for an adolescent are primarily a means of self-exploration and expression. Adolescents are dynamic individuals, constantly growing, changing, perceiving and interpreting the world around them. The art of an adolescent therefore expresses feelings, thoughts, wishes, fears and reactions to the environment in a manner that is marked by images filled with energy, power and change.

Before the industrial revolution, all people were involved daily in creative contact with the world. They built their own homes, made their own clothes, grew their food and made their own entertainment. Today, however, there is little need for such creative involvement. Few people build their own house, make their own clothes, tend their own gardens or make their own animal traps. Entertainment has become a passive phenomenon—flipping through the channels or surfing the internet. Something has been lost, something essentially human.

The therapeutic arts engage the senses. The adolescent touches the materials, sees the colors, hears the music, smells the turpentine. In this era of mass production, virtual reality and cyber-relationships, art therapy has the special mission of engaging the creative sensibilities that Lowenfeld says "make life satisfying and meaningful" (p.13).

The potency and depth of artistic expression engage a sensitivity to the subtleties of color and shade, the emotional undercurrents that flow through line character and the aesthetic awareness inherent in the balancing of weight and mass. Art is always connected to the sensual. The core of our work revolves around sight, sound, movement and touch.

A DIGRESSION

Andy was referred to my private practice office because, as he put it, "Life Sucks." My initial impression was that he was an unpleasant and irritable young man who seemed to be very angry about having been "forced" into therapy by his parents. Andy had been treated for alcohol and marijuana abuse at a residential center for two weeks the previoius year. For the first half-hour or so of our initial session he sat, slumped down in his chair, glowering at the floor. I made several attempts to engage him in art making and conversation, but he deflected my best efforts, so I worked on my own painting. For most of the session he sat in silence as I painted. The image (Figure 10) was of two of my friends and me playing a game of darts.

Figure 10. Throwing darts.

Near the end of the hour, after having watched me for some time, Andy asked, "Why are you painting that?"

I stepped back from my easel but kept the focus of my attention on the painting. "I'm not sure, Andy. I guess I try to paint things that are important to me."

He sneered, "What's so important about darts?"

"Oh, it's not really the darts, Andy. It's the people. We used to be really close."

"Used to be?" He said.

"Yeah, but we seem to have drifted apart."

Andy asked, "Why darts?"

"Well, we used to play a lot of darts, but I think it's also about throwing darts at each other. It's hard to explain."

"But I still don't get it," Andy said. "If this stuff bothers you, why waste your time painting about it?"

"Andy," I replied, "that's just it. You see for me that is what art is all about, painting about my life, the stuff that is hard and the things that are good."

He sat in silence for a few minutes. Then he gestured toward my painting and said, "I've been in places like that."

"Yeah, me too. One thing I like about this painting is that I can almost hear the music coming from the juke box."

"I can smell it," Andy said.

I asked, "How does it smell?"

"Musty and smoky, like it hasn't been aired out in a long time."

I stepped away from the canvas. "Yes, I think you are right. Maybe I should paint an open window."

Andy laughed. "I didn't mean you should change it."

"I know you didn't." I replied. "But it is important to know that I could change it if I wanted to. Painting is a little like life you know, if you don't like the picture you can just paint over it, change it and make it the way you want."

"That's cool."

I painted for a couple minutes before I asked, "Are there any things in your life you'd like to change?"

Andy thought for a moment, "I'm a junior in high school and I have no idea what I'm going to do after next year. I just broke up with my girlfriend, it ain't no big deal, but in general everything sucks."

"Andy," I said, "Sucks is such a harsh word. How about saying that everything inhales deeply." That really made him laugh.

"You paint pretty good man."

"Thanks Andy. Painting helps me a lot. Would you like to learn?"

"Yeah, maybe. I ain't any good, but I could try."

"Andy, most people inhale deeply at painting when they start. Don't worry about it. I tell you what, we are almost out of time today, so between now and next week, I'd like for you to think about what you want to paint."

When Andy arrived for the next session he pulled a piece of paper from his coat pocket, unfolded it and handed it to me. "This is it, this is what I wanna paint."

The image was of a barren landscape. A small leafless tree grew on the rightside of the page. Storm clouds swirled in the sky above.

I said, "All right, looks pretty dreary, sort of like a rainy day. I can almost hear the wind. Would it be a warm day, or a cold day?"

"Cold, I guess."

The image seemed lonely, cold and miserable. I said, "This looks like a hard place to be."

He blew the air, making a whhh sound, like wind.

I placed his landscape drawing on the floor between our two chairs. " Andy, I like your drawing. It gives me a real sense of how things are for you."

Andy looked down at his drawing. "I don't know." He looked around at the paintings that hung on the walls of the studio, the sculptures that sat on the benches, and all the other artifacts of patients past and present that clutter the space.

"So, how have you been, Andy?" I asked.

"Sucky, I mean, life inhales," he said. "Now can we get started on my painting?"

"No," I replied. "All we are going to do today is build the canvas, and if we have time we can get it gessoed."

With something less than eagerness, he said, "So, where do we start?"

I pulled two 2 x 2s from the wood rack and said, "Since this is your first painting, let's make it a challenge. I'd like you to measure two pieces three feet long, and two pieces four feet long." I handed him a tape measure and carpenters pencil.

"That big?" He exclaimed.

"Yes," I said, "I think that will about do it."

When he had finished marking the wood, he asked, "Now what?"

I pointed toward the hand miter box and said, "Set the angle for 45 degrees and cut each end of your 2 x 2s."

I watched as he approached the miter box hesitantly. It was clear that he had never used a miter saw before. He didn't know where to put the 2 x 2 or how to place his hands so that he could both operate the saw and clamp the piece of wood to the metal back wall of the box. He also seemed unsure of how to adjust the angle mechanism of the saw.

I didn't say anything about this, but I moved up beside him and showed him how to change the angle and how to position the wood. I left the sawing to him. He began to pull the saw tentatively. "C'mon Andy, it won't hurt you." I said.

Without looking up he replied, "I never did nothing like this before."

"Don't worry about it Andy. You are doing fine. Just fine. I have faith in you."

A few minutes into the cutting process he exclaimed, "Shit, I got a splinter in my hand."

"Andy, don't make such a big deal out of this. Nobody dies from splinters." When all the cuts on his wood were made, I showed him how to use coarse sandpaper to smooth the edges he'd just cut.

"These aren't going to show, are they?"

"No, nobody will ever see them, but they will fit together better if you do this, and you and I will know you did it right. There is no substitute for quality work."

"This is going to take a long time." He sighed. "I thought I'd be painting something tonight."

I continued to work on the stretcher frame I was building, "Andy, you have got to learn to be patient. Building stretchers is all about patience."

"But don't they sell these in stores? I bet my mom would buy me one that is already stretched if I asked her to."

"But what would you get from that, Andy?'

"A few less blisters maybe." We both laughed.

"Well, Andy, you know if you buy a prestretched, progessoed canvas, you're really cutting yourself off from the process. You miss an opportunity to be in touch with the heart of the painting."

He looked at me a little strangely but kept working. When each of the angled cuts had been sanded, I showed Andy how to clamp two pieces together in order to nail them securely. After he put the last nail in, he held the rectangular frame up for my inspection. He was clearly proud of his work.

"Does the canvas go on now?"

"No," I said. "First we need to check all of the corners to make sure they are square, then we'll make a couple angle braces to make sure the frame doesn't get pulled out of shape when we stretch the canvas. Don't you love the smell of the sawdust?"

By the time we had completed all of this, Andy's hour was nearly finished. In a variety of ways, this session set the tone for the rest of the time Andy was in therapy. Our interactions focused most often on the tasks at hand: stretching canvases, planning paintings, technical details, and finally framing and setting hanging wire on the backs of his finished works. At every step in the process, from gathering tools and materials through signing and displaying his finished products, we paid attention to the sights, smells and feel of the work, as well as the images he created.

He came bearing his emptiness and "sucky" self-loathing. It was critical to help him develop a more positive regard for himself by engaging his senses through doing. The tasks, coupled with self-expression, were the treatment of choice for Andy. The therapy was doing art together. By doing so, Andy got to experience the healing effects of expressive arts processes. In addition, he developed a genuinely more positive internal view of himself as he worked with and gained mastery over materials and procedures.

One of the last paintings he worked on during his art therapy journey illustrates this with potency. It was a small work, approximately 24" X 28". The scene was of an old house, bathed in harsh light from some unseen source. His painting was reminiscent of the building that housed my studio (Figure 11).

Figure 11. Abandoned house.

When I looked at the painting, I felt a vague sense of loneliness, but there was a feeling of anticipation about it, too. "Yowsa," I said, "I love the trees. They really give a feeling of vastness...a depth."

He raised his eyes. "Do you know how long it took to paint all those leaves?"

"No." I said.

"Hours!" He exclaimed.

"It looks like you worked hard, Andy."

"There is no substitute for quality work, Bruce."

Andy worked for several sessions on that painting. He made mistakes sometimes, would get frustrated, but was always able to back up and then rework a section until he was happy with it. I think this describes what Andy was doing intrapsychically also. He was learning to wrestle with thinking about himself as "quality work." He made errors, would become irritated, but was able to stop and gather himself, and remake his self-image. He learned to like what he saw, both on the canvas and in the mirror.

This kind of work could not have been done in verbal psychotherapy. It was imperative that Andy encounter himself through the sensual experience of making art. I don't mean to devalue the therapeutic benefit of the relationship we developed over time and the talking we did. Certainly, these had some healthy impact as well. It is extremely important to stress that my relationship with Andy was inextricably connected to the sensual creative process. It was in the context of the studio that our relationship existed and it would not have been the same without the blisters, splinters, sights and smells.

For Andy, and many adolescents like him, it was (is) equally important that he learn to struggle with style and technique. Throughout the duration of our relationship, I insisted he use materials and tools in a manner that honored them. As an artist-therapist, I worked simultaneously with Andy's senses, his images, the process, the materials and his view of the world. These multiple layers of involvement allowed me to relate to him at various times as his teacher, consoler, beholder, critic and supporter.

Chapter VIII

THE FOUR PHASES OF
ADOLESCENT ART THERAPY

Adolescent art therapy can be understood only if there is an organizing image, or schema, that is specific enough to be directive but broad enough to include a wide range of individual differences. The image I have found very helpful in my own evolutionary process is to envision the treatment journey as being divided into four distinct but overlapping phases. It is, of course, imperative that the reader keep in mind that few, if any, adolescents get better in a linear fashion as these phases imply. In the reality of the therapeutic arts studio there is an ebb and flow among the phases that is rather like a spiral, distinctly nonlinear.

The four phases of art therapy treatment can be labeled in a variety of ways, but I am most comfortable with the following model. It consists of (1) resistance; (2) imagining; (3) immersion; (4) letting go.

Artists I know have alluded to a parallel phenomenon to these four phases that they have observed in their studio work. As the painter faces the blank canvas, she is often overwhelmed by the task. There is a natural resistance, a sense of inertia, fear and worry that accompanies making the first brush strokes. As the work begins, an image emerges on the canvas and the artist begins to have an idea of where the process may lead her. As the work proceeds, she is filled with excitement and energy and as the process nears its end, there is a period of reflection on the work, and a sense of ownership emerges. This is a period of creative immersion in the process. Finally, through the act of signing the finished piece, the artist lets go, acknowledging that this is a partial portrait of her life. Again, this is rarely a linear process for the artist. Sometimes, even after a good beginning the canvas may need to be regessoed. Or just when the artist was about to sign the work a new image may occur and significant segments of the canvas must be reworked.

The course of the artistic-therapeutic journey then may be envisioned as a spiraling path leading through periods of resistance, imagining, immersion and letting go.

THE RESISTANCE PHASE

Artist-therapists who work with adolescents must prepare themselves to work with some fairly consistent forms of resistance which are the hallmarks of the initial difficulties of engaging the adolescent in the treatment structure of the arts studio. Rinsley (1980) suggests that the predictable adolescent resistance can be fully understood only in the context of the predicament of most adolescents in our culture. "namely, that of finding one's self mired between dependent childhood and mature adulthood" (p. 6). This predicament, Rinsley asserts, in turn shapes both the content and the form of the metaphors the adolescent conveys to therapists.

Typically, the *adolescent perspective* on therapy is made up of a collection of beliefs, behaviors and attitudes that can be thought of in the following ways:

First, in my work with hospitalized adolescents and adolescents who came to my private practice, it is generally safe to say that very few of them had a clear sense of why they needed therapy of any sort. In most cases, they had been referred to the hospital or the private practice by their parents, school officials, or juvenile court authorities, and they were usually angry about this. In a very real sense, many teenagers who enter art therapy, or any other form of psychotherapy, have been coerced into doing so. Rinsley (1980) notes that, to adolescents, the notion that they might be sick or mentally ill is abhorrent, and they typically respond with hostility to any such suggestion (p.7). Artist-therapists who intend to work with adolescent patients must be comfortable with the initial hostility of their patients, and develop strategies for dealing constructively with it. Some strategies for working with adolescent resistance are dealt with in the following section of this text. It is imperative that would-be treaters accept the anger of adolescents and not take it personally. Moustakas (1974) takes the position that resistance is a necessary form of protection developed by the patient. Indeed, it can be a matter of some concern if the adolescent is not angry about being in therapy, and initially resistive to it.

Second, it is imperative that the artist-therapist keep in mind that she is an adult. Often adolescents have suffered at the hands of adults and may view all adults as potential inflicters of misery. A predictable aspect of adolescents in therapy is that they will readily view treaters as parental figures and thus project all the difficulties and intense feelings associated with parents and authorities onto the artist-therapist. Additionally, even healthy adolescents tend to believe that their experiences, feelings and thoughts are unique to them and their generation and that adults cannot really understand them. Since the artist-therapist is by definition an adult, this adolescent misconception must be reframed and dealt with. It is essential that eventually the adolescent comes to value the therapist's input. Many art therapists err by altering their behavior or demeanor in an effort to "relate" to the adolescent. However, this attempt is doomed to failure because the adolescent will see through the effort as a shallow manipulation.

Rinsley suggests that adolescent clients will strongly anticipate the recurrence of three major traumas: "(1) The adult will retaliate punitively and hurt him; or (2) the adult will reject or abandon him; or (3) the adult will prove by his actions that he is not a perfect, blameless, omniscient, and omnipotent figure—qualities in which, despite protests to the contrary, the adolescent wants desperately to believe" (p.7).

Third, it is my experience that in order to defend against the recurrence of the three traumas Rinsley identifies, the adolescent will attempt to act in such a way as to defend himself or herself and to discredit, or neutralize, the work of the artist therapist. To that end, the patient will likely see the structure of the therapeutic arts studio as an opponent in a game he or she must win, and the artist-therapist as an adversary who must be defeated.

Adolescent Resistance to Art Therapy

Adolescent patients tend to initially regard both the artist-therapist and the structure of the arts studio as foes who must be conquered. The basic nature of the adolescent's dilemma can be summarized in the question of how to best deal with their adult adversary. To that end, there are some common behavioral resistance mechanisms adolescents employ. The basic purposes of resistance behaviors for an adolescent are to present the self in a manner that denies (1) the existence of disturbing behavioral patterns; (2) the consequences of the disturbing behaviors; and (3) the inner emotional experiences that surround the behaviors.

The most important aspect of dealing with adolescent resistance for artist-therapists is that we regard these behaviors as inevitable phases of the treatment journey. Moustakas (1974) insists that resistance is the psychological protection developed by a patient to preserve an inner sense of ego integrity. While the resistance behaviors are often not particularly pleasant for the art therapist, they are absolutely necessary for the adolescent. It is helpful for artist-therapists to regard these difficult behaviors as if they were performance art events. When one thinks of the teenager's behaviors as being scenes from a drama one is freed to observe and reflect upon the meaning of the performance, without becoming counter-therapeutically caught up in the drama itself.

The second important aspect of dealing with adolescent resistance is recognizing that the patient is, in fact, in resistance and that resistance can often be disguised with a variety of subtle and overt behavioral veneers.

The third most important aspect of dealing therapeutically with adolescent resistance is to be able to identify the primary patterns of resistance, thus enabling the artist-therapist to plan a helpful therapeutic response, or intervention.

Again, if we regard resistive behaviors as being an inevitable component of the treatment journey that is absolutely necessary for the adolescent, and if we think of them as performance art events, then we are free to observe and think about the meaning of the performance without taking the behaviors personally. When Don Jones, one of the pioneers of art therapy in America, was the director of the adjunctive therapy department at Harding Hospital, he repeatedly cautioned the members of the department to, "Always respond, but never react," to patient's behaviors. This is good advice to all artist-therapists who wish to work with adolescents. Robbins and Cooper (1993) suggest that the art therapy studio is an essential holding environment for the patient as s/he learns to tolerate the anxiety of loss.

Rinsley (1980) describes fourteen behavioral devices that hospitalized adolescents use to defeat the treatment structure (pp. 8 - 17). In the therapeutic arts studio, I have observed a somewhat smaller range of typical resistance patterns. Among the recurrent maneuvers adolescents employ in the art therapy studio are the following: The Rebel; I'm in the In-Crowd, You're in the Out-Crowd; Compliant Surrender / I'll Do Anything You Want; Running Away/Catch Me if You Can; and Be My Friend/You Are the Only One Who Understands Me.

1. *The Rebel.* Behaviors that come under the umbrella term of rebellion are perhaps the most prevalent resistance maneuvers. Yet they are also some of the most difficult to deal with in the therapeutic arena because they are not only typical for adolescents in need of psychological care, but are also common in the general population of teenagers. Thus, it is imperative that the artist-therapist make every effort to understand the nature of the rebellious behavior of a particular patient in order to discern those that are especially dysfunctional and those that are relatively normal.

Adolescents who use rebellion in an effort to defeat the therapeutic structure of the arts studio will employ a host of acting out behaviors to create disorder and to disrupt the functions of the studio. These acting out episodes may take the form of destructive outbursts, exaggerated displays of anger, histrionics, dramatic negativism, defacement of the space, aggression toward another and various other dysfunctional forms of engagement. All of these rebellious behaviors may be used habitually, singularly or in swift successive series.

The meta-message to the artist-therapist that the overtly rebellious adolescent sends is, "Through my behavior I will disrupt and disorganize you and the studio and make it impossible for you to maintain your structure, hence I will keep the focus away from my inner problems and therefore I will be in control."

Rollie the Rebel

Initially, Rollie's involvement in the arts studio reminded me of battle. His style of handling paint and brushes was war-like. He would squirt huge amounts of tempera directly onto large 3' x 3' sheets of brown kraft paper. He smeared, pushed, gushed, slashed and absolutely refused to take any direction from me. He worked very quickly and never took his time with anything. As he put it, "I ain't gonna fool around with shit here, so you can jus' leave me alone."

At first I thought Rollie's work was cathartic and the immediacy of his expression might be helpful. But, as the days passed, I began to have a rather different reaction. He had a way of filling up the space around him and not letting anyone get too close. He did this through frenzied activity, messiness and surliness. I noticed that not only was I avoiding his end of the room, but other kids in the space also kept their distance. I also began to see his use of the paint as excessive and wasteful. He was, quite literally, creating a little corner of chaos in the studio in which he was left alone to do as he pleased.

After a couple sessions of this, I decided to intervene. As he entered the studio one afternoon I said, "Rollie, I've been thinking about your art. You know, you really have a way with painting anarchy. But it worries me that you have been working only with tempera paint on paper."

He looked at me suspiciously, "What's the matter with that?"

"Well, Rollie, the tempera is a kind of paint that breaks down over time, and paper is so fragile. I was thinking maybe we could try building a canvas and working with acrylic."

"No way man. I do what I want."

"Rollie, I know that you like to have things your way. But I really believe that artistically speaking it would be better for you to try working with some other kinds of materials."

He sneered, "I said no. Now drop it." And he went to tear paper from the roll.

Rollie's refusal to go through the proper procedural steps of building a canvas, or gessoing the Masonite panels, was clearly resistive. In addition to this, he routinely left his paint-filled brushes in the sink. One day when I attempted to talk with him about how leaving his brushes behind uncleaned would ruin them, Rollie kicked a chair and knocked a coffee can full of water off of the table.

Some time passed without much change in Rollie's engagement in the studio, and no appreciable modification of the behaviors that were responsible for his having been admitted to the hospital in the first place. I began to think about my interactions with Rollie as if they were a performance artwork and to get a sense that I had been missing something important. This rebellious, angry boy was, it seemed to me, creating chaos and isolation through his actions and in his images. I decided to approach Rollie in a different way. I wanted to change my part in the drama. Rather than be the victim of his anger and disruption, I decided that I wanted to play the part of a container and mentor. I wanted to provide him with acceptance, structure and relationship.

The next afternoon as he entered the studio I said, "Rollie, we're going to change directions a little bit here in the studio. I'm not very happy with how things are going for you, so I am going to help you out a little."

"I don't need any help from you," he snarled.

"Well, I don't agree with you, Rollie. But whether you like it or not, I am going to work with you for awhile."

He started gathering paint containers and brushes.

I said, "Rollie, you aren't going to need those things today. You see I've been thinking about you a lot. I think you might have some good skills, but you don't use them very well."

He glared at me. "What are you talkin' about, man?"

"I haven't been keeping score, but I think you've done at least ten or eleven of these splatter paintings since you've been here. Not one of them is, in my view, very well thought out, and technically, you have made a lot of mistakes. You know, you should take a look at the work of Jackson Pollack sometime. But even worse than all that, you seem to just be doing the same thing over and over again."

"Who gives a flying fuck?" He mumbled.

"I do, Rollie," I interrupted. "It's sort of like how I think you'd feel if you let somebody who doesn't know how to play the guitar play your Fender." (I knew his electric guitar was one of the most important things in his life.) "They could strum on the strings and move their fingers on the fretboard, they might make a lot of noise, but it would not be music."

He stared at me. "Is that how you think my paintings are?"

"Yes," I said. "They are okay, but they aren't the kind of music you could make. So let's put the tempera paints away and start to work."

In this vignette, Rollie manifested several rebellious resistance behaviors. He misused media, controlled the space by working in an aggressive and messy manner, refused to take suggestions or support from the artist-therapist, used aggressive and foul language to keep others at a distance, and relied on an artistic style that was safe and repetitive. The underlying intentions of these behaviors were to help him maintain his distance from an adult (me) and to disrupt the therapeutic structure of the arts studio. If he had been successful in his rebellious resistance, he would have been able to keep the focus on his outward actions and away from his inner feelings that were the cause of his hospitalization. It is important to note that while nearly all adolescents expend a tremendous amount of energy in their efforts to defeat the therapeutic structure, it is also true that those same adolescents usually harbor an equally strong desire to be taken care of, contained and won over by the therapeutic structure. This is the paradox of the rebellious adolescent.

2. **I'm in the In Crowd–You're in the Out Crowd.** Adolescents who are in treatment facilities frequently use clique formation as a powerful resistance behavior in an effort to neutralize the therapeutic structure of the arts studio. The In Crowd–Out Crowd resistance involves adolescents in the formation of small, exclusive subgroups within the therapeutic milieu. The primary role of the In-Crowd clique is to impede or preclude patient-therapist interaction and relationship development. Invariably the adolescent employing this behavior places himself or herself in the "In Crowd" while casting the adult artist-therapist in the "Out Crowd." The adolescent then invests his interest and attention (transference) in his peers, thus excluding the adult caregiver. Clique formation may also serve as an expression of territorial needs, and occasionally as a catalyst for group rebellion. The "In Crowd" may be comprised of all adolescents in the studio at a given time, or may be restricted to an exclusive one-to-one relationship. The essential negative quality of the clique is that it creates a confidential group in which important intimacies are shared among members but from which the artist-therapist is excluded.

The "In Crowd–Out Crowd" resistance pattern is based on the adolescent's misconception that adults cannot understand him and will not help him. The underlying message from the adolescent seems to be, "Since I do not trust that adults will be of any use to me, I will relate only to my peers whom I believe can understand me, and I will exclude adults from my life and thereby prove that they are of no help." Artist-therapists who are working in the therapeutic arts studio with groups of adolescents will experience this form of resistance as intensely uncomfortable. They will enter the room and suddenly the group will fall silent. They will be the recipient of cold, rejecting glares and the sometimes subtle, sometimes overt, pressure to "leave us alone" will be intense. In responding to this form of resistance, it is essential that the therapist not personalize these uncomfortable encounters. It is not the specific art therapist who is being excluded but rather, most (or all) of the adult world.

As a general rule, the establishment of cliques, exclusive boy-girl relationships, and intense one-to-one peer relationships in the arts studio should be discouraged by the artist-therapist in most cases, and actively intervened in whenever it appears that these relationships are gaining undue intensity of affect. This is based upon the observation that these relationships interfere with the therapeutic structure of the studio.

The reason for intervening in cliques and exclusive peer relationships is that they represent an effort on the part of the adolescent to avoid the central issues of self-esteem, abandonment and loss of control that are at the core of their need for therapy. Intense subgroups and intimate relationships provide a false deflection from feelings of inadequacy and incompetence. Being a part of an "in crowd" or a boy-girl relationship also serves to defend against underlying conflicts about loss and abandonment. Essentially, these concentrated relationships insulate the adolescent from the pain associated with working through and dealing with the underlying core conflicts that have brought them into treatment.

There are two aspects of dealing with adolescent resistance in the form of cliques and couples that have to be understood in order for the art therapist to deal effectively with these phenomena. I must emphasize that these are minimum things that must be dealt with. When the arts studio is running smoothly, more complex interventions can be made. First, it must be understood and appreciated that clique formation and coupling behaviors represent resistance through symbiosis. Adolescents who may have very different individual issues share the problem of having insufficient strength to cope with the inner turmoil that is stirred by an effective arts therapy treatment program. As adolescents begin to confront their inner life through the images and objects they create and experience the containing qualities of the studio structure, the core issues mentioned above become accessible to both patients and the artist-therapist. In reaction to this the adolescent's anxiety level typically increases to near panic proportions. At this point, the adolescent is most susceptible to using cliques and intense peer relationships to absorb this anxiety. The exclusive relationship(s) become the focal point of their interactions in the studio rather than the core issues of their therapy.

The intense relationships formed both in cliques and in boy-girl sub-grouping serve the adolescent by disguising inner feelings of inadequacy and separation-individuation issues through aggressive dependency. The false security brought on by the belief that "my friends will take care of me" or "somebody loves me" allows the adolescent to ignore the deeper, more painful realities of his or her existence.

Another dynamic often seen as a result of "In Group–Out Group" behavior is that of splitting. The adolescent divides the world into those who are in and those who are out. Often there are sudden shifts where at one moment nothing bad can be said about the members of the clique, then the next moment nothing good can be said. This is because the view of their peers is either idealized or devalued. Typically, the artist-therapist is cast into the "Out Group" on the basis of being an adult, but it is also possible that the idealizing-devaluing phenomena will apply to the artist-therapist as well as to peers.

The second aspect of dealing with clique formation and subgrouping that is necessary for the artist-therapist to understand is in relation to the therapist's own thoughts and feelings about intense relationships. That is, artist-therapists must be aware of their own feelings about inclusion, exclusion and sexuality and how these might influence how they respond to subgrouping in the therapeutic arts studio. When one's own feelings are not dealt with properly, one of two patterns emerge: the artist-therapist engages in either denial or indulgence.

The artist-therapist who is in denial about the negative effects of subgrouping literally does not see what is going on in the arts studio. In this situation, there is a lack of supervision in the studio. A central tenet of dealing effectively with adolescents is, *if as an adult therapist, you do not comment on an adolescent's behavior, the adolescent will assume you approve of the behavior.* But, the artist-therapist who is in denial does not hear or respond in the way she should. The therapist ignores hostile or sexual jokes and comments, and sometimes even participates in them. There is meaning beneath this therapist' denial that is very important. Denial is a fear of the infantile rage that might be expressed by the adolescent if she is asked to put off gratification and is expected to deal with the real underlying issues of self-esteem, loss of control, and loneliness.

Another form of their own denial that artist-therapists must be aware of in relation to the subgrouping phenomenon is related to the severity of illness or dysfunction in the adolescent. Teenagers who are referred to outpatient clinics, or hospitalized, generally have a very long and tough road ahead of them. There are horrible odds against them. Artist-therapists need to be honest in their assessment and aware of their own feelings of inadequacy as a treaters. They must not be seduced by the superficial improvement that comes as the adolescent settles into an "in group" or a "special relationship." Even though the adolescent might be more cooperative or cause less disruption due to finding a "niche," this is not lasting change. To put it another way, if an adolescent is genuinely capable of establishing meaningful relationships with peers, or if an adolescent is really able to be in love, she probably does not belong in the art therapy studio.

In summary, my approach to "In Group–Out Group" resistance behaviors is a conservative one. If I must err, I prefer to err on the side of intervention and interruption rather than overleniency. I know that for many art therapists this is a very difficult area to intervene in because it is an area in which many people have unresolved conflicts of their own. Still, the risks of nonintervention are many. If patients are allowed to focus all of their emotional energy and attention on their friends in the "in group" or if all their concentration is directed toward their boyfriend or girlfriend, then very little therapy will occur. It is imperative that artist-therapists see these behaviors as resistance and actively intervene in cliques and intense one-to-one relationships because, if ignored, the power of these relationships will lead to further acting out behaviors.

Tiffany's Gang

Tiffany entered the studio group after having been in the hospital for several weeks. She was a pretty, street-wise and subtly hostile four-teen-year-old. Before she came into the arts studio, she had remained distant and unattached to anyone on her treatment team. This was not her first hospitalization. She'd been in two other psychiatric institutions before coming to Harding. Her primary difficulties were identified as marijuana abuse, intense dependency on her mother, sexual promiscuity and gang activity. Tiffany had engaged in antisocial behaviors including vandalism, theft and assault.

Her principal modes of relating to the treatment staff and her peers were two-fold. She alternated between angry superficiality and a provocative, seductive style. Both served her well in keeping others at a safe distance from any genuine relationship with her.

On her first day in the art studio, these two behavioral styles were enacted clearly. As I stood holding the door open as the group of adolescents approached, I overheard Tiffany ask one of her peers, "So what do we have to do here to get our way?" As she reached the steps of the studio porch she flashed me a hostile, derisive grin. I introduced myself. "Tiffany, my name is Bruce. I am an artist. Welcome to the studio. Let me get everyone started and then I will give you a tour of the building."

"Oh, don't bother. I'll find my way around." She said.

I did not react to that. In a few minutes I found Tiffany sitting at one of the tables with a group of three or four others. She was using colored pencils to draw a marijuana leaf. Generally, I don't allow adolescents to portray drugs or drug paraphernalia in the studio groups because this sets up an atmosphere of negativity.

As I approached, a hush fell over the table. "Well, I see you found some materials to work with, Tiffany. I'm glad, but I am going to ask you to start over again. You see, out here in the studio we want people to be working on important things."

She looked up at me, "So what important thing would you like for me to do?"

"Well, how about something about your feelings."

This brought a round of snickering from the group. Tiffany glanced around the table at her peers, surreptitiously gathering their support. "What is he talking about?" She asked them. This inspired open laughter from her cohorts. My face flushed and I felt an immediate anger toward Tiffany, and a sense of betrayal by her peers with whom I had already established relationships. It was as if her entry into the studio had brought about a group regression and my hard work was being poured down the drain. I was clearly in the "out group."

The next day, Tiffany was entered into the expressive arts psychotherapy group I co-led with a colleague. The group was comprised of six adolescent girls, my co-therapist, who was a female, and me. The drawing topic for that session was to, "make an image of yourself looking in the mirror." Tiffany quickly gathered chalk and drew a representation of herself standing naked before a full-length mirror (Figure 12). In her picture the figure was holding a towel and appeared to be drying her hair. The image had an erotic and sensual quality. After everyone had finished drawing, the group gathered to share their images with one another. When it was Tiffany's turn to talk about her drawing she said, "Mmm, that looks great! I love to take showers." Then she smiled at me.

Figure 12. Figure in the mirror.

Intuiting that something important was happening, my co-therapist asked Tiffany if she would give her drawing a voice. "What would it say, Tiffany?"

Her smile disappeared momentarily, but she did not respond to my colleague. Instead, she turned to me and asked, "Mr. Artist, what does my drawing make you think about?"

My co-therapist intervened, "Tiffany, you draw very well. I think it is interesting that of all the people in the group you singled out Bruce, the only man in our group, to ask your question of."

"Your point?" Tiffany said derisively.

She responded in a matter of fact tone, "I'm not really trying to make a point. I just think your drawing is rather sexual, and I wonder why you were only interested in what Bruce had to say about it. That's all."

Tiffany turned to her fellow group members, "Do we have to put up with this?" Although none of her peers responded openly to Tiffany's question, it was clear that for the rest of the session they aligned themselves with her. In our postgroup discussion, my cotherapist commented that she had felt as if we were "psycho-dentists" trying to pull the teeth of our group members.

It so happened that I was away on vacation for the next three sessions of the group. The girls seized this opportunity and acted out all of their hostility toward maternal figures on my colleague. This was not an easy time for her. However, it was a crucial opportunity to see the struggles of these girls acted out on the therapeutic stage. Tiffany was the most malicious of the six as she dumped years of rage and frustration on my cotherapist. She became the unelected leader of the resistance movement in the group.

When I returned from my vacation, as I saw each girl in passing, there was a spew of, "Oh Bruce, expressive art group was so stupid... boring"... etc. It was clear that the dynamic of "In Group–Out Group" resistance was in full operation. My colleague had been cast into the out group where she was being devalued and discounted. The patient's sharing of their "boredom" with me seemed to signal that I was being included in the in group, probably in an effort to further exclude my co-therapist.

As my cotherapist and I discussed how we would respond to this form of resistance, we spent much time trying to discern the metaphoric messages that the group members had communicated during my absence. In thinking through the possible meanings of the drama that the girls in the group had enacted, several themes emerged, but the most prominent seemed to be hostility toward female authority figures (mothers) for not providing what they needed. We decided that we would respond to this expression by focusing the next session on the creation of modern fairy tales.

After our initial rituals of closing the door to the group room, sitting in a circle and asking how each member of the group was feeling, I said, "Today I want us to make up and draw a fairy tale. Fairy tales, as you know, are stories about really important things in life that are told to kids as a way to help them get ready for the world." My cotherapist and I then gave several examples of fairy tale themes. I went on, "It is important that you have yourself be the heroine of your tale and that you think about who the 'bad guys' should be."

The girls got to work quickly on their stories and illustrations. After nearly an hour of intense creative work, the girls decided that they should share their stories. It was no surprise that the majority of the tales that emerged dealt with an evil witch-like character who was at odds with the heroine. Initially, there was an atmosphere of child-like playfulness and levity as the members of the group told their stories. But gradually, as story followed story, an undertone of sadness seemed to surface. By the time it was Tiffany's turn to talk about her drawing, the mood in the room had changed markedly. Tiffany divided her paper into four sections in which she portrayed scenes from her fairy tale. The basic jist of her story revolved around a sadistic "rock and roll queen" who commanded all of her subjects to bow down, sing songs and pray to her. The fourth section of her drawing depicted the heroine standing alone on an empty plane, staring upward into a dark star-less sky. In commenting on this section of her drawing, Tiffany said, "It doesn't matter how good you sing or how hard you pray, the bitch never answers your prayers."

My cotherapist gently reached out and touched Tiffany's drawing and asked, "What do you pray for?"

Tiffany sighed, "Just be here."

My co-therapist responded, "Tiffany, I wish I could draw myself into this section. The caption would read, I am not going anywhere."

Tiffany did not, could not, reply, but from that moment on the atmosphere of that group began to change.

The "In Crowd—Out Crowd" resistance pattern was an expression of Tiffany's misconception that adults could not understand her and would not help her. The underlying message from Tiffany seemed to be, "Since I know that adults, expecially adult women, will be of no use to me, I will only relate to my peers because I believe they can understand me, and I will exclude adults from my life. This will prove that they are of no help." My cotherapist and I could never have talked Tiffany out of this stance. However, we were able to adequately understand the metaphoric meaning of her behaviors and to respond with an appropriate artistic activity that allowed her to work through the issues metaphorically.

3. **Compliant Surrender/ I'll Do Anything You Want.** A particularly difficult resistance maneuver that is sometimes used by adolescents is that of compliant surrender. This pattern of behavior is marked by what seems to be an immediate readiness to use the therapeutic structure of the arts studio. These adolescents easily comply with the expectations and rules of the studio, display an eagerness to actively involve and often express an unwarranted sense of gratitude and appreciation of the efforts of the artist-therapist. Such patients attempt to mirror the values (artistic and otherwise) of the art therapist. The adolescent engaged in compliant surrender resistance presents particular difficulties for an artist-therapist. On the one hand, they seem to do everything that is expected of them and seldom do anything that requires redirection or confrontation. On the other hand, they are often part of a milieu in which there are other adolescents who are indeed acting out in negative, disruptive and easily observable ways. The art therapist may be tempted to leave well enough alone—to not stir up anything with the compliant, surrendering patient In a sense, unless the art therapist is experienced and knowledgeable, she may become the unwitting ally of the patient's resistance. It is as if the adolescent has learned to beat the therapeutic system by "out-adulting" the adult treater. Needless to say, if such resistances are not dealt with effectively, the adolescent remains untouched by the therapeutic agents of the studio.

When an adolescent is engaged in compliant surrender, it is of the utmost importance that the art therapist work toward helping the patient discover and understand the meaning of his or her compliant surrender. This, of course, involves exploring with the adolescent the ways he or she uses the yielding behavior to obscure deeper emotional issues and to manipulatively soothe the artist-therapist. Rinsley (1980) notes that a danger in moving in on the adolescent's compliance is that the child's initial response is often expressed by the message, "So, you want me to be bad eh?"(p. 10). In response, the adolescent is quick to deduce that any therapist who would want her to be bad must be crazy and therefore cannot really be of much help.

Connie and Her Ugliness

One such adolescent, a fifteen-year-old "perfect" patient, entered the hospital because she was having extreme difficulty with her eating behaviors. She was a gymnast and who had been harshly criticized by her coach for gaining too much weight in the off-season. Due to her deep commitment to her sport, Connie had immediately placed herself on a strict diet. This eventually led to excessive restricting of her food intake and eventually to vomiting after meals.

In the arts studio, she was the epitome of the cute, pleasant, sweet, witty and outgoing girl. At the end of her first session in the studio, she thanked me profusely, told me what a good experience it had been and that she was really looking forward to tomorrow because she knew she was going to learn so much about painting from me. As the days passed, she was the model student. She quickly adopted an artistic style similar to mine, complimented me on my work and commented, "surely you must have studied with Edward Hopper." I was, of course, pleased by her artistic prowess and flattered by her appreciation of my work. Beneath the surface, however, I sensed there swirled ever-mounting currents of self loathing, rage and hostility.

On the unit, Connie was also a "favorite" child, until the day the nurse discovered she had been lining her clothing with lead fishing sinkers in order to fool the scales during the daily weigh-in. It was discovered that she had in fact been consistently losing weight while in the hospital. At the next treatment team meeting, I shared with my colleagues how Connie had been doing very well in the arts studio, but that I had a vague feeling that hidden behind her sweet facade there were some very powerful and sour emotions. Other members of the team recounted similar stories and reactions to Connie's compliance. It was evident that the entire team had been bamboozled by Connie's surrender. The doctor who served as the team leader suggested that we all needed to rethink our involvement with Connie and make efforts to help her get in touch with the deeper emotional issues.

The next day, as Connie entered the art studio and after we had exchanged greetings, I said to her, "Connie, I've been thinking a lot about what your next project should be."

"Oh, but I already know. I want to..."

I interrupted. "I know, we talked about your wanting to paint a unicorn yesterday, but I have a better idea."

She looked at me suspiciously but said, "Okay, whatever you say."

"Good. What I'd like for you to do is create the ugliest painting you can imagine. Just use lines and shapes and colors, no objects."

"Bruce, I don't want to do that." She smiled. "I want to do the unicorn so I can give it to my little sister. She loves unicorns."

"Well, maybe you'll get to that later, Connie. But for now, I want you do the ugly painting."

With persistent and consistent interventions directed toward her compliant surrender, Connie developed into an openly manipulative girl who was adept at getting her peers caught up in the drama of her rage.

The painting she created in response to the "ugly assignment" was indeed an unpleasant image. She covered her Masonite board with thick globs of brown, black, red, and blue paint. Over these she used red to make slashing, fiery lines. Connie added sawdust to her wet paint in order to give it a coarse texture. She incorporated coffee grounds and at one point hissed that she was going to bring flecks of vomit to add to the piece. Throughout the process, she became increasingly vocal in her anger at me for "making her do this damned thing."

One day several of her peers approached me and asked me to "back off" Connie and let her do what she wanted. Later in that session, I overheard her ask another girl what my reaction to that had been. When her peer told her I had simply reminded them that I was the art therapist and that I would decide what was best, Connie said, "Maybe I have to up the ante."

At that point I made my presence known and said, "Connie, don't you have some ugly work to do?"

Connie worked on that painting for a couple weeks. One afternoon, as she was nearing completion of it, I noticed she was using a thin white wash to make small droplets on the surface. Although by that point our relationship was considerably less congenial than it had been, I said, "Yowsa, Connie, that stuff you are doing now looks very different than the rest of the painting."

Figure 13. Connie's ugly cum.

Without looking up from the canvas she said, "It's cum" (Figure 13).
"Hmmm," I said. "Sort of an odd place for it."
She turned toward me, glared, "It is saying FUCK YOU!"
I responded. "Connie, you sure are angry. I think that's good. I don't exactly know why, but it seems to me like you have a lot of things to be angry about."
"What would you know about it?"
"Well Connie, I know that if you keep starving yourself that eventually you will die. How much more angry can you get? And, I believe everything we create is a partial self-portrait. So, what I mean is, if all that stuff wasn't inside of you, you wouldn't be able to paint it."
Subsequent work in the art therapy studio helped Connie get in touch with and express the rage she felt toward her parents, teachers and coaches for having made her try to be a combination "Barbie Doll and Kerrie Strug all rolled into one." Much later in Connie's therapy she unearthed anger specifically directed toward her mother for hav-

ing used her to be what mother had failed to be in her life, and as a result disrupt her normal development as an adolescent girl.

Again, none of these issues could have been dealt with had the resistance pattern of compliant surrender not been identified and worked through. In the arts studio, thinking of her journey as a performance art event helped me to weather the ugliness that lurked beneath her pleasant surface.

4. ***Running Away/Catch Me If You Can.*** Running away from home is a fairly common behavior in many of the adolescents who are in need of therapy. When we think of this behavior as a performance, we are reminded of the dramatic intensity of the adolescent's feelings. Of course, not every episode of runaway behavior is the same, and indeed there are at least two forms of running away resistance: (1) Literal and (2) Metaphoric.

The literal process of running away from home can be a relatively benign reaction to a specific conflict or event, as when the adolescent runs away to the neighbor's house. It can also be an extremely destructive overreaction that places the adolescent in dangerous circumstances, as when the child accepts rides or a place to stay from exploitative adults. Although few adolescents can articulate it, one of the underlying messages of running away is that it is often an event aimed at determining whether or not the parents or the therapist really care about them. The running away drama insures that the adult world will take notice. At the same time, the adolescent may unconsciously hope he will be found and that the circumstances that prompted the episode will be effectively attended to as a result of the runaway drama. It is imperative that artist-therapists respond to the drama by making efforts to understand the storyline of the performance, rather than reacting to it in a punitive manner.

The metaphoric process of running away is seen in those adolescents who, despite their physical presence in the arts studio, consistently keep themselves "not there" in relation to the structure of the artistic milieu. Metaphoric running away may take one of many forms ranging from passive nonparticipation, to provocative negativism, to daydreaming, to outright refusal to attend the session. It is my experience that in the arts studio, one of the most prominent underlying purposes of metaphoric running away behavior is that of helping the patient figure out if the artist-therapist is being genuine when expressing concern for the adolescent. If the art therapist reacts to the patient's resistance in a retaliatory manner, then the adolescent can rest assured that the art therapist can be of no real help to him.

The Franky Walk

Franky was thirteen years old when he was admitted to the hospital. During the admission interview, his parents told the social worker they were very worried about him because he had been having a lot of difficulties in his new school, a middle school. They said that while he had never done very well in school due to his learning difficulties, he had not been a behavioral problem until that year. They also shared that over the past couple of months he had run away from home three times. The last time he had hitched a ride with a trucker and had wound up in Georgia. It was this last runaway episode that had prompted the parents bringing him to the hospital.

Unfortunately, Franky's family had very little in the way of insurance resources and so it was clear that he would be in the hospital only for a few days. During that time, Franky basically coasted, doing the bare minimum required to get along but not really engaging in any meaningful way in anything.

On the second day of his hospitalization, I administered a projective art assessment with Franky. Although he did not involve enthusiastically in the process, he did enough work so that I was able to write a credible narrative report that poetically described how I thought Franky saw the world. The most telling of his drawings in the assessment session was in response to my request that he portray a good and a bad memory from his life. Using colored pencils, he divided his paper in half with a thick, multicolored line. On the left side of the page he drew a sketch of himself lying on a grassy hill. A bright yellow sun was in the clear blue sky above him. Beneath this drawing he printed, "July 14, 1995 - GOOD."

On the right side of the paper he used brown, black, blue, and purple to draw a simple schema of his school building entrance. In front of the large doors he added a small red stick figure with a cartoon dialogue bubble above the head. In the bubble he drew question marks, exclamation marks, stars, and X's. Surrounding the red stick figure he then added fifteen dark blue stick figures. Below this drawing he printed, "Sept.6, 1995 - BAD!" (Figure 14).

Figure 14. Franky's good and bad memory.

When I asked Franky if he wanted to tell me a story about his good and bad memory drawings, he merely shoved the paper across the table toward me and said, "You figure it out." I made a couple other attempts to engage him in talking about his work, but he consistently deflected my efforts.

The following is a brief excerpt from the Projective Art Assessment Narrative Report I wrote about Franky:

For his second artistic task, Franky was asked to create an image of a good and a bad memory from his life. He chose to use colored pencils for this task. The colored pencil is a medium which affords the artist much control and can lend itself, in a somewhat restrained manner, to emotional expression. This selection, as opposed to the rather inhibited media he used for his first drawing, may suggest that good memory/bad memory topic holds more emotional energy for Franky. Clearly he invested more energy in this drawing process than in any other task during the ssessment session.

It seems significant that the two memory images he drew are both quite recent. It also may be important that his drawing style was markedly different in the two images. The good memory image is done in a manner that is typical of children in the Pseudo-Naturalistic developmental stage, i.e., appropriate for his chronological age. The bad memory image is suggestive of the Schematic developmental stage generally associated with children ages 7 - 9 years. This may suggest that Franky's response to the feelings associated with the bad memory may be expressed in age-inappropriate behaviors.

For his good memory image, Franky drew a picture of a human figure, perhaps himself, lying in the grass on what appears to be a warm summer day. The colors he used are in the warm range and the overall emotional tone of this image is pleasant, peaceful and relaxed. Symbolically, this drawing raises themes of tranquillity, summer, freedom from school, solitude and isolation. He labeled the drawing, July 14 - GOOD, which may denote the approximate middle of summer vacation.

For his bad memory image, Franky drew what appears to be an image of the front of a school building. The focus in this drawing is on two large doors with several stick figures in front of them. One of the figures is drawn with red, the others are done in dark blue. The red figure, perhaps representing himself, has a cartoon dialogue bubble above its head filled with punctuation marks, stars and X's. These are presented in such a way as to suggest inner confusion or disorientation.

The emotional tone of this image is rather painful, confusing, overwhelming and lonely. Symbolically, the fact that this drawing is done in a style typical of children much younger than Franky suggests that his experience of entering the school is a difficult, overwhelming and disorienting one for him. This may be confirmed by his labeling the drawing Sept. 6, 1995 - BAD, which was the first day of school this past fall. His difficulties may be due to his having entered middle school this year and therefore having to navigate a number of classrooms and teachers as opposed to being held in one classroom, as was the case in elementary school. Franky's artistic developmental style in this drawing might also suggest that he has some learning difficulties.

In the summary of the narrative report, I commented that my encounter with Franky, coupled with my sense of what he had expressed in his drawings, had left me feeling that Franky was a pretty lonely boy who felt quite ill-equipped to handle the pressures of middle school. His feelings of inadequacy were, I suspect, exacerbated by the physical changes that were occurring in him at that time and the emotional confusion that so often accompanies the hormonal explosion of early adolescence. I also suggested that, "...his inner feelings of frustration and his negative sense of self might lead to increasingly dangerous episodes of acting-out behavior if they are not attended to in a psychotherapeutic context."

Two or three months after Franky was discharged from the hospital, his father called me to ask if I knew of any art therapists practicing in their community, or if I would be willing to see Franky as an outpatient. The family lived in a very rural part of southern Ohio, and unfortunately there were no art therapists in the town closest to them. Despite the fact that they were over two hours away from my studio, the father made an appointment for four o'clock on Wednesday of the following week. "Things just aren't going well," he said. "We have to do something!"

Wednesday came, four o'clock came...four-fifteen...four-thirty. My telephone rang. Franky's mother was on the line. "I am very sorry, Mr. Moon, but we can't find him anywhere."

I offered her my support and told her that if there was any way I could be helpful I would be glad to do so. "Do you want to make another appointment?"

"Yes, let's hope for the best and try again for the same time next week."

I received a call later that week from Franky's father assuring me that he would be at the next appointment.

When 4:00 Wednesday arrived I was mildly irritated that again Franky did not appear at the studio. However, at about 4:10 I heard a car horn honking outside. I went to the door and could see Franky sitting in the back seat of his parents' car, looking straight ahead. His mother appeared to be scolding him from the driver's seat. When she saw me looking out through the doorway she beckoned me to the car. As I approached, she lowered the window and with an exasperated tone she said, "He won't get out of the car!" She added, "This is so embarrassing."

Keeping in mind that I was witnessing a performance art event, I suggested she pull into the parking lot. As she parked the car, I went back into the studio and gathered two sketchbooks and some pieces of charcoal. By the time I rejoined them, Franky's mother had exited the car. I said, "I know this must be hard on you. If you'd like, why don't you go have a cup of coffee in the waiting area and try to relax."

She glanced toward the car, "What are you going to do with him?"

I replied honestly, "I am not sure. But first I think I will just try to be where he is."

She grimaced. "Emotionally, you mean?"

"No," I said. "I am going to get into the back seat with him."

As Franky's mother headed off to the waiting room, I climbed into the back seat of the car. "Hey Franky, long time no see."

He shifted his position slightly and said, "You are wastin' your time. I don' wanna be here."

"Yeah, Franky, I sorta got that idea last week. Where did you end up this time anyway?"

He half-smiled, "Not far really. I was trying to get to the Eastland Mall in Columbus."

"Hmmm, now that's interesting."

"How so?"

"Well, it is interesting that your parents wanted to bring you to Columbus to see me and you decided to run away to Columbus."

"Just a coincidence," he grunted.

I offered him a sketch pad and charcoal. "Well, as long as you are here, do you want to do some drawing?"

He looked at me as if I was nuts. "In here? My mom will shit a brick if we get chalk dust on her seats."

"Franky, it seems like you aren't interested in going into the studio. So as long as you are here I figured we might as well do something."

"I told you, I am not gonna do anything."

"Okay," I said. "I tell you what, I think that I will just do a drawing of you then, if you don't mind." With that, I began to draw.

We sat in silence for a few minutes. Then Franky said, "This is stupid.

I'm gonna take a walk." He got out of the car and began to walk toward the wooded ravine that runs through the hospital grounds.

I put down my pad and followed. He glanced back over his shoulder every few moments, but whenever I tried to quicken my pace to catch up with him he would match my speed. Franky did not try to run, or even walk fast enough to lose me in the woods, but he did keep his distance. So, for the rest of the hour I followed him around. At one point in our follow-the-leader session I could almost hear the Dave Clark Five singing, "Here they come again, hmmm, Catch us if you can, hmmm."

The next several sessions went much like the first. Each time I would begin to make a sketch of Franky and he would then evacuate the car and walk. What was especially interesting to me was that our walking time gradually decreased and my drawing time increased. It was imperative during these walking art therapy encounters that I made every effort to accept Franky's behavior and not react in a punitive or shaming manner. It seemed evident to me that something important was happening, even though I did not know what that something was. Eventually he began to draw for a little while himself. We would sit in the back of his mother's car, draw for a bit, talk very little, and then walk. The drama Franky enacted was really about testing the adult, me, to see how I would respond to him. Would I reject him, or try to have him rehospitalized, or would I go along on the journey with him? After several months he allowed me to walk beside him through the ravine and eventually he abandoned the car altogether and our sessions would begin in the art studio.

What Franky had been running away from, of course, were the potent feelings of self-loathing, frustration, loss and anger that had been brought on by the transition from elementary school, to middle school, coupled with the emotional turmoil that accompanies puberty. In the relatively small and contained classroom atmosphere of elementary school he had been able to cope with his learning difficulties and receive enough individual attention from his teacher that he was able to get by, both academically and socially. However, in the larger middle school, where he had to change classrooms every forty-five minutes, learn the whereabouts of each room, and establish relationships with several different teachers, he had been completely overwhelmed. One particularly poignant drawing Franky did about these issues portrayed him standing in the school hallway, a huge clock falling from above as if to squash him.   As he talked about this drawing, he told me a story about getting lost in the school during the first week. "I knew I was going to be in a lot of trouble, but I just couldn't find my way. I hated it, I felt so stupid."

It is important to remember that Franky used both *literal running away* and *metaphoric running away* resistance patterns. Both forms of running away served to protect him from the pain and confusion he was experiencing related to his difficulties in school. For me, the critical therapeutic tasks were to first be clear that this was a resistance pattern and not juvenile incorrigibility, and second to develop a therapeutic stance that regarded Franky's runaway behaviors as if they were performance art events so that I could freely observe and reflect upon them without becoming controlling or punitive. Third, I had to plan a helpful, therapeutic response that would honor the running away as a significant and inevitable component of the treatment journey that was absolutely necessary for Franky. When it became clear to me that his performance art event was all about running from himself, then I was able to genuinely attend to him and care for him regardless of whether we were in the arts studio or walking through the ravine.

5. **Be My Friend/You Are the Only One Who Understands Me.** The attempt to make the adult art therapist into a "best friend" is another form of resistance often observed in the arts studio. This is a difficult resistance pattern for many art therapists to confront, because we all naturally want to be liked by our patients. Also, due to our background in the arts and our basic sense of ourselves as nonconformists, art therapists tend to want to establish a nonauthoritarian, nonhierarchical relationship with patients. However, we must keep in mind that a professional treatment relationship is not synonymous with personal friendship. When adolescents use you are my friend as a resistance maneuver, the underlying purpose is to devalue the art therapist, who is then seen as being no different than the patient and therefore of no potential benefit.

Shannon's Gift

Several years ago, an art therapy student I worked with developed a special relationship with Shannon, a seventeen-year-old patient. Jill, the art therapy student, was only twenty-two years old herself and inexperienced, so she viewed the establishment of a friendship with Shannon as a natural and positive occurrence. Shannon was laudatory in her praise of Jill as being "the one person on the staff that she could really trust and talk with."

The relationship might have gone along benignly had it not been for the following event. During an expressive arts group therapy session, Shannon revealed to the group that her adult boyfriend worked at a popular bar and restaurant on the campus of Ohio State University. After the session, as Jill escorted Shannon back to her cottage, Jill ill-advisedly mentioned that she often frequented the establishment where Shannon's boyfriend worked. Later, Shannon talked with her boyfriend about Jill and the boyfriend commented that, "Oh yeah, she's a big Wild Turkey drinker."

A few days later, Shannon asked Jill to take her on a walk around the grounds. As they were walking, Shannon presented Jill with an unopened bottle of Wild Turkey as a gift of appreciation for all Jill had done for her. Jill was taken aback, but did not know how to handle the situation. She did not want to alienate Shannon or damage the relationship, but she had a very bad feeling about accepting the liquor. Jill was clear that the rules of the hospital strictly forbade alcoholic beverages on the hospital grounds. Not knowing what to do, Jill stashed the bottle in her coat pocket, hoping no one had seen it.

The next week things were not going well for Shannon. She had had an ugly argument with her parents during a family therapy session, and she was having conflicts with her peers on the unit. During an art therapy session she confided to Jill that she was having suicidal thoughts again. Still, as Jill was escorting Shannon back to the cottage after the session Shannon asked her to "tell the treatment team that I am doing good enough to go on an off-grounds pass this week end. I really need to get away from here for awhile."

Jill replied, "But Shannon, you just told me you were thinking about killing yourself. I couldn't tell the team that you should go off grounds."

Shannon stopped walking, "Oh yes you will, Jill. I need you to."

Jill said, "But I can't."

Shannon said, "Either you do what I ask, or I will tell my doctor about the Wild Turkey I gave you. That wouldn't look so good for you now, would it?"

Jill was shocked.

Later that afternoon, Jill tearfully approached me with the story of the alcohol and the demand from Shannon. She was very hurt by Shannon's manipulation and felt both embarrassed and betrayed. She had learned a hard lesson about the difference between professional and personal relationships.

Other examples of adolescents' attempts to make the art therapist their friend rather than their therapist can be observed as patients attempt to engage the artist-therapist in social banter, or in off-color joke telling, or when they ask personal historical questions of the therapist. An illustration of the latter of these resistance maneuvers comes from an art therapy studio session: Several adolescents and I had been talking about rock and roll music. One boy asked if I liked Jimi Hendrix. As soon as I said yes, he loudly suggested that, "Bruce, you

look like you were a child of the sixties, you must have smoked a little weed in your day."

Many inexperienced art therapists get caught in such traps. As a
therapist, regardless of what one's personal history is with such issues,
one must always ask a couple questions. "How can I respond to such
a query in a manner that is therapeutically beneficial to the patient?
What is the patient's motivation in making such an inquiry? Should I
tell the truth? Can a lie be therapeutic?"

My response to the patient's attempt to cast me in the role of a
friend rather than as an art therapist was to say, "It's nice that you are
interested in my life, but really here in the arts studio my past is not
the issue. Your feelings and your experiences are what are most important here."

My colleague, Debbie DeBrular, used to handle such situations
more bluntly. She would simply say to the patient, "Let's be clear, I am
your therapist, not your friend."

Regardless of how an individual art therapist chooses to respond to
this resistance maneuver, it is most important that they clearly identify the patient's urge to friendship as a resistance. One simply does not
do therapy with one's friends. Therefore the adolescent's efforts to
engage the art therapist in a "friendly relationship" are inevitably
efforts to defeat the therapeutic structure of the arts studio.

SUMMARY

As a general rule, it is safe to presume that adolescent people who
are experiencing inner emotional turmoil so intense it manifests itself
in behaviors that parents, or teachers or friends regard as dysfunctional will tend to initially regard the artist-therapist and the structure of
the arts studio as adversaries who must be defended against. Such adolescents are almost always struggling with how they can best deal with
the adult world. As a way of coping with the struggle, disturbed adolescents can be expected to be resistive in the arts studio milieu. The
art therapist working with adolescents must keep in mind that the
basic purposes of resistive behaviors are to present oneself in a manner that denies (1) the existence of disturbing behavioral patterns, (2)
the consequences of the disturbing behaviors and (3) the inner emo-

tional experiences that surround the behaviors. It is essential for artist-therapists to honor the adolescent's resistance behaviors as an inevitable phase of the treatment journey. While it goes without saying that dealing with resistance is often a difficult and unpleasant process for the art therapist, it is absolutely necessary for the adolescent.

In my work with adolescents I have found it extremely helpful to think about resistance behaviors as if they were performance art enactments. When I am able to do this, it frees me to observe and reflect upon the meaning of the performance without becoming enmeshed in the drama itself. Thinking in this way also helps me to remain somewhat detached, to not take personally the overwhelming anger and resentment that often accompanies adolescents in therapy.

It is utterly imperative that art therapists understand that adolescent resistance is often disguised with a variety of subtle and overt behavioral veneers. One must be able to identify the primary patterns of resistance and plan therapeutic response to it. If the adolescent's resistance is not identified and worked through, no genuine therapy will occur. Resistance is inevitable and absolutely necessary for the adolescent. Artist-therapists working with adolescents should strive to always respond but never react to their patients' resistance behaviors. By doing so, art therapists metaverbally assure the patient that (1) they see the patient for who she is; (2) they understand; (3) they will not abandon the adolescent in mid-journey. The artist-therapist who is successful in therapeutically responding to the resistance of the adolescent inevitably is rewarded by the establishment of a solid foundation of trust from the patient.

THE IMAGINING PHASE

The second stage in my model of adolescent art therapy is the imagining phase. Again, it is important to keep in mind that this model of understanding is meant to serve only as an organizing image, or schema, and that there is a constant ebb and flow among the phases. The imagining stage of art therapy with adolescents is interdependent with the preceding resistance phase, and with the following immersion phase of the treatment journey. The hallmark of the imagining phase is a certain sense of sadness and discontinuity that arises as the adolescent begins to come to grips with an awareness of the meaning of the earlier resistance behaviors. This sadness, or what others describe as "therapeutic depression," is healthy; it sensitizes the adolescent to his or her own needs. These needs include a deep longing for support, containment, stability, predictability, and emotional safety. During the imagining stage, the purposes of the therapy gradually dawn upon the adolescent. The adolescent begins to let go of his or her denial of the presence of disturbing behavioral patterns, their consequences and the inner emotional experiences that have surrounded these behaviors. During this phase of treatment, the solid foundation of trust the patient and artist-therapist formed as they weathered the resistance phase together provides a powerful base for *imagining* a different way of being in the world for the adolescent. This imagining a new way of being engages the adolescent and the art therapist in a process of joint consideration of the essence of their work together. As a result of imagining, the adolescent and the artist-therapist develop a sense of their relationship as being a team. During this phase they work together to clarify their purpose, essential values, core beliefs and a sense of the future. As a part of this process, the adolescent and artist-therapist team works to identify the adolescent's current reality from a more ideal reality, or vision, that the adolescent holds for the future.

The imagining phase of the adolescent art therapy journey has two primary but conflicting emotional tones. The one, as I mentioned earlier, is sadness; the other is wonder. Accompanying both of these emotional states is an intensified sense of enlivenment that is a refreshing change from the heaviness and deadening negativity so often present in the resistance phase.

The hard work that being in therapy entails can be tolerated only in the context of a solid relationship foundation. In order for the adolescent to re-imagine her life, to have purpose, she must be able to transcend the self.

The making of art is a transcendent process that depends utterly on imagination. In nearly every circumstance, adolescent artists are interested in the reaction their work will inspire in others. This interest is motivated by the longing for contact with others, for support, stability, predictability and existential and emotional validation.

The structure of the therapeutic arts studio is deeply committed to the establishment of relationship through the process of making art. In Chapter IX, I will discuss this at greater length. A central thrust of our work is promoting relationship, both in our approach to the patient and her art, and in our therapeutic goals and objectives. Making art is a process concerned with community, with deepening relationships. The community of the arts studio invests the artist-therapist with a degree of authority to work with the imaged burdens that the adolescent patients bring. Through the rituals of creating art we engage in a process of acknowledgment of the way our lives are. The most profound aims of painting out the painful pieces of self are to empower the adolescent to grasp the full meaning of current images and to help them re-vision a future.

The imagining phase of the adolescent art therapy journey has three distinct aspects: (1) The denial of disturbing behavior and feelings is gradually abandoned; (2) A solid relationship based on trust and mutual engagement in art making is established; and (3) A healthy vision of how the adolescent might be in the future begins to be formed. This is the work of the imagining phase of the art therapy journey.

Lannie's Vision

Lannie, a sixteen-year-old, had been coming to my outpatient studio art group for a couple of months. She had been a difficult patient to work with because she often skipped her weekly sessions, and when she did attend, she would complain loudly, to anyone who would listen, that she was "B-O-R-E-D!"

My response to her lamentations was always the same, "Lannie, I believe that boredom comes from a lack of quality relationships. I wish you would let yourself not be bored here." I must have said this at least twenty times to her.

At this, Lannie usually scoffed, "Oh my God, you are so predictable. Do you know how boring that is?"

So, I was somewhat surprised when she told me one afternoon that she wanted to make a painting. Before this she had refused all of my efforts to engage her in painting, preferring instead to do small pencil sketches in her diary.

The painting seemed harmless enough. Lannie had covered the canvas with a dark umber. Then she used black, blue and white to depict several pairs of hands placed randomly about the surface.

That session of the outpatient studio group had been a rather wild one. One of the girls had come to the group directly from a family therapy session. Another was all wound up, in anticipation of his first "big date" that weekend. He'd been working up his courage to ask the girl out for weeks. The other five adolescents in the studio were, in varying degrees, depressed, angry and resistive. It was one of those days when I felt I'd earned my salary just by keeping the studio from being demolished.

So, Lannie's low-key work on her painting had not demanded much attention from me. As we were cleaning up she approached me and said quietly, "I'm not sure about this, but before we leave would you take a look at my painting?"

"Of course, Lannie. Just let me make sure I get the tools accounted for and that everybody gets out of the building okay. Did you drive yourself today?"

"Yeah," She replied. "I'm not in any rush today."

When the other patients had left I approached Lannie and her painting.

She looked at me, "I wasn't sure I'd say anything about this to you. It's hard for me to look at."

"Yowsa, Lannie, it doesn't look like you were bored today. You know you don't have to say anything about it if you don't want to."

"I know," she replied. "I've heard you say that stuff enough times."

"I just want you to know that what's most important is the art. It's ok to talk but it's not the main thing here."

"Yeah, I know. But I want to, okay?" She paused. "This is a picture about my family (Figure 15). They are all reaching out, or holding things." She began to cry. "I used to think . . ." More tears.

Figure 15. Lannie's hands.

I reached for the box of tissues from the counter and offered it to her.

"I haven't been very nice to you." She sobbed.

"Lannie, it is okay. I know that being in therapy is hard. Nobody really wants to do it. I am used to people not being very easy to deal with."

She looked at her painting. "Before they got divorced, my mom and dad used to get into these huge fights. They'd scream and call each other horrible things. I had to choose sides...I was afraid . . ." Her body shook with tears. Oh God, it makes me sick."

"You've been through a lot, Lannie."

Silence

"These hands," she said, "are like them. Sometimes all I want is for them to hold me. Other times, I just want them to leave me alone."

Speaking gently to her, I said, "Lannie, sometimes I am absolutely in awe of what happens here in the studio. It is an honor for me to be with here with you."

Lannie said, "This hurts so damn bad. It just makes me want to hurt everybody else."

"Lannie, as you know, I believe a painting is sort of like a self portrait. I also know you can change the picture if you want to."

She dried her eyes and gave me a skeptical look. "What do you mean?"

"You can change the painting, Lannie. You don't have to be held prisoner by the hands. You can change them around on your canvas any way you want.

You can paint fists, paint caresses, paint them waving good-bye or hello, anything you want."

"No, they are the way they should be. But maybe I will do another painting of them."

"I guess I'd better go now. Thanks for listening." With that she left the studio.

In the months that followed, Lannie painted a number of "hands" paintings. They changed in color. She rendered them as fists and gestures of welcome and rebuke. In one of her later works she extended them, as if in a gesture of waving good-bye.

The imagining stage of the art therapy journey is a transitional stage during which we help our patients make images of the way their lives are and encourage them to imagine the way their lives can be. We do not ask them to do this work alone. We accompany. The imagining phase of the adolescent art therapy journey is marked by the conflicting emotional tones of sadness and wonder. Accompanying these emotional states is an intensified sense of being alive that is markedly different from the burdensome negativity of the resistance phase. It is during the imagining phase that the adolescent begins to partially understand the meaning of her past behaviors and current images, and begins to develop a new vision of how she might be in the future. The artist-therapist can be assured that the adolescent has begun to move into the imagining phase of art therapy journey when the patient ceases to deny the presence of disturbing behaviors, is able to graphically express feelings about her behaviors, is able to relate in a trusting manner to the art therapist, is able to meaningfully engage in art making and is able to envision how life might be better for her in the future. This is the work of the imagining phase of the art therapy journey.

THE IMMERSION PHASE

The third phase, Immersion, is heralded by the adolescent patient being able to connect to his or her own inner experiences, and to consistently assume ownership for present emotional and behavioral difficulties. This does not mean the patient will necessarily be able to put these things into words. In fact, more times than not, the immersion phase will be most clearly expressed through actions and images. This is a period of very hard work for the adolescent. The patient in this phase of the art therapy journey gradually lets go of old, negative and defeating self-views and in turn develops new and more positive ones. During this phase, there is usually a marked change in the image content of the adolescent's artistic products.

At first glance, the changes in imagery that occur during the immersion phase may appear to be problematic, if taken out of context. An example of this was seen in the work of a 14-year-old boy who during his resistance phase used his artistic skill as a clever defensive ploy. He was a masterful cartoon and charicature artist who had charmed his peers and the staff with his witty portrayals of life on the unit. As he entered the imagining phase of therapy, he continued to make funny images, but their frequency diminished. The immersion phase, for this boy, was marked by images of loneliness and sadness. This prompted a nurse to comment, "I liked his art a lot more when he first came here." To the untrained observer, the boy's art seemed to become more sullen and depressing as he progressed in therapy. However, in reality the feelings of loneliness and sadness his pictures portrayed were exactly the feelings he needed to express. There would be plenty of time later in his life for caricature and humorous cartoons.

Again, entry into the immersion phase of the art therapy journey is often a stormy period that places much stress on both the adolescent and the artist-therapist. Real immersion into the work of the therapy forces the adolescent to let go of many of the images of self that he or she has grown accustomed to. Generally, during this phase, the patient comes into close contact with the anxiety and guilt that his or her disturbing (resistance) behaviors had held at bay. The art therapy journey engages the teenager in a process of mourning the loss of the "bad" self-view, for no matter how dysfunctional it may have been, at least it was a known entity. Typically, during this phase of art therapy with adolescents, the content of images will either metaphorically or directly relate to evil, badness or destructiveness. It is critical, during the immersion phase, that the art therapist maintain a consistent attitude of acceptance and support. The artist-therapist must be aware of the potency and importance of the turmoil the adolescent is experiencing. Furthermore, the art therapist needs to be always on the lookout for opportunities to promote new and positive self perceptions in the adolescent. If the patient is able to successfully traverse the immersion phase, he or she will emerge with a clearer sense of who he or she is in the world, complete with both positive and negative attributes.

Corey's Dark Place

I was writing in a patient's medical chart late one afternoon when I overheard two nurses talking about a patient I'd been working with for some time. One of the R.N.s handed me a piece of wadded-up lined paper. "Do you approve of this?" she asked.

I opened the paper and found a distorted portrait of the patient Corey. The image was rather disturbing, but I could see she had really put some time into the drawing. It was done with pencil, and the line character, shading techniques and attention to detail were all pretty well done. I knew this patient had been practicing her skills.

The nurse explained that the drawing had been picked out of the trash by one of the housekeeping personnel. She went on to say that the patient, Corey, in her view, "was going downhill fast." Apparently there had been some disruption on the unit earlier that day, and Corey had been really angry and combative.

"So what do think about this drawing?" she asked.

"Well, it's a pretty unsettling picture of Corey, but you have to admit that she is getting better and better with the pencil." I said. "Do you mind if I hold onto this drawing?"

"No, you can have it. I was going to throw it away," the nurse muttered. It was evident from her tone of voice that she had no use for Corey's drawing.

A few days later Corey arrived for her usual appointment in the early evening adolescent art studio. (It should be noted that at this time Corey and I had already worked the Resistance Phase, and it was my sense that the Imagining Phase was blending into the Immersion

Phase. The drawing of her distorted self-portrait, which was markedly different from her previous artwork, seemed to suggest that a transition was occurring.) In planning for this session, I established the following goals for her studio art experience: (1) develop a more positive self-view through mastery of task; (2) expand expressive skills, both graphic and verbal; and (3) promote therapeutic alliance through shared task involvement.

She entered the studio, arms held tightly at her sides, head down, her long dark hair falling across her face. There was always a lot of art hanging on the walls. The studio milieu is a little disordered but stimulating as well. The walls are covered with patients' works, and my colleagues and I also hang our paintings and drawings. The effect is mildly chaotic, resourceful and infectious. At times, the space is cluttered and messy, but this sets the tone for the creative process because it is always in a constant state of reorganization and structuring. In a phenomenal sense, the studio space is a symbol of the role of the arts in therapeutic work, which is the endless process of making sense out of chaos, order from disorder.

"Corey," I said, "any idea of what you'd like to work on today?"

She shrugged but said, " I think I want to try those paint sticks you've been talking about, and some of that big roll of black paper, okay?"

"Sure," I replied, and I helped her gather the materials she'd asked for. We cut a 48" X 48" piece of black kraft paper, and opened a new set of oil paintstiks. She chose to work at the table nearest to where I had set up my easel.

As she settled in, I asked, "So, what you are going to draw?"

"I'm not sure, Bruce. You know I don't really like this black paper, that's why I want to use it."

"What do you mean?"

"I'm not sure. My doctor kept asking me questions the other day, you know stuff about the past. Usually I get so pissed off when he does that. But, for . . . I don't know . . . I didn't get mad. I still didn't answer him! I just sat there like I always do. He thinks he can make me talk . . . he's got another thing comin'. But I wasn't mad, just sort of empty. Not mad. Not sad. Not anything. It was weird."

I started to work on my painting. "Corey, I guess black is a good background color for not feeling anything."

"Yeah, I guess."

"All right," I said. "Let me know if you need anything."

Saying no more, we began to work. As I worked on my painting, I paid close attention to her progress. Corey began by using a dark green oil stick to cover nearly the entire surface. She followed this by adding a layer of deep blue, again over the entire page. Over the deep green and blue she added yet another layer of dark red. She worked with great force, pressing the oil into every pore of the black paper.

By the end of the session the paper was covered with a thick coating of deep color. In the next session she continued to work earnestly on her drawing. She seldom spoke to me or her peers in the studio.

As the days passed the image of a room began to emerge on the page. It was a subtly disquieting image that seemed to evolve out of the intense mottled darkness (Figure 16).

Figure 16. Corey's dark room.

As she was working one evening, she gestured to me and asked me to come over to the table. As I approached she said, "I think I'd better leave now." She looked at her paper.

"What do you mean?" I asked.

Her elbows rested on the table, she cupped her hands and held her face. "I can't look at this anymore."

"I know that feeling," I said. "Sometimes I feel like my paintings are just staring at me, waiting for me to do something."

"No, that's not it, Bruce!" She pulled her hair away from her eyes. "There isn't anything I have to do to this. It is done."

"Hmmm. So, what's the problem?"

She frowned. "There ain't nothing in there."

"Yowsa," I sighed. "That is hard." An odd look came over Corey's face, but she did not respond. Corey said no more for the rest of that session. She mechanically cleaned up, put her drawing away, and left the building at the end of the period. She did not attend the next scheduled session, so I did not see her until two weeks after the events above.

She entered the room.

"Hi Corey. Long time no see."

She said, "I brought some drawings with me for you to look at, Bruce." She placed her sketchbook on the table beside my easel. There were several pencil drawings inside the book. The first was another rather distorted self-portrait. The figure huddled in a corner, its arms wrapped tight around the knees. A second showed a room with a bare light bulb casting harsh light onto an empty table. Another appeared to be a detail of Corey's hand with the middle finger upraised in a well known gesture.

"Yowsa," I exclaimed. "You have been busy."

"Yeah." Corey said quietly.

These sessions marked the beginning of major changes in Corey's life. She
embarked on a graphic journey which laid to rest many of the negative and self-defeating images of herself that had been so engrained in her. This was a very difficult period for her. Internally, she had to wrestle with who she would be if she was not the marijuana smoking, hostile, self-described "loser" who entered therapy. In a metaphoric way, her drawings and paintings chronicled the death of one Corey and the birth of another. Ugly and disturbing images were seen time and again during the journey. Over time, her images changed, they softened a bit, and became less empty and painful. Corey's creativity brought light into her rooms and breathed life into her countenance. Parallel to the changes in her images were similar changes in Corey.

As she mastered materials, she enlivened herself and developed more positive self-views through the artistic tasks. The mastery of media promoted an expansion of her expressive skills, and the therapeutic alliance with me grew strong as we shared the work.

Some would suggest that Corey's drawings and paintings did little more than document the work she did in her psychiatrist's office. But I know she maintained her stance of, "He thinks he can make me talk . . . he's got another thing comin'," throughout the time she was in treatment with the psychiatrist. I would argue that any therapy she was able to do in other venues was made possible through the creative metaphoric work that took place in the art studio.

The immersion phase of the art therapy journey is often a turbulent and painful period that challenges both the adolescent and the artist-therapist. Genuine immersion into the art therapy process helps the adolescent let go of old images of self. During the immersion phase, the adolescent may appear superficially to be getting worse when in fact she is getting better. This is caused by the anxieties and guilt inevitably brought to the surface as the resistance behaviors are abandoned. The art therapy journey involves the adolescent in a metaphoric process of death and resurrection as the "bad" self-view is exchanged for a more positive sense of self. The content of the adolescent's images during this phase metaphorically and/or directly relate to old self-images that are bad. During the immersion phase, the artist-therapist strives to maintain a consistent attitude of acceptance and support, and of attention to the importance of the turmoil the adolescent is experiencing. Furthermore, the art therapist needs to always be on the lookout for opportunities to promote new and positive self-perceptions in the adolescent.

THE LETTING GO PHASE

The letting go, or termination, phase of the art therapy journey is a process, not an event. The feelings and phenomena of this phase of the journey are captured in the following poem that was written by an anonymous adolescent in preparation for discharge from a psychiatric hospital.

> As I look back, inside the facts
> of the time I spent with you

memories fade like crayon shades
written in red, black and blue
I was so lonely, so enraged
I wrote you once, but I tore the page
as I look back upon the tracks
of the time I spent with you

It's not my way, words are hard to say
when and why things rearranged
the hate collapsed, seasons passed
one by one the colors changed
I hated doors and locks, hated letting go
I hated looking inside, I s'pose you know
as I look back upon the tracks
through the time I spent with you

Here I go, say hello
to all the people I once knew
and if you can, make 'em understand
I just did what I had to do
now I'm not one to say what's inside
but tell 'em I said thanks, at least I tried
I look back upon the tracks
through the time I spent with you.

(Anonymous)

The letting go phase of the art therapy process with adolescents is a period of internalization and consolidation of the gains made during the treatment process. It is a readying to leave the artistic journey, to take a different path which inevitably separates the adolescent from the artist-therapist. This is a time when the adolescent struggles with the concept that the most meaningful relationships in life are those that are not dependent upon space and time. This is to say, the adolescent learns that he can take the relationship with him in the form of memories and experiences he has shared with the art therapist. Ideally, the adolescent has a sense that he or she can recreate the experience of the relationship with the art therapist by creating new quality relationships in other, nontreatment settings.

During the Letting Go Phase, the arts provide the adolescent with a means to express the sense of loss that is experienced as the relationship with the art therapist comes to an end. These feelings are often too difficult for the adolescent to put into words but are usually profoundly expressed in images. In addition, the artifacts of the journey: the sculptures, paintings and drawings, serve as tangible objects that adolescents take with them from the experience. These are the observable external representations of invisible internal experiences.

Phenomenological psychotherapist Clark Moustakas (1995b) describes the final phase of therapy in this way: "The aim is to bring together the *what* of the person's experience and the *how* in such a way that its nature and meanings are embraced" (p.211). Such work demands that the adolescent patient and the art therapist put much effort into understanding the essence of what their time together has meant. This is not a simple process of summing-up but rather a creative and intuitive *image-ination* of the core meanings of their journey together.

It is imperative that artist-therapists maintain an attitude of support, neutrality and acceptance of the inevitable end of the relationship during the Letting Go Phase. It is reasonable to assume that most adolescents who are in therapy will not have had successful termination experiences in their past. It is more likely that they will have experienced pathological versions of the saying good-bye process. Their past will have been littered with clichés like: "We aren't really saying good-bye," when in fact a relationship really is ending; or in reference to a deceased grandfather, "He isn't really gone," when in fact he really has died. So, the adolescent is typically inexperienced in dealing with healthy endings. The last major piece of work between the art therapist and the patient is the crafting of a healthy process of letting go.

Kyla's Road

I'd been seeing Kyla in weekly art therapy sessions for almost two years. She had grown up in a very wealthy family. She had told me once that, "everything I ever wanted has always been mine for the asking." To most people, I am sure that Kyla must have looked like she was happy. Her family loved her, all her material needs were supplied, she was a good student, she had a good life . . . and yet shortly before I met Kyla, she had tried to kill herself. That brought her to the hospital for a short crisis-stabilization stay, and eventually into my private practice art therapy studio.

Kyla liked almost every art material, but she was especially adept with clay. During our time together, Kyla worked on sculpture after sculpture, each new one delving deeper than the last. It was as if working with the clay was like a metaphoric onion for her. Each new creative act peeled away another level, revealing ever more precious aspects of her complex self. Figure forms of grace and brutality gave way to fuming volcanic fires. These were extinguished by shallow pools held by wishing wells. Layer after layer, form upon form, the three-dimensional person that she was emerged.

As her inward journey unfolded, I had to do very little. Kyla did all the hard work. She'd been attending sessions regularly for nearly twenty months when she brought a small statue to the studio of a person sitting hunched over on a bench. The figure had a tired and forsaken quality.

As she worked on this sculpture, she said that it reminded her of a man she had seen in a small village in Northeastern Pennsylvania, where she used to live. She remembered walking along the sidewalk with her mother and seeing a man sitting outside a barber shop.

"Kyla," I said, "I wonder what it would be like to go back there someday?"

"You mean back to Union Dale?" She asked.

"Yes," I replied. "What would that be like?"

She grimaced. "I don't know. There is no one there that I know. It'd be really lonely, I guess."

Kyla was quiet for most of that session. She asked for my help with one small section of the piece, but I don't think she really needed my assistance. In the silences, I was aware that something had happened between us during the interaction around the figure, but I wasn't clear just what it was.

I took my notes from the session to my next meeting with my supervisor. I described the long silences, reconstructed our conversation as best I could, and tried to describe the little sculpture Kyla was working on.

When I'd finished telling the story, she asked me how I felt about what had occurred. I told her I had a warm but lonely feeling. "Maybe Kyla is trying to let you know she's almost ready to leave therapy," she said. As soon as these words left her lips, I had a feeling she was right. I asked if I should raise the subject with Kyla at our next session. My supervisor suggested that I just keep going with the warm and accepting, neutral stance I had maintained during the course of Kyla's therapy. "Trust the process, Bruce. She will let you know somehow when she is ready."

When Kyla returned to the studio the next week, she brought only an unopened box of Sculpy. Sculpy is a polymer-based modeling compound. I asked her where the figure she'd been working on last week was and she remarked in a casual manner, "I broke it."

The sculpture, however, reappeared a couple of weeks later. Kyla had added details to the man's clothing and to the texture of the bench, and she had subtly altered his posture. I could see no sign that it had been broken. It appeared as if the man was looking away, toward some distant place.

"I see you've been working." I said.

"Yes, I had this sitting on my dresser for a long time. I didn't touch it. Then, the other day, I just decided to work on him again." She pointed.

"He's looking at something?"

"Yes," she sighed.

The rest of the session was spent in random discussion of modeling techniques and how things were going for Kyla at her part-time job. At the end of the session, as I was filling out an appointment reminder card for her, Kyla said, "Maybe we should not meet next week, I am really busy."

"That's fine," I said. "How about the next week?"

"No," she said. "I was thinking I'd just give you a call when I need to come."

A few weeks later, Kyla called to set up another appointment, but then canceled our session the day before. She scheduled an appointment for the following week.

When she arrived for the session, the sculpture was in much the same condition it had been in three weeks prior.

"I really haven't done anything," she lamented. "I can't seem to get his eyes right." She pointed toward the face. "Could you sit that way for a minute and pose like that, Bruce?"

I turned toward her. "I've wondered if maybe that figure wasn't supposed to be me." Kyla didn't say anything. She kept her attention on the clay before her. "Okay," she said, "I'm done."

"You missed last week."

"I know, stuff came up, I'm really busy."

Later, when I approached the table where she was working I noticed that the figure seemed to have very deep set eyes. Kyla put her tools in a water container and looked at me.

"You may be right, Bruce. Maybe this guy is you. I think he's watching me say good-bye to him."

I shifted my gaze to the figure. "I wonder how he feels?"

(Dialoguing with the statue in this way was quite familiar to Kyla, so she easily slipped into the imaginal story.)

"Oh, I think he's pretty sad."

"Why is that," I asked.

She paused. "He's sad because he might not get to see someone anymore. But he's happy for her, too, because she is happy."

"I see. Why can't he see her anymore?"

"It is time for her to move on."

She shifted in her chair. "Bruce, I think it's about time, I think I'm ready."

"Everything ends, Kyla. Maybe we should talk about your stopping therapy?"

"I think I'll just work on this."

Over the next few weeks, the sculpture continued to change. Details were added. For the most part, Kyla and I spoke of artistic techniques, how to create 3-D shadows and highlights. The figure and bench became a symbolic object, an icon of sorts, representing our relationship. It contained memory images of pain, sadness, anger, loneliness, joy and finally hope. It was, in a subtle way, an imaginal map of our journey together. Several times Kyla wondered out loud what I would do if she "just quit coming." At each of these moments, I reminded her that saying good-bye is a process, not an event.

Our process ended as Kyla lifted the finished sculpture from the kiln. It was, for me, both a haunting and warmly nostalgic piece. As she spoke of it during our last session together, she recalled moments of intensity and flippancy that had passed between us.

I have wondered, from time to time, how Kyla is doing. I hope that all is going well for her. She deserves good things in her life. Sometimes I feel that I am a professional good-bye sayer. It is almost frightening to me to think of how many adolescents I have established relationships with over the past two decades only to bid them farewell. It is the nature of the work. The whole point of establishing the therapy relationship is to make it no longer necessary.

Chapter IX

THE STRUCTURE OF THE THERAPEUTIC ARTS STUDIO

*I don't think I want any structure in my life. Because if I have structure
I might have feelings. Who needs 'em!*

Anonymous Adolescent

Perhaps the most difficult task of the artist-therapist working with
adolescent patients is that of continually needing to "hook" or
engage the patient in the treatment process, and to keep that involvement active. This is demanding work, because the initial interactions
with the adolescent are often focused on the young person's resistance
to, and resentment of, the therapy process. As discussed earlier, it is
essential that the adolescent's resistance be honored and dealt with
effectively so she can begin to feel that the structure of the therapeutic
arts studio will in some way be useful to her.

Figure 17. The Art Street Studio, Albuquerque, New Mexico.
Photograph by Amanda Herman.

When I discuss the *structure of the arts studio* I will be referring to:
• the presence of artworks on the walls;
• the attitude, enthusiasm, tone of voice, facial expressions, body movements, energy level and charisma of the artist-therapist;
• the range of quality art materials and equipment;
• the rituals of the studio;
• the ambience of the space, the color of the walls, the flooring, the windows, the furniture, the floor plan, the organization of the space;
• the presence of music or absence of music;
• the baseline rules of behavior;
• privileges and restrictions that are associated with the use of specific tools or materials; and
• a host of metaphysical aspects of the studio.

When all of these qualities are added together, they serve as a container for the adolescent's feelings, fears, wishes, ideas, behaviors and fantasies. McNiff (1995) states, "In a therapeutic studio it is the overall presence, the soul of the place, which grows from people and images while simultaneously acting upon them" (p. 182). Another way to think of the structure of the therapeutic arts studio is that it is the sum of all of the overt and covert elements of the artistic milieu.

There are three core principles of the therapeutic arts studio structure that must be in place in order for adolescents to benefit from involvement in art therapy. If these core principles are not present, then no therapeutic work will be done. The three core principles of the arts studio are:

1. The studio must be safe.
2. The studio must be predictable.
3. The studio must be simultaneously focused on
the making of art and the establishment of relationships.

"I love this place. Isn't that odd? It almost feels
like I'm in the eye of a hurricane or something here,
but I am not afraid because I get to make stuff."

(Anonymous Adolescent)

Figure 18. The studio of Vicki Blinn, A.T.R.

The Studio Must Be Safe

Two primary ingredients in successful psychotherapy of any kind, with any population, are safety and anxiety. The patient must have a sense that the therapy context is a safe place in which to explore and share their inner lives. At the same time, the patient has to have a measure of inner anxiety in order to want to make changes in his or her life. One of my students recently used the image of a teeter-totter to express this dynamic. On one end of the teeter-totter is safety, and at the other end is anxiety. In this metaphor, the midpoint, or fulcrum, is the position of the art therapist. As anyone who has ever played on such an apparatus knows, to have a perfect balance between the two ends is rare, and in fact, becomes boring fairly quickly. Someone always leans back in order to disrupt the stillness of the balance.

In therapy with adolescents, it is my experience that they bring all the anxiety the journey demands. Generally, art therapists do not need to worry about stimulating anxiety on the part of their adolescent patients; the teenager will have more than enough of that. So, the art therapist needs to attend to establishing the safety of the journey.

The central psychological task of every adolescent is to become an independent, functional adult. This is referred to in therapeutic literature by many different terms, including separation-individuation, emancipation, autonomy, and identity formation. In the therapeutic arts studio the focus is always on the adolescent's process of separation and individuation and the ways this can be manifested through the behaviors of art making. For adolescents, this is difficult work. In both a very real sense and a profoundly symbolic sense, the adolescent is undergoing a death process. Life as he knows it is coming to an end. Nothing will ever be the same again. He will never again have the luxury of being able to be a child.

In the best of circumstances, children face the difficulties of moving from childhood into adulthood with the support, guidance, containment and best wishes of their parents. However, the adolescents who enter the art therapy journey typically do not have the benefit of optimal parental support. Sometimes the parental alliance has been disrupted through separation, divorce or death. Often, the adolescent's parents are emotionally troubled themselves and have discovered that an acceptable way to seek help for themselves is to enter their adolescent into therapy as the identified patient. Hence the overt desire of parents to have their child treated is in many instances a masking of their own covert wish for treatment themselves. The adolescent, then, is in a very difficult emotional situation. At one level, she is mourning the loss of her childhood, at another level, she may fear that if she "gets better" her parents will get worse, or even worse, abandon her.

For the adolescent, the process of exploring inner feelings in the therapy context is a treacherous task. The dramatic immediacy of the adolescent perspective may push the patient to perceive the art therapy treatment journey as almost life- threatening. Against this backdrop, it is easy to see why safety in the arts studio is the first required ingredient for successful therapy. If the adolescent does not feel that the studio is a safe environment, then no therapeutic work will take place. Regardless of how skilled the artist-therapist may be, or how wonderful the physical facility may be, or how fine the artistic materials may be, if the patient does not feel safe, no therapy will occur.

For the art therapist who wants to work with adolescents, it is imperative to think through how to establish a sense of safety in the art therapy studio or group room. There are countless things an art therapist can do to create the feeling that the studio is a shelter from the storm. In a profound sense, this is the art therapist's primary task.

In *A Sense of Place*, Gussow (1971) says that the thing that changes any physical location into *a place* is the process of experiencing deeply.

"A place is a piece of the whole environment that has been claimed by feelings" (p. 27). The presence of artworks on the walls of a therapeutic arts studio has a permeating influence on the feel of the art-place. Their images, colors, textures, themes and particular energies have strong impact on the atmosphere of the studio. The presence of art on the walls transmits a creative energy that is one of the primary transformative elements in the studio and can be one of the primary conveyors of the message that this is a safe place.

Healing for an adolescent is a process of transforming destructive, self-defeating energy into creative, curative energy. The whole purpose of art therapy with adolescents is the stimulation of the nourishing force. The nourishing force finds its way into teenagers' lives in many different ways and it is impossible to predict accurately how it will manifest itself for each adolescent. Still, after many years of observation, I know the studio works with a kind of mysterious place magic. An important element in the "place magic" is the imagery on the walls of the studio. It is essential that empty wall space, which is often quite popular with housekeeping staffs and administrative personnel, be filled with the paintings, drawings and poems of patients and therapists alike. In a sense, the walls of the studio should be a living gallery, always changing, destructuring and re-forming, thus providing a potent unspoken metaphor of the workings of the place. The studio is a constantly evolving, aesthetic milieu consisting of image themes and patterns that define the adolescent community's creations. Whenever the adolescent enters the studio, he should be greeted by a host of images which, through their very presence, invites him to participate in the healing activity of making art. This does not mean that the images on the walls are always comforting or comfortable. Sometimes it is the presence of disturbing imagery that conveys the message to the adolescent that the studio is a safe place that can hold many aspects of life, both the pleasant and the disturbing.

Since many of the essential curative elements of the art therapy studio are given off by the environment itself, one way to conceptualize the role of the artist-therapist is as a caretaker of the studio. McNiff (1995) discusses being a "keeper" of the therapeutic arts studio. He says, "...my primary function is to kindle the soul of the place, to maintain its vitality and its ability to engage people in highly individuated ways" (p. 180). I often tell my graduate students that their primary job in treating adolescents is to take good care of the studio so that the studio can take good care of the adolescents. As caretaker of the studio, the most significant things the artist-therapist must do have little to do with what is said, but more to do with how one is in the world.

The attitude that the art therapist holds toward the adolescent patient is extremely important. Adolescents, especially emotionally disturbed ones, are surprisingly sensitive to unspoken cues and energies they pick up from the environment. The patient will know immediately if the therapist likes working with teenagers or not. The patient will know, without ever being told, whether or not the art therapist regards adolescents as young persons worthy of deep respect, or as behavior problems needing punishment. It won't necessarily be anything the therapist says; rather, such core attitudes will seep out into the environment in a thousand subtle ways. The attitudes of the artist-therapist are in the air the therapist exhales and in the sweat that emanates from her pores. Ask any high school student to tell you which of their teachers really enjoy working with teenagers and which ones are simply putting in their time, and the student will immediately provide you with a list of both kinds of teachers. The success of art therapy with adolescents is tied inextricably to the attitude of the artist-therapist.

It is my experience that adolescent patients thrive on the commitment and enthusiasm of the artist-therapist. The commitment and enthusiasm I refer to here is in regard to the artist-therapist's own artistic work. If art therapists are actively engaged in their own expressive art tasks, both in the therapy studio and in their own personal studio, this establishes a positive sense of contagion in the environment that is powerful medicine. Creating this sense of artistic contagion is absolutely dependent upon the therapist. You cannot expect a group of emotionally disturbed adolescents to be able to generate much in the way of artistic exuberance of their own accord. By definition, adolescents who are in need of psychotherapy do not feel positively about themselves or others, and therefore cannot easily be enthusiastic about much of anything. On the contrary, the adolescents who most often are referred to art therapy are typically angry, hurt and negative individuals, so the generation of artistic infectiousness is the therapist's responsibility. This is not to suggest that the art therapist needs to be a cheerleader, but rather that she must carry the load in terms of setting a positive tone in the milieu.

Artistic contagion is stimulated by the art therapist's own ongoing commitment to making art, which is not talked about in itself, but rather is lived out in the environment. The way the art therapist uses his or her tone of voice, facial expressions, body movements, energy level, personality and charisma are all important elements in the studio. It is imperative that art therapists exude an amount of excitement, expectation and joy in their work, while at the same time honoring the boredom, pain, sadness and angst that so often accompanies the adolescent in therapy. Unger (1995) notes, "You need to have the right combination of honesty, genuine interest, caring, firmness, flexibility and enthusiasm to pass their [adolescents] test" (p. 132). I am not suggesting here that there is any one personality type for artist-therapists who work with adolescents. There is plenty of room for out-going and gregarious art therapists, quietly gentle art therapists and everything in-between. It is imperative that art therapists working with adolescents develop a degree of personal power and self-confidence if they want to be effective with adolescents. Essentially, this means that one must work with one's own personality traits and develop a therapeutic style that exudes a therapeutic persona. This persona comes in many flavors. I have observed art therapists who are able to fill up a room with their gentle sincerity. Others create a contagiuously benevolent atmosphere through their outgoing warmth and energy. Moustakas (1995) describes such a therapeutic persona as the firebrand. "The firebrand is the person who recognizes what is natural, what is organic, what is alive and vital in life, the person who dares to live, to be and to create" (p. 5). Moustakas describes what I consider to be the essence of what an artist-therapist must be as he discusses *Being-In, Being-For, and Being-With.* The following is a brief integration of Moustakas' ideas with adolescent art therapy. For a more thorough understanding of these concepts, I refer the reader to Moustakas' wonderful book, *Being-In, Being-For, Being-With.*

Being-In is an uncontaminated state that requires that the artist-therapist enter into the adolescent's artistic expressions exactly as they are given. When an art therapist is able to meet an adolescent in his or her way of artistically-being-in-the- world, there is an attempt to understand precisely what the teenager is saying from his or her perspective. When the art therapist is able to genuinely Be-In the adolescent's imagery world, the adolescent feels understood, and this experience initiates new ways of being in the world for the patient.

In Being-For, the art therapist's task is to actively encourage the artistic expressions of the adolescent that will facilitate self-actualization. The art therapist not only accepts the adolescent's images as presented but is clearly and solidly present as an ally. The art therapist *is* for the adolescent, promoting a common purpose, which is the adolescent's recovery of self-esteem and confidence. This, of course, entails making available artistic resources, technical experience, competencies and skills to the adolescent so that she can meet her positive expressive goals.

The Being-With process involves the creation of an I-Thou relationship between the adolescent and the art therapist. The process inevitably stirs sacred moments of life with the adolescent, moments when the artist-therapist and the adolescent are together as a team.

To summarize the attributes of an effective caretaker of the studio, I offer the following principles and values:

· An intentional focus on the part of artist-therapists to live out their commitment and enthusiasm for making art in the presence of adolescents

· A deep desire to enter fully into the adolescent's world as it is presented in the images the adolescent creates

· A belief that within the adolescent there is a wisdom and resource that enables the adolescent to make choices and pursue affirming experiences

· A commitment to artistic intuition, spontaneity and mystery, and a willingness to take creative risks

· A willingness to attend to the adolescent's feelings and underlying meanings that often are unspoken and must be art-ed out

· A commitment to life and the goodness of art making

· An active participation in whatever image and theme the adolescent brings

As the leader of the adolescent art studio, the art therapist functions in the dual role of protector and motivator. The art therapist establishes and holds an artistic community that is bound by the principle of parallel participation in which the isolating "solo" activities of art making are joined with the communal experience of others' creative processes. This sets up a shared energy in which adolescent artists affect and are affected by their own images and the art works of their peers. The leader keeps the structure of the place by setting the tone for parallel participation. The therapeutic style that is most helpful with adolescent patients is one that involves a careful attending to the processes of art making, to the images that arise and to the group process that is revealed in artistic and interpersonal interactions.

When values such as these are embedded in the relationship, they form an unshakable foundation for therapeutic change and growth. They make possible the transition from a troubled life to a healthy way of being, and they help to transform destructive, self-defeating energy into a creative, nourishing, curative force.

Adolescent art therapy literature has, in my view, too often presented the work as if the artistic mediums of choice for adolescents are colored markers and magazine cut-out-collage. In a review of one such source, Spaniol (1989) states, "...the book takes the 'art' out of art therapy, thereby divesting art therapy of a major source of its potency" (p. 119). An important factor in establishing the safety of the art therapy studio is the presence of a range of quality art materials and equipment. Materials play an important role in the design, making and final outcome of any art form. It is a terrible error to regard the media as only a means to an end, i.e., as a way to get the patient to do talk therapy. As Lowenfeld notes, "...thinking with the material itself and developing a feeling for the function and use of materials may well result in changes in design, revisions in original plans, and a greater flexibility of approach." The materials and tools need to be of good quality, or else there is a meta-message conveyed that the process as well as the end product of the adolescent's expression is not really valued. It is probably better to limit the range of materials and tools available than to select inferior products that convey such a meta-message.

Different materials, of course, give out qualitatively different expressions consistent with their inherent structure. As McNiff notes, "The free-flowing nature of watercolor evokes distinctly different psychic states than do thick oil paints. Sculpture made from wood and metal will arouse feelings distinct from a clay construction" (p. 181). The materials are the carriers of the emotional states of the artist. Art therapist Cathy Moon goes well beyond what one might think of as traditional art materials in her own art and in her therapeutic work. Since often the patient (and she herself) is struggling with the broken aspects of life, she encourages her clients to combine shards of broken pottery, shattered mirrors, damaged cast-off furniture, and other found objects, with paint and clay to create multimedia pieces that capture the essence of the patient's experience of life.

The presence of "stuff" in the studio helps to generate the nourishing force of the place. The work of art therapy cannot be confined to colored markers and magazine cut-outs; it must engage materials of many kinds in order to foster the sense of safety and artistic contagion that adolescents so desperately need. As caretaker of the studio, the art therapist must encourage **art** making as the primary vehicle of the journey.

Every aspect of the physical space of the therapeutic studio either helps or impedes the creation of the ambience of safety and creative contagion. The color of the walls, the flooring, the windows, the furniture, the floor plan, the organization of the space, all have the potential to enhance the therapeutic milieu or detract from it. To be sure, some of these physical attributes may be beyond the control of the artist-therapist, but it is still the art therapist's responsibility to make the best use of whatever space he or she has to work in.

In my career, I have provided art therapy services to adolescents in a variety of studio settings, ranging from a brand new, consciously designed creative arts building to a windowless 12' x 12' concrete basement cubicle, and from an old funky cottage-like structure to an open modern cafeteria setting. I have run expressive arts groups in plushly carpeted, pristine group rooms and in a converted unit bedroom. In each of these instances, there were aspects of the space that were unchangeable, whether it be the size or shape of the space, or the color of the walls, or the quality of the lighting. Regardless, it was my responsibility to transform the space into a creative and safe place.

One physical attribute of the studio which is of particular interest for art therapists working with adolescents is the lighting. Many institutions and offices use fluorescent tubes because they are economical and energy efficient. This environmental element is often overlooked or taken for granted. Research has shown that the rapid flickering of some fluorescent lights has a negative and agitating effect, particularly upon adolescents who have attention deficit disorders or who are hyperactive. Furthermore, some fluorescent lights affect color perception, and this can make working with paint and other color media difficult. Whenever possible, art therapists should try to locate their studio spaces in rooms that have ample window light with northern exposure. If that is not possible, then it is preferrable to have adequate incandescent lighting and/or full spectrum fluorescent lighting.

There is no "perfect" art therapy studio or group room. In fact, the places where art therapists work are often quite unpleasant. An example of such a place was the windowless 12' x 12' concrete basement cubicle I referred to above. Still, even that dark, damp and initially disturbing environment was able to be transformed. Through the parallel participation efforts of the hundreds of adolescents who cycled through the groups I led there, and with the aid of the images they made, that dank room was transformed into a safe, creative place that was nicknamed "The Bomb Shelter."

Adolescent patient-artists continually remind me that if I provide a committed, soulful presence in the studio, it does not matter where the work is being done. While I favor working in the best location possible, I know that the therapeutic efficacy and spirit of the studio has much more to do with creative parallel participation and my presence than with the physical characteristics of the space.

To have music or not to have music, that is the question. As I have traveled around the country visiting treatment facilities for adolescents, I have been struck by how strongly individual therapists feel about one side or the other of this question. Some art therapists say that in their view music detracts from the therapeutic environment. Others say that since adolescents often cannot agree on what kind of music to listen to or which radio station they want, it is easier to simply not have a stereo available. One therapist I interviewed regarding this question said she felt that allowing patients to listen to music set up a "too-comfortable environment." She wanted her patients to "work in, not enjoy" the studio.

I have never experienced adolescent patients having too much fun in a therapy setting. On the contrary, many adolescents who require therapy feel as though the process is a form of punishment for their badness. So, I do not worry that I may make the studio too enjoyable. I believe that including music, in some form, in the art therapy milieu can be very helpful in establishing the creative and expressive qualities that are essential in the healing work of the studio. Music is one of the most common and natural languages of the adolescent, and it seems silly to ignore or restrict such a potent element. I do not mean to suggest that I abandon all control of the music that is present in my studios. For instance, I pay close attention to the volume level on the stereo. It is important that the music not be so loud that conversation is impeded. If I happen to leave the room and someone turns up the volume in my absence, when I return, I invariably turn off the radio for a short period of time. This gives the adolescents and me a chance to talk about the value of trust and negotiation. I tell them how important I think it is that they trust me enough to negotiate turning up the volume a little, rather than to take matters into their own hands while my back is turned. Of course, one of the adolescents immediately wants the music back on and asks to do so. This gives me the opportunity to talk about logical consequences to behavior, and I ask the group if they think the music should be turned back on. Generally, I accede to their judgment and the music returns. Through this quick interaction, I model my willingness to talk things through and the group experiences their communal power to negotiate in a reasonable fashion.

I also give close scrutiny to the emotional tone and the messages conveyed by the music the adolescents listen to. At times, if a particular song or station is offensive, I make the decision to change the station. This, of course, always draws a reaction from the adolescents in the studio, and that gives me an opportunity to engage in a dialogue with them about what was offensive, or to discuss socially unacceptable themes in the therapeutic environment. An example: There was a song a few years ago that had a chorus which suggested that the main character of the song was a loser and should be killed. Whenever that song came on the radio, I would drop whatever I was doing and go change the station. An adolescent would say something like, "Hey, I was listening to that!"

My response, "I am sorry. But you know, that song is about pretty negative feelings and violence. I know everyone in here has already had enough hard things happen in their lives. We don't need to listen to that."

The adolescent replies, "Yeah, but I like that station."

I reply, "We can turn it back in a few minutes if you'd like. For now though, is there another station you'd like to listen to?"

Again, this little interaction has provided the adolescent group with several important messages.

1. I am paying close attention to what goes on in here.
2. I care about this environment and I will protect it.
3. I care about you and I will protect you.
4. I am in authority here, but I will listen to and respect what you want.
5. I try to understand how you and others in the group feel.

The same kinds of interactions often take place in relation to the chatter of disk jockeys. For instance, it is fairly typical for teams of DJs to make sexual innuendoes a part of their "routine" between songs and commercials. An example of this occurred when the afternoon D Js at a radio station sponsored a contest during a live broadcast that encouraged listeners to call in to the show and share their "favorite thing to suck on." The winner of the contest would receive a new vacuum cleaner as their prize. As the calls started coming in, I changed the station. One adolescent boy said, "What did you do that for?"

"Well," I replied, "I don't think we need to listen to a contest that is sexually degrading."

The boy, feigning innocence asked, "What do you mean? I didn't hear them say anything about sex."

I responded, "I was born in the morning, but not this morning. Of course it was about sex, but that's not what I object to. It's the way they were talking about sex that I think was devaluing."

"I don't get it. Maybe you are just a dirty old man."

I said, "I think sex can be a beautiful thing. But hearing people call in to a radio station and talk about how much they like to suck bananas, or whatever—that to me sounds cheap. And, I know there are folks in here that would find it hard to listen to that sort of thing."

"Yeah, but I liked hearing those suckers."

At that point, one of the girls in the group spoke up. "Give it up. Bruce is right; that was disgusting."

Once again, this interaction provided the adolescent group with several important messages.

1. I am paying close attention to what goes on in here.

2. I care about this environment and I will protect it.

3. I care about you and I will protect you.

4. I am in authority here, but I will listen to and respect what you want.

5. I try to understand how you and others in the group feel.

If there was no radio in the studio, then such interactive opportunities would be lost.

If one decides to have music in therapeutic arts studio, it is imperative that the art therapist stay in touch with the music trends of the adolescent culture. Musical awareness and knowledge about current groups and individual artists can be a point of contact between art therapists and adolescent patients. Being able to identify a musical group and speak intelligently about it can be of great value, particularly in the early stages of relationship formation. Likewise, the art therapist who makes no effort to be attuned to teen culture can unwittingly build unnecessary walls between herself and her patients. Furthermore, the art therapist who can, at the appropriate time, quote the lyrics of a currently popular song in response to something an adolescent has said or done will have a powerful therapeutic tool at her command. There are few things an art therapist can do to hook an adolescent into engagement more surely than demonstrating fluency in his or her cultural language.

Example: A fifteen year old girl is crying, having just done a drawing about her parents getting divorced. She says, "I want everything to always be like it was. I hate this!"

The art therapist responds, "Your drawing reminds me of that Counting Crows song *Anna Begins*, *'Oh,' she says, 'you're not changing.' But we're always changing."*

The girl says, "Yes, that's it."

Finally, sometimes the addition of live music to the art studio can serve to deepen the soul of the place. Shaun McNiff nearly always plays his drum in the background as participants in his studios work. I have sometimes brought my guitar to sessions, and I have encouraged adolescent patients to bring musical instruments to the studio. Depending upon the individual musician's comfort and skill level, the introduction of live performance into the space stimulates the ongoing stream of creative expression. A song often incites movement, movements induce poems, poems encourage visual images and on and on the circle spins. I find that inviting music and sound into the studio gives adolescents permission to be deeply affected by their own images and those of their peers.

As the keeper of the adolescent art studio, the art therapist must protect the place by establishing baseline rules of behavior and assigning any privileges and restrictions associated with the use of specific tools or materials. The art studio is not a democracy, and in order for it to be a safe place there must be some rules or principles of behavior. I have visited many adolescent treatment facilities and have been surprised at the variety of approaches to rules. Some treatment centers have page after page of single-spaced, small-type rules. Other facilities operate with a minimum of written dos and don'ts. There is a rules continuum, with one end representing a lengthy code of behavior and the other pole representing anarchy. My advice to art therapists is to stand somewhere near the middle but lean toward as few rules as possible.

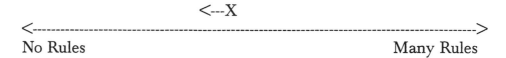

<----X

<-->

No Rules   Many Rules

I keep the rules in my studios as simple and clear as possible, because I have found that clarity and depth are closely tied to one another. If the rules of a space are overly complicated, they inevitably interfere with the creative process. Also, the greater the number of rules, the more the art therapist has to either concentrate upon them or ignore them. Neither of these is a good option. If the art therapist spends her time policing and enforcing a battery of rules, she does not have the time to make her own art or engage in genuine relationship with her patients. If she ignores the rules, she gives off the message that she regards authority as irrelevant, and ultimately the adolescent will translate that to mean the art therapist (as an authority) is also irrelevant, of no use to the adolescent. It is also my experience that art therapists who make up too many rules do so in order to mask their sense of inadequacy in relating to teenagers. In these instances, the rules become the focus of interaction rather than the relationship. It is easy for adults to engage with adolescents around a rule; it is hard work to engage in a genuine relationship.

My experience tells me it is important to keep the rules in the arts studio to a minimum, and to keep them simple. I offer the following examples of rules that have worked well in my adolescent art studios:

1. Use whatever you need but don't waste materials.
2. Take care of tools, brushes, and furniture.
3. Respect the rights of others.
4. Be positive.
5. Express yourself.

There are few, if any, situations that arise in the therapeutic arts studio that cannot be governed by these simple rules. Note that they are each stated in the positive.

There are, of course, some exceptions that must be made from time to time in response to particular situations. For instance, if an adolescent patient in the studio is actively suicidal, it is important to be very cautious regarding the use of some tools. An adolescent who is in the midst of extreme stress and emotional pain can often act impulsively, so it is important that her access to potentially dangerous tools or materials be restricted, or limited. The art therapist may not, for example, allow a suicidal patient to have free access to a mat knife while the therapist is occupied with another matter. Generally, it is my experience that such restrictions on materials and tools are viewed by adolescents in two ways. At a superficial level, this gives the teenager an opportunity to complain about authority, but at a deeper level, the patient feels cared for and protected by the art therapist's vigilance. This is true not only for the patient who is the object of the restriction but also for other adolescents in the studio.

Figure 19. The Studio of Lou Powers, A.T.R.

The Studio Must Be Predictable

In order for adolescent patients to successfully engage in the difficult work of being in therapy, it is necessary that they experience the art studio as a safe and predictable place. In fact, the predictability of the place is a prominent aspect of its safety. To some degree, this principle is paradoxical for I find that I am always being surprised by the mysterious and unexpected outcomes of adolescent's work in the studio. There are certainly repeating patterns and themes in adolescent's art works, but the effects of their creative processes are impossible to know in advance. In some ways, I never know what will happen artistically for an individual patient and yet I am deeply committed to constructing and maintaining a consistent, predictable container that is capable of holding the surprises of the adolescent's artistic efforts. The paradox is that while I never know what will happen artistically within the studio, I am very clear about how I, as the keeper of the studio, will be. I am also very clear about how the studio space itself will be.

There are many ways that an art therapist can establish herself and the studio as predictable elements in the life of an adolescent. The art therapist can promote an atmosphere of predictability by: always being on time; always welcoming the adolescent into the space in the same way; always having the necessary material supplies and tools available and well organized; being consistent in her own affect and attitude; always having her own ongoing art as an element in the studio; consistently responding to negative behaviors in the same way; and developing rituals of beginning and ending sessions.

I do not want to unduly belabor these points, but I will offer a brief discussion of them and their relevance to adolescent art therapy. It is important to keep in mind that many adolescents who enter art therapy will bring with them a long history of adults in their lives being unpredictable and untrustworthy. Therefore, the simple act of the art therapist always being on time is a potent metaverbal message to the adolescent about the art therapists' commitment to the process and about their trustworthiness. Punctuality is not always a virtue that artistic people come by naturally and so this may be an aspect of the art therapist's life that must be worked with. I have had the experience of having a patient tell me, after nearly two years of therapy, that my keeping my promise to be at every session when I was supposed to be was the single most important thing that had transpired between us. I cannot overstate this. If a patient has to stand at the door to the studio and wait for the art therapist to arrive, regardless of the reason, this is a powerful message to the patient that they are not a top priority in the art therapist's life.

In my art therapy studios, I always welcome adolescents into the space in the same way. I greet the patient (s) at the door and say, "Welcome to the studio!" This simple phrase, uttered in the first few seconds of our encounter, sets the tone for the adolescent's entry into the studio space. I convey a sense of excitement about the work ahead, and there is a quality of enthusiasm and genuine pleasure that they are here. This is an essential, subtle way to begin to establish the creative contagion that I want the adolescent to participate in.

It is very important always to have the necessary material supplies and tools available and well organized before the adolescent enters the space. This means that I spend time before sessions making sure that we have what we need, and that I monitor the "stuff" of the space. If we are beginning to run low on gesso, or 2 x 2s or clay, I know that it is time to reorder supplies. There is nothing more deadening to the creative urges of adolescents than running out of a particular medium and having to delay the process.

As difficult as it sometimes is, I work very hard at being consistent in my own affect and attitude. This means that sometimes I have to be a "therapeutic actor" because there are some days when I don't feel well, or when I have just come from a particularly stressful meeting or when my wife and I had an argument before I left for work that morning. Regardless of the reason why, it is imperative that I put aside my own life circumstances in service to the adolescent patient. I almost never share my own particular life circumstances with an adolescent patient because to do so would place an unnecessary burden on the youngster. There is nothing that the adolescent could possibly do that would ease any of these situations, and that is not why they are in the studio. The adolescent is in the arts studio in order to receive the therapy he requires and therefore it is my responsibility to always give him my undivided attention and effort.

I always have a "painting in progress" as an element in the studio. My commitment to and enthusiasm for artistic expression fills the air and becomes a nearly irresistible unspoken force in the place. Henley (1995) notes, "By working in the presence of clients, the art therapist models important art making behaviors which clients can begin to identify with and incorporate" (p. 190). Often my work becomes a vehicle for ritual greetings with particular adolescent patients. The patient enters the studio and asks, "What are you working on now, Bruce?" This affords me the opportunity to model involvement in self-exploration and expression in a profound way with the patient.

It is also very helpful to art therapists working with adolescents to develop consistent responses to negative behaviors. Some examples: A new patient enters the studio and angrily uses a swear word. My response is always to exclaim, "Strike one!" They look at me like I am crazy. I then ask them if they know anything about baseball. Then I say, "It is really important that we have a safe and comfortable atmosphere out here in the studio and swearing makes things feel a little edgy and unsafe. Now, I know that you are new here and, of course, I know that everyone slips now and then, so I developed the three-strike rule. You just got strike one, but I know that you don't want to have to go back to the unit, so you get two more strikes, or warnings."

Another example of a predictable response: An adolescent complains, "I'm bored." I respond, "You know, boredom comes from an absence of quality relationships. Think about it. You could go to Coney Island and if you were with people that you don't have a good relationship with you would probably get bored. On the other hand, you could sit in a white room all day with people that you have quality relationships with and never get bored. I hope you will work on developing some quality relationships here."

A third example: The patient says, "This place sucks." I respond, "Ouch, sucks is such a harsh word. How about saying, This place inhales deeply. That gets your point across without the harshness."

I've had these three experiences many times over and I always respond consistently, so consistently that other patients in the room will mimic my reactions. I always regard their mimicry as a high compliment because it affirms that they can predict how I will be in response to negativity. This is a subtle and yet crucial process that strengthens the bond between the adolescent and me.

I also work consciously developing rituals for the beginning and ending of studio sessions. As I mentioned earlier, I am always at the door to the studio waiting for patients to arrive. My, "Welcome to the studio," provides a ritual of entry. Following this there are rituals of gathering tools, materials and work in progress. Near the end of each session I announce to the group, "Five minute warning!" And when it is time to prepare for leaving, I again announce, "Time to clean up the mess, young Americans." Now, in each of these instances, the specific words are not all that important, but what is important is that I say them the same way each day, with the same tone of voice.

Each of these things, and many more, serve to give the adolescent a sense that the studio environment is a safe and predictable place. They know in advance what will be expected of them, and how I will be in relation to them. These elements of predictability establish the boundaries of the studio container which holds the surprising, mysterious, and awesome contents of the adolescent creative process.

Figure 20. The studio at Kids Peace National Hospital.

The Studio Must Be Focused on Making Art and the Establishment of Relationships

The greatest gift that art therapists have to give to the individual adolescent patient and to the larger adolescent treatment community is art making. There are many therapy disciplines that endeavor to treat adolescents. Among these are psychiatrists, psychologists, social workers, pastoral counselors and substance abuse counselors. While each of these professions has a contribution to make to the treatment of adolescent patients, they also have limitations that stem from the verbal nature of their approach. Art therapy has the unique advantage of being able to engage adolescents visually, tactilely, kinetically and aurally. In addition, art making involves the patient and therapist in tasks that utilize ideas, feelings and physical sensations. None of the verbally-oriented therapy disciplines have such easy access to as wide a range of possibilities.

The unique characteristics of the *art as therapy model of art psychotherapy* that our work with adolescents embodies is inextricably tied to art activity. Therefore, as one considers the configuration of an art therapy studio, special attention must be given to insuring that the studio is conducive to making art while at the same time is also focused on experiences that foster relationships. I want to be very clear about this point because I am convinced that much of our art therapy literature has missed the mark in this regard. The *art as therapy model of art psychotherapy* with adolescents, as I have practiced in art studios, places equal value on both the art process and the relationship that grows from the shared experience of making art in the company of another. Too often, art therapy authors have described art making as if it were only a means to an end, the end being the establishment of a therapeutic relationship. This, in my view, is a terrible error and a misunderstanding of the powerful therapeutic value of artistic activity. Making art in the therapeutic studio is not merely a means to establish relationships, it is the ground from which relationships grow without conscious manipulation. In other words, I do not form relationships with my adolescent patients because I am skilled in verbal articulation. I build relationships because I am willing to engage in doing things with the adolescent. The things that I do are artistic. There is a mutuality of purpose that is of great value here. On the one hand, art making creates an arena in which relationships grow. On the other hand, my relationships create an arena in which images emerge. Neither component of the studio, the art or the relationship, is of greater weight in this process than the other. I find that when I focus too exclusively on the relationship, both my art and the relationship suffer. Likewise, if the art takes too much attention, the relationship and the image suffer.

The model I am describing here challenges the western binary thinking that has prevailed until very recently in the art therapy profession. In the traditional ways of thinking about art therapy, authors have defined their focus as either focused primarily on the therapeutic relationship, or primarily on the art process. I believe that the studio should not be an *either - or*, but rather, a *both - and* venue.

Chapter X

SIX RECURRENT FEATURES OF THE ADOLESCENT ART THERAPY JOURNEY

Six themes of the adolescent art therapy journey that present with some frequency are identity confusion, risk-taking, suicidality, self-loathing, intense anger and fear of abandonment. Artist-therapists who work with adolescents need to consider these six themes as a part of their understanding of the patient, regardless of what the primary psychological diagnosis may be. The following are case examples to illustrate each of these themes.

IDENTITY CONFUSION

As noted earlier in this text's brief discussion of the developmental tasks of adolescence, this is a period of unparalleled change. It is a time of exploring strengths, acknowledging weaknesses and forming hopes for the future. Ideally, the process should result in a relatively clear internal image of who one is and hopes to be. The teenager gradually develops the capacity to reflect upon her life with both honesty and realism. The changes that occur in thinking processes during adolescence allow most to accomplish this task. However, it is also during adolescence that issues of identity occasionally become evident in dysfunctional behaviors.

Major shifts in the adolescent's sense of self often occur as a common part of successful art therapy. These changes, though, are typically experienced as anxiety-producing and scary. Oftentimes the adolescent is tempted to go back to the way she used to be because she feels ill-equipped to handle the unknown aspects of her own development.

Jenna

Jenna, a sixteen-year-old girl diagnosed with Major Depression, was initially referred to the art studio when she was fourteen. She had been in outpatient art therapy ever since, although the frequency of her sessions had decreased significantly over the past year. Preoccupation with her school performance and appearance had not been an issue for her for the past year. In school, she had been getting acceptable grades and she had developed a close circle of friends. In the arts studio, her drawings had focused on issues such as conflict with her parents, getting her driver's license and dating. Jenna had been able to address each of these problem areas in a positive manner, both artistically and behaviorally.

Three things happened, however, that stimulated a studio art session in which Jenna seemed intensely depressed and preoccupied with her inadequacy, concerns that she had not raised for several months. She had passed her driver's examination, a boy to whom she was attracted had made a sexual overture toward her, and she had received four A's and two B's on her report card.

The drawing Jenna did that afternoon portrayed a small figure carrying a large overstuffed bag while balanced on a tightrope stretched above a deep gorge. As she talked about her drawing, Jenna expressed the feeling that these recent successes would lead to ever-increasing demands. "More things will get stuffed into the bag and I will lose my balance." She was afraid she would not be able to control the expectations of her parents or the boy and that she would ultimately fail and "ruin everything."

It was my sense that Jenna was feeling torn about her successes and overwhelmed by the responsibilities and freedoms that accompanied them. Her newly acquired driver's license had symbolically given her autonomy and independence from her parents. Jenna's good grades brought a sense of competence and expectation for continued positive academic performance that was new to her. I also wondered if she was interpreting the decreased frequency of her sessions in the art studio as an indication that I no longer cared about her. In response to these events she had become increasingly anxious and briefly regressed to her former identity as a sad and inadequate person who blamed all her troubles on her depression.

Jenna's vignette illustrates some of the common problems that arise around identity for an adolescent. She was aware that her old identity as an inadequate, unassertive and underachieving young woman allowed her to show only limited sides of herself. Although she was not content with such an existence, she also could not cope with the stress of simultaneously becoming more independent, sexual and competent in others' eyes. In response to these stresses, Jenna briefly retreated to the safety of her known misery, the familiar depressive identity.

I responded by suggesting that for a month or so we go back to having weekly art studio sessions so that she would feel supported by me as she struggled with her fears. After several weeks of artistic exploration of her fears and insecurity about her own competence, Jenna got back on track with her journey toward health.

RISK-TAKING

For art therapists and other treaters, one of the more disturbing aspects of working with adolescents is their tendency to want to push the limits of their developing physical attributes, skills, and abilities. An adolescent boy once confided to me that, "It doesn't matter how fast I drive, I know my reflexes are quicker than the car." This statement underscores a disturbing sense of invulnerability and immortality that often accompanies adolescence. Risk-taking and experimentation are constants in some teenagers. In fact, these may be ingredients for further development and growth. It is evident that adolescents who avoid experimentation and risk also tend to constrict the evolution of their own independence. Art therapists who work with adolescents must prepare themselves for the anxiety that patients' experimentation may generate in them, be willing to set appropriate limits on their patients' behaviors when needed, and accept the role of supportive consoler when the adolescents' risks bring painful results. The art therapist must always comment on risky behavior, for if one does not comment, the adolescent will assume that his behavior has the blessings of the art therapist. This does not mean that the art therapist always intervenes or seeks to block experimentation. Sometimes the adolescent needs to feel the sting of the consequences of risks. Still, the art therapist should always comment whenever unhelpful risk-taking or experimentation is brought up in the session.

Diana

Diana, a fifteen-year-old girl, had come to the hospital the morning after having been sexually assaulted by several older boys. The previous evening she and two of her girlfriends had attended a football game. During half-time the girls were invited to accompany the boys to a secluded spot underneath the stadium to drink beer and smoke some pot. Diana had never drunk a beer before and certainly never smoked marijuana. For whatever reason, on that particular night, the riskiness of the boys' offer was appealing. The older boys encouraged Diana and her friends to drink not just one, but several bottles of beer each. When the girls were quite drunk, they forced them to perform fellatio, and one of them raped Diana.

In the projective art assessment session I had with Diana, she told me she had been "sort of excited by the danger, but I didn't think anything bad would really happen." She said she had always been regarded by her friends as a "Miss Goody Goody" and it was evident that she had romanticized the antisocial adventures of her peers.

I responded, "Your drawing seems painful. I know that it is hard to always be good, but it can be just as hard to take risks too."

"Oh yes." She replied.

In this vignette, the risks Diana took, as is often the case with adolescents, proceeded from one step to the next. First she followed the boys to the secluded location, then accepted the first beer, then drank the second. Each step placed her in more danger with the exploitative boys. The most common risk-taking behaviors adolescents engage in involve new, pseudoadult-oriented activities such as drinking, driving, sexual acting-out or performing dangerous stunts. Usually, the risks start out as minor but escalate in small incremental steps.

Compounding this problem is that adolescents often have the experience of taking small, unnecessary risks without any negative or damaging consequences. Fearful adult reactions to these small risks serve to solidify the adolescent's view of parents and authority figures as unreasonable worriers who have no clue about the realities of the adolescent world.

Art therapists who are working with adolescents engaged in risky behaviors need to give consistent, clear and repeated feedback to their patients regarding the dangers of risk and experimentation. Emphasis in these interventions should be placed on a calm, artistic response to the risky behaviors. The art therapist can be quite helpful to the adolescent by keeping attention on the phenomenon of escalating or accumulated risk. It is my experience that such encounters with adolescents are best reserved for individual sessions, rather than group situations. When it is just the adolescent and the art therapist in the studio, the patient is much more likely to be able to reflect rationally on his behavior than when he is surrounded by peers for whom he feels he must perform or keep up his image.

SUICIDALITY

A very alarming aspect of emotional dysfunction in adolescents is the potential for serious self-harm, suicidal ideation and suicidal acting out. Suicide is one of the most prevalent causes of death among teenagers. Steiner (1996) notes that suicidal thoughts triple in frequency in youths between the ages of eleven and fifteen (p.16).

Self-harmful and self-destructive behaviors represent a continuum of actions and thoughts. Basically, suicidality may be assessed along two dimensions: (1) intentionality–the degree to which the patient wants to be dead and (2) lethality of method–what is the method's known efficacy?. A superficial cut across the wrist, for instance, may suggest a relatively low intentionality for death, whereas a deep cut that follows the direction of a major vein or artery may be quite lethal. Multiple suicide attempts by an adolescent are often misinterpreted by inexperienced art therapists and mental health clinicians as indicative of manipulation on the part of the patient. In actuality, the evidence indicates that lethality rises as the number of attempts increases. Art therapists must pay close attention to the symbolic manifestations of a suicide attempt. The patient who takes a relatively mild overdose of aspirin is expressing one thing about her life, while the adolescent who lies down on the tracks in the path of an oncoming train is saying something very different. The art therapist must attempt to discover the meaning of the drama, the performance event, that the patient is enacting. I have thought a lot about this topic over the years and generally, I think that there are fairly clear precipitants before a suicide attempt. Typically there is a period of gradual social withdrawal during which there are usually indirect, metaphoric warning signals left by the adolescent for others to find. Frequent precipitants include the sudden break-up of an intense relationship with a member of the opposite sex, the coming to light of inappropriate antisocial episodes the adolescent fears will lead to social repercussions or legal interventions, or the experience of a profoundly disappointing failure.

David's Death

David, a fifteen-year-old, had been having difficulties in school for a long time. His grades were poor and he was often belligerent toward his teachers and other school officials. Many people who came into contact with him had the feeling that something was not right. One morning, after his parents had left the house for work and his siblings had boarded the bus for school, David took his father's 12-gauge shotgun down from the gun rack, put a shell in the chamber, and shot himself in the head. The news of David's death spread like wildfire through the school later that day. He was well known to the high-school authorities. He had always dressed in black and had pierced his ears, nose and eyebrow. David had been diagnosed with learning disabilities and attention deficit-hyperactive disorder. He had often been accused of using drugs. He smoked, and was often at the center of acting-out behaviors at school. His family was a conflict-ridden one, and each of his older siblings had also had behavioral problems.

The night before he killed himself, he had called several friends to warn them that he was going to "do it at last." Unfortunately, none of them said anything about his intention until it was much too late. David had cried wolf many times before, and they assumed this was just one more in a long series of attention-getting threats.

After his death, some of his friends showed David's parents drawings that David had done of the grim reaper, caskets and decapitated human figures. Several of his friends became quite depressed, overwhelmed by the burden of the guilt they felt.

David's death, in many ways, is a classic example of adolescent suicide. He had manifested a combination of difficulties, including learning problems, disturbed conduct, drug use and depression. Additionally, David lacked the support he needed from his family and other adult authorities. Clearly, his first suicidal gesture was intentional and quite lethal. He wasn't kidding.

The guilt and depression that some of David's friends felt is a fairly common response that sometimes leads to what is described as suicide contagion. Art therapists and other mental health clinicians need to be especially vigilant after a successful adolescent suicide in order to contain the potential epidemic reactions of affected peers.

In the arts studio, one may often see images that raise the specter of suicidal ideation. I believe that whenever the thought crosses the mind of an artist-therapist that a particular adolescent patient may be contemplating suicide, the therapist must respond to this suspicion. Now, I want to be clear that I am not suggesting there are image formulas or set graphic clues regarding an adolescent's suicidal thought process. In fact, I find problematic interpretive theories that propose that specific images always symbolize suicidal ideation. For instance, an image of a road that disappears into a dark chasm may indicate suicidal thoughts, or it may indicate confusion about the future, or it may denote fear about how a date will go this weekend, or it may connote worry about one's parents who are considering divorce, or...or...or. Still, whenever I am looking at a particular adolescent's image and I have a fleeting thought that this kid may be thinking about suicide, I take that as a powerful sign that demands follow-up. The follow-up may take one of many forms. I might engage the adolescent in a shared artistic task in order to get a clearer sense of how he or she is functioning that day. I might engage the patient in a poetry exercise geared toward artistically responding to his visual image through verbal metaphors. I might decide to pay particular attention to the patient and watch for other possible clues about suicidal thoughts. I might simply tell the patient that her image stirs up the theme of death for me and see how she responds to my statement. I might ask the patient if she had been thinking about death. I might engage in a dialogue about the image to see what her interpretation of the picture is. I might notify other members of the treatment team (if one exists) of my concerns and ask if others have had similar suspicions. I might feel compelled to share my concerns directly with the patient. I might feel the need to notify the patient's parents or other custodial authorities if my concerns are strong enough. I might do any one or several of these things. All of these responses are possible interventions in response to the potential suicidal thought process of adolescents. I would always seek supervision from a respected colleague or other authority in order to help me clarify my feelings about the patient and the issue of possible suicide.

SELF-LOATHING

Throughout many years of clinical art therapy with inpatient adolescents, day treatment patients, and outpatients, I never encountered an adolescent who did not, at least to some degree, express a disturbing sense of self loathing. For the adolescent, this self-loathing has multiple possible meanings. It may mean "I feel lousy, depressed, like a failure," or "I am a bad person, I have caused harm to people I care about," or "I could hurt you," or "I could ruin everything for everyone," etc.

Susan

Susan came into the hospital with a long history of antisocial and destructive behaviors. She had been engaged in drug use and distribution, vandalism, theft and truancy. Her mother, a single parent, had lost all control of this hard and incorrigible girl. Susan was remanded to the short-term adolescent crisis stabilization unit by the juvenile court system for a diagnostic evaluation and treatment recommendations. This was the fourth time Susan had been involved with the juvenile court, and the judge was concerned that her recidivism was an indication of chronic criminality warranting long-term incarceration. She was currently facing charges related to an alleged assault on a male peer. Her file indicated that the boy was a former boyfriend who had broken up with her. Susan had confronted him with a knife on the school bus. A struggle had ensued, and the ex-boyfriend had received a serious puncture wound.

Before her entry into the expressive arts psychotherapy group, a member of the nursing staff telephoned me to warn me to be particularly careful with this girl. "I wouldn't turn my back on her; this is a dangerous kid," the nurse said. "And make sure the door is locked. She'll run if she has half a chance."

I assured the nurse that I would take every precaution possible.

Susan entered the group room quietly. She was 15 years old, but looked closer to 25 than 15. Her eyes were dark and sullen. She had a tattoo at the base of her neck and a nose ring that gave her a hard appearance. As she came into the art group room, her eyes were downcast, her hair greasy and unkempt, and her clothes smelled of cigarette smoke. "Hello," I said. "You must be Susan. My name is Bruce, welcome to expressive arts group."

"Yeah, whatever."

She looked around the room. Her eyes then focused on a drawing that had been left hanging on the wall from an earlier group. The image was of a red, open wound surrounded by black and blue lines. "Did you draw that?" Susan asked.

"No. That was drawn by one of the kids in the morning group."

Susan looked at me suspiciously. "Why is it still there?" There was an acidic quality of defiance and hostility in her voice.

"Oh, lots of times kids decide to leave their work hanging up for awhile," I replied. "She could have taken it with her, but she decided to leave it hanging here in the group room for awhile."

"Why'd she do that?"

"Well, Susan, you'd really have to ask her to know for sure, but I think it was because she felt pretty good about the drawing and she just wanted to leave it up so others could see it."

She grimaced. "That's fucked up. Who the hell feels good about anything here?"

Steve, a boy who'd been in the art group for a couple weeks overheard this. He said, "I have."

Susan turned toward him. "Who gives a shit?" She sneered.

"Susan, I'm going to have to ask you to not swear while you are in this group. It really makes the atmosphere unsafe and I can't have that here."

Steve shifted in his chair uncomfortably. "Maybe nobody gives a blankety -blank. But I heard what you said to Bruce. When I first came here I felt the same way you do. But Bruce told me making art would help me. I thought he was nuts."

"Sounds pretty screwy to me." Susan exclaimed.

Susan, I said, "You'll get out of this place what you put into it. Nothing more, nothing less."

Susan yawned. "Oh that's an original line. Tell me something I haven't heard before, I'm getting bored," she sighed.

I said, "You know, Susan, boredom comes from an absence of quality relationships. Now, let's get to work."

Dealing with adolescents who feel so badly about themselves requires that artist-therapists have a firm conviction that what we do is both curative and good. When we have faith in the power of the creative process and trust it, our faith will be infectious. At the same time, we have to be willing to accept the adolescent's view of herself and not attempt to prematurely argue with the patient that she is not really that bad. For an adolescent who is caught in the midst of self-loathing, adult attempts to point out the patient's good qualities are interpreted as evidence of the therapist's stupidity or phoniness. Obviously, if the adolescent regards the artist-therapist as stupid or inauthentic, they will have little reason to take the therapy process seriously.

The artist-therapist, rather than attempting to persuade the patient that he or she is not bad, should endeavor to engage the adolescent in using the self-loathing as the subject matter of the art process. One such intervention that was successful with Susan was the drawing task of portraying "The Enemy." Susan's image depicted a monstrously ugly figure whose goal it was "to ruin everything." In dialogue with the image, Susan expressed the notion that the monster was the way he was because he had been treated so cruelly by the world. This, of course, was the beginning of Susan's process of metaphoric introspection and reflection. It eventually led to her being able to understand her own self-view and to rework her self-image in a more positive manner.

Making art is a transcendent activity. Often the patients art therapists treat are ruthlessly self-critical and negative. Their negative self-absorption takes the form of hopelessness, self-defeating behaviors, antisocial actions and an inability to maintain authentic relationships. Since personal meaning can be found only in self-transcendence, it is a crucial aspect of the art therapy journey to engage the patient in situations that involve a thing outside the self. In the expressive group therapy context, transcendent absorption is the norm. Patients respond to each other, and to each other's art, as Steve did in the earlier illustration. In this way, an air of unspoken contagious benevolence is established that begins to cut into the adolescent's self-loathing.

Frannie

Frannie had been in the expressive group for five sessions. She was a thirteen-year-old girl suffering from anorexia nervosa. A precise, controlling and cold girl, her drawings in the group had been rather rigid and constricted.

Bruce: (to the group) Today, I want us to begin by drawing seven circles on your page. Put your name at the top the page. Now, I'd like us to move around the room to others' pages and draw a symbol of your impressions of that person in one of their circles.

This is an exercise adolescents invariably enjoy because of the intense focus on themselves that they experience as their peers in the group share their images of them. This exercise fits the developmental dynamic of intense interest in how their friends view them.

Frannie: Oh, I don't think I should do that. I really don't know these guys that well.

Peer: It's okay, Frannie. You've been here a bunch of times. You know us as well as we know you.

Bruce: Just do the best you can, Frannie. I'm sure everybody will be very interested in how you see them.

Frannie: Well, I'll just put a smiley face on everyone's page. Will that make you all happy? (glaring)

I chose not to respond to Frannie's provocative bait. The group members moved around the room working on their images of one another. In the discussion period following the drawing portion of the session, when it came time to discuss the images drawn on Frannie's page, the atmosphere of the group grew heavy. An air of tension filled the small group room.

Tom: Frannie, I drew a sledge hammer for you. You seem to beat on yourself all the time. You never ease up. At least I don't see it.

Frannie: You don't even know me, Tom. And from what I see you are not all that perceptive.

Patty: Did you hear what Tom said, Frannie?

Frannie: I heard exactly what he said.

Patty: I drew the—they are supposed to be—soup cans. They are all the same kind'a soup. They are all lined up in order, but something looks wrong.

I'm not sure what I meant, Frannie. Maybe it's something about how you eat.

Frannie: How I eat is none of your . . .

Jamie: I just filled in your circle with white. I couldn't think of any thing very colorful to draw about you.

Tears welled up in Frannie's eyes. She tried to fight them.

Bruce: It's alright, Frannie. Let those tears come. Nobody wants to hurt you, here, just let them come.

They came. Years of tears ran down her cheeks. As they poured from her, Patty offered her the box of tissues. Jamie leaned over and gave Frannie an awkward hug.

In the art studio and the expressive group room, patients struggle with their feelings of self-loathing and badness. Through the processes of art making, they share these feelings with others and simultaneously experience the curative effects of responding to, and giving to, others. Sometimes the gifts are painful ones, but sometimes they are gentle and supportive. For adolescents who are caught in the emotional entanglements of self-loathing, making art is a treatment of dysfunction by functioning. This is potent medicine for adolescents who feel badly about themselves.

INTENSE ANGER

Nearly every adolescent who enters into an art therapy treatment context shares the common feature of intense anger. To be sure, each individual is angry at different things—parents, school, peers, authority figures—but the underlying experience of nearly uncontrollable anger is ever-present. The adolescent's anger confronts artist-therapists with particular challenges, for the anger is inevitably directed toward the art therapist. The art therapist must recognize and acknowledge the patient's anger and respond to it appropriately but not punitively. When an adolescent senses that his or her capacity to contain anger is breaking down, the adolescent becomes very anxious. If the artist-therapist fails to provide artistic tasks and materials that respond to the adolescent's anxiety effectively, the adolescent is likely to be overwhelmed by various forms of panic that are brought on by unneutralized aggressive and erotic feelings. The result of this failure on the part of the therapist is usually an episode of destructive and aggressive act-ing out. It is important to underscore here that the adolescent will always provide signals to the art therapist regarding his anger. Typically, these warning signs will take the initial form of mild misbe-haviors which, if the therapist does not respond to them, escalate in form until they simply demand intervention. It is imperative that art therapists respond to the earliest signals in order to reassure the ado-lescent that he is understood and will be contained, that is that they will not be allowed to get out of control. Although the adolescent typ-ically reacts in a negative way to such early interventions, they also, at a much deeper level, are very grateful for the support and control the art therapist's intervention affords them. I have received anecdotal evi-dence that supports this belief from former patients who have shared with me, years after the fact, their appreciation of my efforts to help them keep their behavior under control, even though at the time they resented my interventions.

The following are brief examples of how adolescents signal their fear of losing control of their anger.

A fourteen-year-old boy entered the studio and immediately began shadow boxing. When the art therapist did not comment on this, he escalated by involving a peer in light sparring. Again, the art therapist did not make any effort to contain this behavior. Soon after that, a fist fight broke out between the boy and a male peer, both boys being romantically interested in the same girl.

Early in one session, a seventeen-year-old girl was observed draw-ing on the surface of a work table in the studio. Later during that same session, she used an X-acto knife to carve her initials into a window sill. On the unit that evening she used a broken light bulb to assault a female peer.

In an expressive group psychotherapy session, a sixteen-year-old boy preceded a panicky, rageful, psychotic episode by using increas-ingly vulgar and hostile language directed toward the hospital staff.

In each of these instances, the art therapist working with the patient failed to respond to the early signals the adolescent gave. Thus, the patient became more anxious and "upped-the-ante" until their actions became so apparent and inappropriate that the staff had to intervene by physically restraining the patient. Physical restraint as an interven-tion is often an indicator that the therapeutic staff has failed to attend to the early signals of the patient. It is likely that each of the situations discussed in these brief examples could have been avoided if the artist-therapist had intervened with appropriate artistic tasks and materials earlier in the escalating progression of signal behaviors.

Example: The fourteen-year-old boy who entered the studio and immediately began shadow boxing and then escalated by involving a peer in light sparring. The art therapist, at that point, should have said something like, "Wow, you really have a lot of energy. How about helping me nail together some canvas stretchers today?" By doing so the art therapist would first, acknowledge and comment upon the behavior, and secondly respond by providing an acceptable aggressive outlet for the boy. These simple interventions would have likely prevented the fist fight between the boy and his peer.

Second Example: At the beginning of the expressive group psychotherapy session, when the sixteen-year-old boy uttered his first vulgarity, it would have been helpful for the art therapist to say something like, "Oh John, please don't use language like that here. Swearing makes the group unsafe and negative. It is really important that we all respect one another here. Now, if you would like to do a drawing about how angry you are right now, that will be fine." By doing so the art therapist would have provided the patient with needed limits, and also given direction as to how the patient could discharge some of his negative feelings in a socially appropriate manner. The combination of containment and expression may well have helped the patient manage his thoughts and feelings in such a way as to preclude the psychotic episode.

As is discussed elsewhere in this text, if an adolescent is engaged in any behavior or conversation that the art therapist regards as negative or destructive, the art therapist *must* comment on this or the adolescent will interpret the therapist's silence as permission to continue the behavior.

Art therapists who work with adolescents must be prepared to engage with images and behaviors that emerge from the angry and ugly, dark corners of human existence. Adolescent rage will often be directed at treaters and it is crucial that art therapists not take these expressions personally. It is important to regard the patient's anger as a gift, for this is really an expression of where the adolescent is. One cannot encourage self-expression without accepting the forms it takes.

FEAR OF ABANDONMENT

While each of the aforementioned features of adolescence are expressed repeatedly, it is perhaps the fear of abandonment that I have seen most graphically. The very act of the parents or guardians of an adolescent insisting that their child enter into therapy, whether it be in a residential setting, or to a lesser degree in an outpatient studio, is in some ways a symbolic act of abandonment. Entering into a therapy relationship is often, in and of itself, a traumatic event in the life of a teenager. In most instances, patients are unclear about why they need to be in therapy. They resent the implication that they are *sick*. Generally, the adolescent perceives adults as punitive, and he expects that the adult art therapist will inevitably hurt him. Ultimately, the teenager who is suffering enough to warrant therapy imagines the therapist will eventually "give up" and abandon her.

The fear of abandonment underlies many of the other fears and disturbing feelings that are expressed by adolescents. Usually, due to the depth of this fear of abandonment, the adolescent expresses it through metaphor rather than through direct communication. Rinsley (1980) notes that a cluster of associated themes make up his understanding of the adolescent's fear of abandonment. "Fear of a lack of understanding by the adult. Fear of retaliation by the adult. Fear of lack of control by the adult. Fear that the adult will condone being bad. Fear of one's own instinctual demands. Fear of one's dependency, which places the child in the vulnerable position of helplessness if abandoned" (p. 19).

Carolyn

The processes of art-making with adolescents often leads to metaphoric expressions of their awareness that they are ultimately alone. Carolyn was sixteen years old when she was entered the hospital. The admitting physician diagnosed her as suffering from Major Depression 296.3 (Recurrent/ Severe). She had been abandoned by her parents when she was four years old. Since that time she had lived with different sets of relatives and been in two foster homes and three residential care facilities. She'd been "on the streets" for the several months prior to admission to the hospital.

She told the doctor that there was nothing she was interested in, and that she saw "no hope" that things would ever be better in her life. The behaviors that led to her hospitalization included sexual promiscuity, alcohol abuse, and episodes of self- mutilation. Her arms and legs bore gruesome testimony to the despair she felt within.

Carolyn's treatment team decided to schedule her into Recreation Therapy, Current Events Group, and Communication Skills Group. By the end of the first week, Carolyn had managed to have herself sent back to the unit from each of the activity areas as a consequence of her refusal to participate in the sessions and her hostile and defiant attitude toward the staff.

In Recreation Therapy, she got into fights with her peers. In Current Events Group, she taunted her peers and devalued the notion that anything happening in the world had any relevance to her life. In Communications Skills she picked at her scabs and ignored the therapists and others in the group. This, of course, set her apart from her peers and reinforced her negative self-view.

After a week of such self-defeating encounters, I was asked to consult with the treatment team about this patient to explore how the milieu could become more helpful to her. As I read Carolyn's chart and social history, it seemed to me that there was a consistent pattern of inconsistency. She had attended four different elementary schools and three different high schools. She'd lived in many different places and been in treatment with several therapists. I tried to imagine how the world looked to her. Images of chaos, turmoil and fear came to my mind.

I suggested to the treatment team that they limit Carolyn's activities and relationships. In a sense, I hoped they could make her world a little smaller and more secure. I thought Carolyn desperately needed the stability that consistent and predictable relationships could offer her.

The team agreed to my suggestions and Carolyn was taken out of her activities. A small group of nursing staff were assigned to be her primary caregivers. I was asked to provide her with individual art therapy sessions on the unit.

Initially, Carolyn was very resistant to working with me. During our first session, she stood in a corner with her arms crossed, head down, ignoring me. In her second session, she got angry at me, threw a full can of paint at the wall, and knocked over a table that I'd set up with art materials. I tried, as best I could, to view these sessions as gifts that she was offering. They were dramatic performances, enactments of her inner feelings. Her crossed-arms-ignoring-me stance gave me a glimpse of her vulnerability and her wish to block out the realities of her life. The angry outburst presented me with a dance, of sorts, whose theme was the rage and inner mess of Carolyn's life.

As I spent more time with her, I began to get the sense that Carolyn had never experienced herself as having either freedom or responsibility for anything in her life. She had always been at the mercy (or lack of it) of others. As this idea developed, I began to form a therapeutic plan.

I met Carolyn at the unit. "Carolyn, I'd like us to go to the Creative Arts Studio today."

She frowned. "Can't. I'm on Special Precautions. The staff says I am unpredictable and a potential danger to myself. They won't let me outta their sight, 'cause I might run away ya' know," she sneered.

"I still want you to come to the studio," I replied. "Let me talk to the nurses about this."

It took some convincing, but I eventually got clearance from the head nurse to take Carolyn off the unit. As we walked out the door, she turned to me and asked, "So what will you do if I take off?"

"Carolyn, why in the world would you do that?"

"Just to get the hell outta this hole."

"I guess I don't blame you," I said.

"What?" Her jaw dropped.

"I don't blame you for wanting to run away. If I were in your shoes I might want to do the same thing, but I hope that you don't. You've had enough running."

It was a cold February day, and a few snow flakes drifted through the air. Carolyn shivered and pulled her coat tightly against her. She said, "You didn't answer my question. What would you do if I run?"

"Well, I guess I'd run with you."

Then she asked, "You wouldn't try to grab me or make me stop?"

"No, Carolyn, I wouldn't."

"But...so why would you run with me?" She wanted to know.

"Well, I think that you should be free to do what you want to do, but I am free to do what I want to do also. I want to work with you, Carolyn. So I'll run."

She did not say anything more until we got to the creative arts studio. As we entered the building, I directed her to the painting area. Earlier that day, I had cut a large square of canvas, approximately four feet in diameter. I gave Carolyn a coffee can full of gesso and said, "Let's get this canvas ready to paint on."

"What do I do?" she asked.

"We have to cover the whole surface with gesso," I replied.

"And then what?"

"That will be up to you, Carolyn."

"What?" she asked again.

"You can do whatever you want to do on this canvas, Carolyn. I'll help you any way that I can, but you will have to decide what you're going to do for yourself."

"Yeah, right," she sneered. "What if I want to make like a billboard that says "Fuck the world!"

"Well, if that is what you really want to do, but I'd like you to try to be a little bit more creative than that. Anybody can say F.T.W."

When the gesso was dry, Carolyn said, "I need some paint." I showed her the cabinet in the main studio area where acrylic paint was kept. She selected bottles of red, blue, and black and an assortment of brushes.

Carolyn used a pencil to rough-in the outline of her caption in large graffiti-like letters. She kept looking at me out of the corner of her eye, as if she was just waiting to see how I would react to her graphic profanity. I did not comment on the content. I did suggest to her that the F and W needed to be capitalized.

"Are you really going to let me do this?" She asked.

"Yes, Carolyn. I told you that this piece of canvas is yours to do with as you wish. I do not approve of what you are doing and I will ask that we put your work away in between sessions. I guarantee that I won't hang it on the wall here, but I won't stop you from doing what you feel you need to do and I will not reject you."

So, Carolyn began to paint the F black. By the end of the session she had painted the first and second words. As she painted, I worked on a painting of my own. My image was of a stone wall. Behind the wall there was a turbulent background of intense colors. Inscribed on individual stones were the names of people, old friends of mine whom I've lost touch with.

Carolyn put down her brush and sighed, "I'm getting tired. What's your painting about?"

I thought for a moment. "Well, Carolyn, I've been thinking about how my life has changed. I'm not sure that I like all of the changes. Anyway, I wanted to do a painting about the people I've lost over the years. I guess this is a way of saying good-bye."

She looked back at her canvas and the words she was painting. "Make's my painting look ugly."

"Carolyn," I said, "I know that being here in the hospital is hard. It's okay for you to be angry at the world. It's okay to be angry at me. But I have to tell you, I love making art in this place."

"I don't love anything!" she said.

"Carolyn, I don't believe in accidents. You must have a lot of reasons to not love."

She looked at her black lettered "FUCK," then quietly said, "Oh fuck it! Can I start over again?"

"Carolyn," I said, "you can do anything that you want, absolutely anything. Art is like life. If you don't like the picture, paint over it. If you don't like your life, back up, gesso over it and start again. I will stick with you, I am not going anywhere. You can change the painting."

She gathered the gesso and recovered her canvas.

What emerged in the following sessions was an intriguing image of fear and hope. Carolyn covered the left side of the canvas with dark blue. Then, over the blue she applied red, and purple slashing lines. She said that each line represented "somebody who left." She covered the right side with a pastel yellowish green. It had a soft, cool, glow. She told me that the right side of the painting was, "something about trust."

* * *

Art making gives adolescents a way to metaphorically express their deep fear of abandonment and their longing for attachment. Making art in the presence of an art therapist affords teenagers the opportunity to express this fear in a safe way, while at the same time developing a relationship. It is only through relationships that adolescents are able to have reparative experiences. Through shared art experiences adolescent patients are able to become accountable for their lives, that is, to become the creator of the meaning of life. Along with this come the burdens of responsibility and freedom. At a deep level, freedom is responsibility. To become aware of responsibility is to be aware of the capacity to create one's story, purpose and destiny.

The implications of such a view of our work are profound for art therapists. Let us return to the metaphor of the work of art in progress. Carolyn had the ultimate freedom to do anything she wanted with the piece. Initially, she chose to do what was comfortable, to be negative and angry. As our relationship developed she also came to accept responsibility for her work. No one else could take the credit if her art-work was successful. No one else would take the blame if it turned out poorly. Carolyn's artistic freedom was inextricably bound to her responsibility. There was no escaping the anguish that came from her awareness that she was unconditionally accepted in our relationship and that I would stay with her regardless of what she did. I would not abandon her.

Art therapists working with adolescents come into contact daily with kids suffering from identity confusion, risk-taking, suicidality, self loathing, intense anger, and fear of abandonment. These are the painful, heavy and burdensome themes that are the content of the art of adolescent patients. The great strength of the art therapy profession is that at every turn of human history, it has always been the painters, the poets, the playwrights who have been willing to struggle with what they see around them in the world. The artists have always been the ones willing to be wounded as they wrestle with the loneliness, rage, ugliness and longing of existence. Making art can ease the suffering of adolescence. I have seen this time and again in my clinical work. I have seen kids in great emotional pain create metaphoric images of monstrous fear and I've watched as their heroic, creative selves emerge to form lasting relationships. I have listened to their stories and I heard them let go of their meaningless blaming of others, wel-coming a courageous acceptance of responsibility for their own lives. At my best, I participate in helping them tell their stories and I act as an artistic midwife in their rebirth labor. Sometimes, I have been a temporary adversary with whom they do creative, healing battle. At other times I have been an attentive member of the audience who is interested in understanding the meaning of the images that unfold before me. Sometimes the monsters are too powerful and the drama ends in tragedy. Sometimes their triumph is celebrated. Regardless of the outcome, I am repeatedly awed by the effort and courage of my adolescent artist/patients.

The crucial point of this for artist-therapists is that we can deal with the ugly ruined parts of our adolescent patients by knowing and accepting that these can be changed by art. Making art can help to solidify identity, encourage acceptable risks, lessen suicidality, trans-form self-loathing, soothe anger and ease abandonment fears. Hope is there for adolescents if they are willing to create it.

Chapter XI

ART AS THERAPY IN ADOLESCENT GROUPS

In this chapter, I will review the basic principles of art therapy group work with adolescents and discuss the special clinical advantages of the *art as therapy model of art psychotherapy* in relation to group work.

In the life of an adolescent, there are few things that are more important and influential than how one is regarded by one's peers. The power of acceptance or rejection by friends and acquaintances cannot be overstated. The central psychological task of adolescence is to become an independent, functional adult. In order to accomplish this task, it is necessary that adolescents successfully separate themselves from the secure confines of their families. She must break away from parental control in order to establish a sense of individual identity, but this can be a terrifying task. It is certainly an emotionally overwhelming one that must be approached in gradual steps. Hence, as a way of easing the terror of independence and freedom, the adolescent supplants her dependence upon parental and familial support and approval with dependence upon her peers. Art therapy groups can be an important treatment component for many suffering adolescents because they combine the safety, structure, and benefits of artistic self-expression and peer interaction with the acceptance and guidance of the artist-therapist.

How do art therapy groups help adolescent patients? In some ways, this is a simple question, yet if it can be answered with any sense of clarity, then we art therapists who work with emotionally disturbed teenagers will have a significant organizing principle from which to chart our approach to the intense and disturbing dilemmas of working with adolescents. The role that art-making in groups plays in the process of facilitating therapeutic change forms a basis from which art therapists may develop artistic treatment strategies and plans.

The course of change for an adolescent in therapy is an intricate and nearly indefinable process. Change happens in the context of a complex interweaving of relationship and experience. In the adolescent art therapy group milieu, the relationships are multiple: patient to materials, patient to peers, patient to therapist, patient to tools, patient to images, as well as therapist to patients, materials, tools and images. The experiences in group art therapy sessions are also multiple, tactile, visual and process-oriented. The intersections among relationships and experiences are the locations where the curative aspects of art therapy groups are formed.

In an effort to describe the treatment process, I have offered the metaphor of a carpenter attempting to describe the process of building a house (Moon, 1994). In its entirety, the explanation would be overwhelmingly complex and technical. "However, if the same carpenter explains the use of two-by-fours in the construction of walls, the description will be relatively easy to digest and understand. Whenever attempting to describe the complicated, it is helpful to explore first the simplest building blocks. An intricate whole may best be understood through its basic parts" (p. 115). Following that logic, I will turn to discussing the curative aspects of art as therapy in adolescent groups.

The curative aspects of adolescent art therapy groups, in my view, may be described by the following ten factors:

1. Art as the Natural Language of Adolescence
2. Art as Engagement with Stuff
3. Art-Making as Existential Expression
4. Art-Making as Personal Metaphor
5. Art-Making as Relationship
6. Art-Making as Structure and Chaos
7. Art-Making as Empowerment
8. Art-Making as Reparative Experience
9. Art-Making as Self-Transcendent Hope
10. Art-Making as a Way of Being with Adolescents

ART AS THE NATURAL LANGUAGE OF ADOLESCENCE

For many adolescents, even happy and healthy ones, reflecting upon and sharing their inner emotional life with others is quite difficult. It has been suggested that the ability to articulate deep feelings is developmentally atypical for most, if not all, in early adolescence, and that such communication skills do not generally emerge until early adulthood. For that matter, deeply emotional verbal communication is often difficult for many adults. Bly (1995) notes that men in our culture have a particularly hard time expressing feelings directly. The inability to express feelings with words presents a host of problems for the treatment staff members of facilities that focus on the care of adolescents. The question for therapists and staff members is how to help the adolescent express deep feelings when this capacity is developmentally inappropriate via verbal format. The answer to this question is found in the fact that teenagers are adept at expressing their feelings through actions, images, metaphors, music and dance. Art is the natural language of adolescence. In many ways, an adolescent's life is a continuous performance event. The meanings of the event are revealed through behaviors. The adolescent "tries out" for different parts within the drama. They are the main character in the play and are also in charge of casting, set design, costuming, music selection, script revision and choreography. Each of these functions serve as metaphorical expressions of the inexpressible.

Art therapy groups offer adolescent patients the opportunity to enact the themes that are central to their existence within the safety of artistic processes and structures. Simultaneously, the teenager experiences the benefits of self-expression and peer interaction, coupled with the acceptance and guidance of the artist therapist.

During my career, I have visited many treatment facilities where the staff failed to understand the developmental inability of adolescents to express feelings in words. Such facilities attempted to treat adolescent patients through traditional talk-therapy modalities and inevitably found that their patients resented their efforts. Emotionally suffering adolescent patients are not merely younger versions of emotionally disturbed adults. While verbal group psychotherapy approaches may be a successful treatment modality for adults, art is the natural language of adolescent group therapy.

ART AS ENGAGEMENT WITH STUFF

In Bob Ault's (1986) wonderful video, *Art Therapy: The Healing Vision*, psychoanalyst Paul W. Pruyser, Ph.D., observes that, "the wo~'

is made of stuff." This simple observation embodies one of the greatest advantages that art therapy groups have over verbal treatment modalities. They involve working with the "stuff" of the world. Engagement with artistic processes and materials involves the adolescent patient in what Yalom (1985) refers to as "working in the here and now" (p. 135-98). The here-and-now process in art therapy groups operates at two interrelated levels. The first level has to do with the things that happen within the session: the members of the group, including the art therapist, make art; they develop feelings toward their image, the media, the process, their peers, the group leader and the group as a whole. "The thrust is ahistoric: the immediate events in the meeting take place over events both in the current outside life and in the distant past of the members" (Yalom, p. 135). The second level of the here-and-now process in art therapy groups occurs as the members of the group reflect upon the images that have been created during the art-making experience. In a verbal group therapy session, what is left after a word has been spoken? Nothing beyond subjective memories. But, in art therapy groups, the images, the products, the artifacts of creative work remain in the here-and-now, providing an objective thing to be reflected upon.

Thus, in art therapy groups the effective use of the here-and-now is profoundly dualistic: the group engages with "stuff," actions are taken, images are made; it then reflects upon the artifacts of what has occurred in the here-and-now. The beauty of this is that adolescent patients can create an image related to an event from their past, and through the here-and-now artistic process, it ceases to be a distant memory, but rather becomes a live, present-tense phenomenon. Any verbal articulation related to the image then is not about the past event, but rather focused on the messages of the image that is in the room at the moment.

In my art therapy groups, I always maintain a profound respect for all aspects of the work. This reverence is applied to the image, the artist and to my efforts as therapist. I encourage the patients in my adolescent art therapy groups to work constantly toward mastery of materials because of the sense of adequacy that comes from this. The mastery of artistic techniques and media is inextricably linked to self-discipline, which inevitably leads the adolescent to positive self-regard. From this comes a passion for life. This passion is disclosed through authentic, creative and vital interactions between the adolescent and others in the group. Such interactions are inherently connected to the artist's skillful use of media. The success of art therapy group work depends equally upon the metaphoric expression of feelings and the capable handling of materials.

It is unfortunate that much of art therapy group literature has focused heavily upon the temporary cathartic aspect of the work. While cathartic expression is certainly one helpful element of group art therapy, it is in my view a relatively minor one. More important are the formal artistic procedures and the quality of expression. In adolescent groups, careful attention must be given to the constant evolution of mastery of art processes. These are as important as the development of interpersonal relationship skills and communications skills.

In a profound sense, learning to master art materials may be thought of as the ability to organize and transform raw materials and experiences. The significance of art work in the group therapy setting is found as an adolescent transforms powerful destructive inner forces into constructive, meaningful objects. The process of making art is a process of organizing chaotic emotional material into a coherent, restructured product. The adolescent's turbulent swirl of feelings, sensations, actions and relationships is the marker of mental and emotional distress. The arts offer hope for clarity and balance by alleviating the distress through the work itself.

As the teenager's sense of mastery grows in relation to specific artistic tasks there is always a corresponding increase in confidence and self-esteem. A reciprocity is established among the artist, the task and the product that is intrapsychically contagious. As the adolescent artist experiences success in his or her ability to handle media and solve artistic problems, the capacity to deal with other aspects of life is also enhanced. Art therapists working with adolescent groups should take the quality of patient's artwork, and their own, seriously. At every opportunity, it is important to encourage the patient to express feelings, and to do so in a skillful and artistically articulate manner.

I have worked with many adolescents who initially seemed to view the arts studio as a depository for the feelings they did not want to have. These kids often slopped their way through group sessions with no regard for the aesthetic aspects of their work. Their finished products were often reminiscent of chaotic mud. In such instances, my response is to insist that they slow down and learn the mechanics of a given task. Sometimes this means helping the patients learn about mixing color, or sometimes it means giving a quick lesson in one- and two-point perspective. These artistic disciplines help the adolescent patient structure and organize his expression in a way that enhances his attachment to both the process and the final product. This is not to say that I insist on pleasant or pretty pictures. On the contrary, most times the images that are born in the art therapy group are painful and raw, but I do insist on attention to quality in the work itself.

My position that attention be given to the quality of the art produced in adolescent art therapy groups is based on the belief that mastery = care. If I encouraged adolescents to simply slop paint onto a canvas, with no regard to the quality of the work, the meta-message would be that I have no genuine investment in their art, and therefore no real interest in them. Likewise, if I approach my own artistic efforts in the art therapy group with anything less than a focused care in relation to quality, I would be modeling inattention to self.

I do not expect adolescent patients to become accomplished artists, but I do expect them to learn to care about quality in their lives. I ask them to do the best work that they can, and I look for ways to help them be better than they believe they are capable of being.

ART AS EXISTENTIAL EXPRESSION

Adolescents who enter art therapy groups are nearly always in the midst of painful and frightening life crises. The particular events and circumstances that lead, or push, an adolescent into an art therapy group are as diverse as the individuals themselves, but there are some common threads that appear time and again. Existentialists describe these as the "ultimate concerns of existence." Prominent among these are: freedom, aloneness, guilt, each person's responsibility for his or her own life, the inevitability of suffering and a deep longing for meaning.

In adolescent art therapy groups, the focus is often on metaphorically addressing the patient's anxieties and struggles that form in response to an awareness of the ultimate concerns of life. The work in the art therapy group is always tied to the creative struggle with the core issues of meaning, isolation and freedom. These issues are expressed subtly and overtly by adolescents in the following ways:

> Life is not fair;
> I don't want this pain and discomfort;
> I feel so lonely;
> I am not responsible for my life.

Artists have long known that an important source of their creative work is the emotional turmoil that is stimulated by their struggle with the ultimate concerns of existence. A central principle in art therapy group work is that adolescents relate to these issues either by attempting to ignore them, or by living in what Yalom refers to as, "a state of mindfulness." It is the awareness of one's capacity to be self-creative in the state of mindfulness which promotes the ability to change. The arts are natural activities for expression and expression leads to mindfulness.

The major thrust of my work with adolescents can be conceptualized as going on a shared journey with the patient. The purpose of this journey is to discover the meanings of the patients' life as they emerge in artistic processes and products. Metaphoric expressions of the unfairness, the struggle, the loneliness and responsibility are always found in the images my patients make. I guard against temptations to interpret or diagnose. Rather, I encourage the adolescent to tell his or her own story, for it is through the telling of the tale that understanding comes. It is through the experiences of being understood and understanding that healing comes.

Throughout history, the arts have always dealt with the ultimate concerns of existence. It is this tradition of struggle that is the extraordinary gift of the artist therapist to the adolescent milieu. Artists have always struggled with issues of meaning, isolation, death and creative freedom. As art therapists, it is our mandate to do the same in the company of our fellow travelers. Making art is a process of dealing with existential concerns.

ART MAKING AS PERSONAL METAPHOR

The classic understanding of metaphor is that it is a manner of *speaking* in which one thing is described in the terms of another. The bringing together of the two sheds new light on the character of that which is being described and holds in tension the possibility of multiple interpretations. In relation to art therapy group work, it is important to think of metaphors not only in terms of words, but as *images and actions* as well. Metaphors are enactments and images that hold symbolic meanings, both conscious and unconscious, for the artist. The purposes of action and image metaphors are to articulate, express, free and define their maker. This is an essential aspect of our work with adolescents in groups.

Metaphoric images have an inherent quality of comparison in which one thing (the art object) is used to shed new light on the character of the adolescent artist. Just as verbal metaphors hold the possibility of many divergent interpretations, so it is with visual and action metaphors. The art therapist can never **know** exactly what the image metaphor means. The best that we can do is engage in imaginal interpretive dialogue with the adolescent in an attempt to help them discover their own meanings.

Art therapists are in an extraordinary position to see and respond to the metaphoric creations of adolescents. We must not attempt to enslave it through our vocabulary. Rather we should promote appreciation and awe, and dedicate ourselves to the notion that images can and should *just be.*

Every image that the adolescent creates in the art therapy group is a partial self-portrait. I do not mean to imply that this is all images are, but it is one important aspect that is of deep therapeutic interest to art therapists. We need only to look at, and be with, our patients' images. We hardly need to talk at all. The need that some therapists seem to have to put an adolescent's images and experiences into words makes me uncomfortable, for it implies a distrust of the image to convey its own meanings. It is fundamental that art therapists working with adolescents value the communication that is presented in the artistic process and product. This is so despite the fact that metaphoric images hold the potential for multiple interpretations, leaving us with only ambiguous, mysterious and unconfirmed ideas about meaning. Making art is making personal metaphor.

ART MAKING AS RELATIONSHIP

For an adolescent, there are few things that are more important and influential than how he or she is regarded by peers. The power of acceptance, or rejection, by friends and acquaintances cannot be over-stated. As William James (1890) said, "No more fiendish punishment could be devised, were such a thing physically possible, than that one should be turned loose in society and remain absolutely unnoticed by all members thereof" (p. 293).

In order to accomplish the basic developmental tasks of adolescence, it is necessary to break away from parental control in order to establish a sense of individual identity. This is terribly difficult work that can be done only with the aid of other relationships.

No matter where one looks in the history of humanity, it is clear that relationships between individuals are of critical importance. Whether one examines the development of a single person or the evolution of a group, nation or entire culture, it is clear that one's relationship to others is a central phenomenon. Simply put, people need people, in order to survive and in order to thrive. As Yalom states, "No one—neither the dying, nor the outcast, nor the mighty—transcends the need for human contact" (p. 23).

I have often encountered adolescent patients who proclaim that they do not care what others think of them. As one fifteen-year-old girl said in reference to her peers in the art therapy group, "They don't mean shit to me. What do I care what they think?" My experience has been that if I can get an adolescent to attend at least two art therapy group sessions, then a very different persona will inevitably emerge. Adolescents are intensely concerned about how group members feel about them. Teenagers almost never feel indifference toward their peers. They are never bored by being in an art therapy group. They may feel scared, panicked, anxious, disrespectful, shamed or enraged, but they are never indifferent.

Given the intensity of adolescent feelings, the question for group therapists is how to hook the adolescent into the process. I contend that the quickest and most efficient way to form a solid therapeutic alliance with adolescent patients is through making art rather than through discussion. By making, the adolescent artist takes images from within and spreads them in the world. This is an act of acknowledgment of the "others" beyond the boundaries of the self. The others are the beholders, the audience, the peers in the group.

Few things are more painful to the adolescent psyche than loneliness. Hence, the importance of art therapy groups. Personal meaning can be found only in the context of relationship. The self must be transcended for purpose to be present. The creative process is most clearly manifested in the domain of relatedness. Art is inspired in the territory of interpersonal connection which is the shared human experience.

Through the process of making art the adolescent offers his view, his unique response to the world. The community of the art group receives the imaginal offspring of the artist's struggle. It is only in the context of relationship to the community that the artist establishes his particular self. The others in the group give witness to the uniqueness of the adolescent artist. The artist creates, the community responds, the artist makes again and the community attends. On and on the creative relating circle spins. Art making is relating.

ART MAKING AS STRUCTURE AND CHAOS

Adolescent patients have often told me that the hardest day in the art therapy group was their first one. They stood staring at the blank, empty piece of paper and were overwhelmed by all the possibilities and all of their insecurities. There were so many options available to them when the paper was untouched. The potentials were endless and their feelings were chaotic.

Every decision that the adolescent artist makes, beginning with the size and shape of the paper they will use, limits their options and brings order to the disorder. As the teenager selects the chalk that she will use, she closes the door on other possibilities—the acrylics, the watercolors and the tempera. Through the countless decisions that she makes, subtle and dramatic, overt and covert, she brings form to the chaos of endless possibilities. The decisions the artist makes relative to size, shape, form and media are analogous to the internal process of filtering image and content possibilities. Exactly how this thematic fermentation happens is a mystery. In *Existential Art Therapy: The Canvas Mirror*, I (Moon, 1995) used the image of a boiling pot of sea water to describe the process. As the water boils and turns to steam, it leaves a residue of salt. The salt was always there, but it took the boiling to make it visible. The same thing happens within the adolescent artist. Feelings, images, themes, conflicts and powerful forces simmer, eventually turning into the artist's "salt," as the artwork is completed. As adolescents make art they bring structure to the chaos of their lives. Whatever needs to be expressed will be expressed. Creating art is a process of constantly moving back and forth between order and disorder, spontaneity and composition, chaos and structure. This process is analogous to the journey through adolescence in that the individual is continuously moving between the order and security of the family and the spontaneity and experimentation of the peer group and the larger community. Thus, art making provides an essential action metaphor of the way life is for the adolescent.

ART MAKING AS EMPOWERMENT

The adolescents who come to the art therapist as outpatients or who are hospitalized in a residential treatment facility, whether for psychiatric or physical reasons, often bring with them a disturbing sense of vulnerability and powerlessness. Their faith in personal power has either never fully developed or been severely wounded. They have often been victimized by family, friends or the world itself. It is an essential task of the art therapy group to work with adolescent patients to develop their awareness and belief in their own power.

This is an aspect of art therapy group work that, in my view, cannot be accomplished through talking alone. There have to be experiences that foster the development or reclamation of personal power and the responsibilities that accompany it.

As art therapists, we are in an ideal position to empower our patients by virtue of our own experiences with art making and imagery. Every art therapist has experienced firsthand the healing and transformative nature of artistic work through our own empowering involvement with media and processes. Art making has brought meaning to our lives by transforming our conflicts and ennobling painful struggles. These experiences are what initially called us to the art therapy profession.

Struggle is a universal element of human nature. The collision of internal forces is what brings about the creative actions of art. One of the primary tasks in adolescent art therapy groups is to inspire in the patient the desire to create out of his or her discomfort, rather than be abused by it. Artistic acts of empowerment help the adolescent to transform himself from victim to hero/survivor.

Adolescents are a conglomeration of opposing forces, inconsistencies and contradictions. They are in a state of continual change; therefore conflict and struggle are inevitable. There is a core tension within the teenager that is most clearly expressed by polarities. Art making does nothing to lessen the tension; on the contrary, it often accentuates it by using the energy in empowering actions. In the group context, adolescent artists discover meaning in their lives as they shape and color the disturbing disharmony within them. Creation does not banish pain or discomfort but rather ennobles it. Through the creative process of artmaking, contradictions and conflicts are brought into clear focus that makes nonlogical sense. The empowering nature of art making in adolescent groups does not seek to cure. It accepts and uses. Art brings the adolescents' deepest fears, loneliness and anguish close to the surface in a safe and structured way. It does not rid the patient of these difficulties. It enables them to live courageously with them.

The process of creating art in the therapeutic art group is a metaphor for life itself. As the artist works, she has ultimate power to change the picture. She can add new elements; she can darken or highlight. The artist can, if she chooses, draw over a section and start again. This is an allegory of life itself. It can be changed if and when the individual decides to change. Many times the adolescent does not believe that she has such power over the course of her own life. So the doing of art becomes an introduction into free will and the power of choice and creation. Making art in adolescent groups is an empowering experience.

ART MAKING AS REPARATIVE EXPERIENCE

Alexander (1946) described the basic principle of psychological treatment as, "to expose the patient, under more favorable circumstances to emotional situations that he could not handle in the past. The patient, in order to be helped, must undergo a corrective emotional experience suitable to repair the traumatic influence of the previous experience." Alexander's basic principles of individual therapy support my own conclusions, based on clinical experience, that an intellectual understanding or insight on the part of the patient is insufficient to bring about lasting change. There must be an emotional and behavioral component to the therapeutic experience in order for the patient to effect lasting change. In fact, I would argue that lasting change for adolescents comes most often through reparative experiences, and seldom through classic psychoanalytic insight.

These basic principles of therapy regarding the importance of the emotional experience in the therapy context and the patient's validation of these experiences through behavioral implementation are equally important to art therapy group work. The art group setting offers many opportunities for reparative experiences. As adolescents engage in artistic work within the confines of the therapy group, they inevitably create a social microcosm that reflects their interpersonal sphere. The relationship tensions that have been contributing factors to their difficulties outside the group will almost immediately emerge. In other words, the adolescent will quickly display her dysfunctional behaviors in the group; there will be no need for her to verbalize her maladaptive patterns (which they would resist doing anyway) because these will surely be enacted within the group. In the adolescent art therapy group, there are many built-in relationship tensions: sibling rivalries, sexual attractions, competition for the group leader's attention and approval, domination of others, etc. These inherent tensions provide the group with opportunities to repair the trauma of past experiences by transforming maladaptive behavioral reactions into healthy responses via artistic working-through activity. In order for such transformation to occur, the members must feel safe within the group and there must be honest reflection on the images that emerge during the session.

The most common reparative artistic experiences that I have observed in art therapy groups involve the adolescent's graphic expression of intense feeling toward the leader of the group or toward another member. In either case, the structure of artistic processes and the culture of the group allow adolescent patients to express feelings metaphorically or directly without incurring any negative consequence. In fact, with the aid of the graphic image as an objective force that is continually referred to during the group session, the adolescent often experiences a feeling of joyous relief that is quite exhilarating. In my closing comments after such sessions, I regularly ask the members of the group to check their wrists to make sure they still have a pulse. "You see," I tell them, " you have been able to be honest with one another and nobody died." These are truly reparative emotional experiences.

ART MAKING AS SELF TRANSCENDENT HOPE

Hope is an essential element in every form of psychotherapy. As the leader of an adolescent art therapy group, the therapist must have hope for the patient and ultimately the patient must have hope for himself. If there is no hope, there will be little or no therapeutic progress made. Of course, it is to be expected that the adolescent's hope may be an "endangered species" at the time of admission into the group. Therefore, the art therapist's hope must be solid and unshakable. Hope requires faith. The patient needs to have faith in the art therapist. The art therapist must have faith in art making, in group process, in herself and in the essential goodness and value of all the members of the group.

Making art is an expression of hope. In an entirely unspoken way, engaging in creative activity is an act of self transcendence: i.e., a giving to others beyond the self. In order to do this one must believe that the other is worthy of the gift.

In my clinical work, I have seen this principle enacted again and again in art therapy groups. Adolescent patients who have been in the group for a while subtly welcome and initiate newcomers. The seasoned patient demonstrates to the new member that the art therapy group experience can be a good one. This happens behaviorally, symbolically and verbally. Patients often want their drawings to be left hanging on the walls. Their images stimulate the environment. Whether the new patient knows the artist or not, there is a powerful message inherent in seeing the gift of someone else's art hanging in the group room. If these drawings could speak, I believe they would say to the new patients, "Have faith, have hope."

Critical in this hoping is the art therapist's firm conviction that what we do is healthy and curative. Our belief is contagious. Likewise, any doubt we have regarding the integrity of our contribution to the therapy process will infect the air of the group room. Such messages, whether positive or negative, are not a matter of verbalization. They are subtle and covert.

In art therapy groups, adolescents also find that their needs can be met as they give to others. These same kids feel empty and barren in the early stages of therapy, as if they have nothing of value to offer to anyone else. Adolescents are of tremendous support and help to each other in the art therapy group. They encourage one another, critique one another, share artistic techniques, make suggestions and listen to one another. Huestis and Ryland (1990) found that the relationships among patients that are formed in the context of the treatment situation have as much or more to do with the eventual success or failure of the therapy as do the professional therapists.

The making of art is an activity of self-transcendence. Adolescents in a psychiatric hospital are often morosely self-absorbed. Such absorption takes many forms, yet it is clear, as Viktor Frankl (1959) discusses, that meaning can be found only in the context of relationship and in transcending the self. The doing of art invariably absorbs the patient in a thing outside, beyond the self. In the art therapy group, this transcendent absorption is a public act. Patients respond to the art work of other patients. There is a contagious benevolence that infects the air of the group room. Creating art in a group context is a declaration of faith and hope.

ART MAKING AS A WAY OF BEING WITH ADOLESCENTS

Art making is a way of being with adolescents. I want now to explore the basic tasks of the art therapist in relation to group leadership. It is important to keep in mind that a consistent positive relationship among art making, the patient and the art therapist underlies all of the tasks of the art therapist. The position of the art therapist is always one of concern, acceptance and genuine willingness to engage with the adolescent in his pain, his struggles and his risk-taking, as he attempts to find the meaning of his life. As art therapists, we must never attempt to force our own system of beliefs upon the struggles of the adolescent. Our task is to accompany the teenager as he discovers for himself the point of his journey. The best that an art therapist can do in a group setting is to model artistically, behaviorally and verbally a sense of faith that the suffering, anguish and insecurities of the adolescent patient are of value.

The basic tasks of the adolescent art therapy group leader are threefold. The first task is the setting up and maintenance of the adolescent art therapy group. The second is the establishment of the group culture: a code of conduct, rules of behavior, routines and norms that guide the artistic interaction of the group. The third task is to keep the focus of the group to "the here and now."

Now, let me discuss how I think about these three leadership tasks in relation to adolescent expressive art therapy groups. I am referring here to group experiences that are intensely focused on utilizing art processes in conjunction with group psychotherapy techniques. Expressive art therapy groups are thereby substantively different than the open studio experiences I have discussed in other segments of this text. First, the art therapist establishes the time and frequency of sessions. In fulfilling this function, I must make sure that adequate art materials are available and that the group has an appropriate amount of time in the studio space. Generally, I am the one who sets the theme of the day for the artistic task. I also have to control the number of patients in the group.

As the culture builder, I symbolically hold the values of the group. One way to envision this is to think of a vessel that holds water. Inside the vessel the water may sometimes be perfectly smooth. At other times the water may be swirling or choppy. Sometimes the water might freeze. At other times it might boil. Regardless of how the water is, the vessel that holds it remains the same. The vessel contains whatever is happening in the water. As the culture builder, I also shape the mores and expectations of the group, both implicitly and explicitly. For instance, I want the members of a group to value our time together. One subtle way that I can have an impact on this is by seeing to it that the group starts promptly. I give a powerful implicit message by consistently being punctual and ready to work at the prescribed time. The group learns through my example that I value our time together and generally this translates to their valuing it also.

One aspect of the culture that I make explicit is the expectation that confidentiality will be maintained by the adolescent members of the group. This is extremely important to the safety of the group. I always let the adolescents know that, "What you say in here stays in here." I also explain that as the leader of the group, I may, at times, share information from the group with my colleagues on the treatment team, particularly if I am concerned that a group member may be considering harming themselves or someone else, or if I think that I have information that will be beneficial to the group members' overall treatment program. I stress that it is not fair for an adolescent to talk about what happens in the group to other people who are not members because this could damage the sense of safety and security within the group.

The culture is built and reinforced by my modeling. My investment in the art process, my beliefs that making art is important and that life has meaning, my punctuality and my openness to the process all have tremendous effect on the tone of a session.

The culture is enriched as the adolescents assume a more active role in imparting the history of the group or explicit rules, etc., to new members. In this way the group maintains its own culture. Another way that the group tends to itself is through the imparting of traditions. It never ceases to amaze me that contributions made by patients from years ago live on in the group mind. An example: Several years ago a tradition of smudging the cheek of a new group member was started in a group of adolescent girls. The smudging served as a ritual of initiation to that group. Although the original "smudgers" had been discharged years earlier, the dirty cheek remained as a sign of warmth and acceptance for a long time. A boys group established the tradition that when a member was discharged, the peer who was closest to him would take over the drawing place and sit in the chair of the one who was gone. Such traditions indicate that a positive culture of ownership has been established within the group. I watch for this sort of indicators and regard them as powerful symbols of alliance between individual members and the group as a whole.

The culture of the art therapy group is strengthened whenever a powerful self-disclosure event occurs. These events involve here-and-now sharing of the feelings stirred by the image metaphors created in the group. Often these events lead to poignant moments of vulnerability and openness. Inevitably, at such times, the adolescent group members rally to the support and aid of their peer, enhancing the cohesiveness of the group and fostering the sense of safety that is required to face the suffering and struggles that each member brings to the group. At such times, my role is akin to being an honored guest. In another sense, I provide a container (the group culture) in which such things can occur and therefore serve as host.

Finally, I encourage the shaping of the art therapy group's culture through consistent adherence to procedural rituals. Every group begins as I close the door and sit down. Every group session consists of four events. First, there is a brief period of checking in with each individual. Second, there is a period of making art. Third, there is a period of reflection on the images that have been made, and finally there is a brief closure process. I never make exceptions to these procedures. The flow of the session becomes ingrained as part of the experience of the group. The predictability of this structure can be most reassuring to the adolescent patient who is caught up in the intensity of his or her pain. The patient knows that there will be an opportunity to wind down, to compose himself before he walks out the door. This frees him to experience his feelings more fully.

The third task of the art therapist is to keep the focus of the group in the here-and-now. As I have stated elsewhere in this text, I believe that all things we create are partial self-portraits and therefore one task of the art therapist is to empower the adolescent to own what they have created in the present. Adolescent patients often attempt to distance themselves from their graphics by describing them as representing historic events in their lives that no longer affect them. The power of the art image is that it is a present-tense object that represents how a person feels right now.

An example: Stanley, a thirteen-year-old boy, was asked to draw a picture of "me and my family." He drew a picture of his mom, dad, and sister sitting in front of a television set playing a Nintendo game. He told the group that he had been given the game for his eighth birthday but that his family had played with it more than he had. As Stanley shared the story, he laughed about his parents playing with the game. It was tempting for me and the group members to simply regard this image as a drawing about a funny historic event. But, when I asked Stan to imagine that the Nintendo game had a voice and to speak for it in the here-and-now, the game expressed outrage at being taken over by Stanley's mother and father. The game angrily said, "I was supposed to be Stan's." One of his friends in the group asked, "Stan, you were supposed to draw about yourself and your family?" Stanley had chosen to portray his mother, father and sister, but not himself. The group members got into this story and dialogued with the game and later with the image of Stanley's sister who held the remote control device. Stan became aware of his present-day feeling that he was excluded from his family. Without the rubric of keeping the content and process in the here-and-now, the significance of Stan's drawing might have been lost in what seemed at first glance to be a humorous drawing of an old event.

Staying in the here-and-now is quite easy in art therapy groups as long as the art therapist keeps referring to the image that the adolescent has made, rather than to the history of events depicted.

The tasks of being with adolescents in art therapy groups are multilayered and require intense energy and concentration on the part of the art therapist. While the art group leader is attending to her own artistic work, she must also attend to the individual patients and all of the graphic communications that take place within the group.

Again, it is essential to keep in mind that underlying each of these tasks is a consistent involvement with art making. As art therapists, we are always focused on maintaining an attitude of concern for the adolescent, acceptance of all his or her feelings and genuine willingness to be with the adolescent. Adolescents who require art therapy will bring their pain, struggles and their risk-taking behaviors. In the context of the art therapy group, we encourage them to use art as a way to find meaning in their lives. We do not try to force our beliefs on them, but always work to accompany the patient as she discovers the meanings of her journey. We do this through our own artistic efforts in the group, through our behavior toward the adolescent patients and through the things that we say during the session. In every way possible, art therapists need to exude a faith that the suffering, anguish and insecurities of the adolescent patient are of value and can be eased through making art in a group setting.

These elements describe different aspects of art therapy group work. Some of them refer to specific actions or attributes of the process of change, while others might more accurately be characterized as catalysts or mediums in which transformation occurs. While I suspect that these curative aspects are operative in other therapeutic modalities, I believe firmly that the art therapy group is an ideal milieu for their enactment by adolescent patients.

This listing of the curative aspects of art in adolescent therapy groups has evolved from many years of clinical experience. It is, to be sure, only a partial inventory of the therapeutic characteristics of art processes in groups, but it has emerged out of encounters with real live adolescents who are struggling with their lives. Having observed many kids get better as a result of art making in groups, these are the aspects that I find common among them.

Chapter XII

PORTRAITS OF THE CURATIVE ASPECTS OF ART AS THERAPY IN ADOLESCENT GROUPS

In this chapter I will discuss again the ten curative aspects of art as therapy in adolescent expressive art groups. The reader is reminded that the experiences described here are in relation to intensive therapy groups utilizing art materials and group psychotherapy techniques. Again, adolescent expressive art groups are quite different than the adolescent studio art experiences referred to in other sections of this book. I want to take the reader into the expressive art group room in order to give you the "feel" of these curative aspects at work. I hope I can convey to you the atmosphere of these interactions: the sounds, the smells, the tastes of the places. I have done my best to bring you into the intriguing world of the adolescent art therapy group in progress.

The vignettes offered here are brief. It is my hope that they will point the way for the reader to grasp the concepts of the ten elements in such a way as to enable you to identify them at work in the other, more lengthy illustrations offered in various segments of this book. Although in other chapters I do not refer directly to these ten aspects, I believe that you will see their healing effects at work in the vignettes.

ART AS THE NATURAL LANGUAGE OF ADOLESCENCE

Gina did not talk very often. She had been viciously abused and emotionally neglected for much of her fifteen-year-old life. She just did not have a lot to say.

When she was referred to the adolescent art therapy group I was a little worried about how helpful it would be for her. During her first session, as I explained the group structure to her, Gina made hesitant eye contact with me and her peers in the group, but would quickly look away. "Gina," I said, "this is a group where we use drawing as a way of expressing feelings. You don't have to be Picasso or Michelangelo, or anyone like that. Whatever you do here will be okay. I do ask that when other people are talking about their artwork that we all pay attention. I know that everybody in this group has a long history of people not taking their feelings seriously. I promise you that in this group we will always take your feelings seriously. Welcome to the group, Gina, I'm glad you are with us."

Gina didn't say anything.

The beginning ritual of this group is to sit in a circle and quickly share the feeling that each member is entering the group with that day. As it came Gina's turn she quietly mumbled, "I'm okay." She held her arms tightly against her body and looked at the floor.

When everyone had shared their feeling, I said to the group, "Today, I want us to think of all the different kinds of trees there are in the world. You know, there are apple trees, and oaks, hickories, evergreens and cactus trees. Given the sort of a person that you are, and the kind of life you have had, I want you to imagine what you would look like if you were a tree. When the image comes, try to draw what you see."

In that expressive art therapy group we worked with vivid colors of poster chalks on large sheets (3' x 3') of brown craft paper that were hung on the wall with masking tape. Without hesitation, Gina moved to a place at the wall and began to draw. She covered the paper quickly with blue and purple. She then used black to sketch a primitive-looking leafless tree. The tree was standing by itself in a clearing. Behind it there was a forest. Nestled against one of the exposed roots of the solitary tree there was a huddled figure curled against the rough bark.

When all of the adolescents in the group had finished their drawings, we sat back down in the circle and each patient had the opportunity to tell the story of his or her tree. One of the girls, Alie, had drawn the stump of a large tree. She told the group about how, "some guy came along with a chain saw and cut the tree down for no good reason."

Jeff drew a maple tree with leaves that were brown and dead, leaves that were brightly colored and leaves that were brand new. He said, "I got no clue why I did any of this. It just seemed right."

Al said, "Looks like a good trip, Jeff."

Jeff responded, "Everything looks like a trip to you!" And the room was filled with laughter.

When it came time to discuss her image, Gina looked away. She huddled in much the same position as the figure in her drawing.

In some ways, this first session symbolized Gina's entire journey in the art therapy group. She seldom had much to say, but she always portrayed people and places from her life. The scenes were often hauntingly lonely, sometimes disturbing, and sometimes stark and painful. She did not have to say a lot about them; her peers in the group seemed to understand. By making art about these places and events Gina told her story. Her images were never direct portraits of the people who had treated her so inhumanely, yet they were metaphorically profound. By making art she creatively transformed herself from being a victim, to being the heroine of her image-stories.

On one especially remarkable day, Gina drew a picture of a bull-dozer that was about to demolish an old dilapidated house. Jeff reacted, "Gina, that 'dozer looks like it's gonna put a serious hurt on that house!"

Gina turned to Jeff and replied, "Yea, that place deserves it."

I always end adolescent art therapy sessions by ritualistically asking each member, "What are you leaving with today?"

Gina made a mechanical roaring sound and then said, "I have work to do."

* * *

For many adolescents, talking about their innermost feelings is quite difficult. The ability to articulate deep feelings is a skill that often does not develop until early adulthood. The inability to express feelings with words need not be a problem for art therapists who care for adolescents, because the tools of our trade are action, image and metaphor. Art is the natural language of adolescence. Art therapists should keep in mind that in some ways an adolescent's life is a continuous performance event and that the meanings of the event are revealed through behavior. The adolescent is the main character in the performance.

Art therapy groups allow adolescent patients to enact safely through artwork the themes that are central to their existence. The teenager experiences the benefits of self-expression and peer interaction coupled with the acceptance and guidance of the artist therapist.

Some would say that since Gina so seldom talked in the group, my imaginings about her pictures and my presentation of her work as an example of the natural artistic language of adolescence is invalid. To such colleagues I would respond, with all due respect, *I was there.* I watched as Gina used the natural language of art to tell her tale. I saw her heal herself through the mysterious power of art.

ART AS ENGAGEMENT WITH STUFF

Art therapists working with adolescents must maintain a marked respect for the "stuff" of the group. In the expressive art therapy group, "the stuff" consists of being with others, engaging in the work and mastering art processes. The patients, the images, the procedures and the quality of craftsmanship all can be equally embraced by artist therapists. Mastery of materials and the techniques of handling them promotes a sense of inner adequacy that is deeply therapeutic for adolescents. Mastery of process and media is linked inextricably to self-discipline, which is likewise connected to self-esteem. When art therapists approach artistic group work with adolescents from a perspective that values quality equally with expressive content, an identification with the work is affirmed. From this grows a new and enriched regard for oneself, and for others. Positive regard for self fosters authentic, vital and creative interactions with other people. An adolescent artist's engagement with media and process is such an interaction.

The engagement with stuff—mastery—that I want to describe has to do with the process of organizing raw materials and events by working creatively with them and transforming them into objects and meaningful experiences.

* * *

Riane 's early sessions in the adolescent art group were chaotic at best. Her style of using materials and tools was haphazard. She slammed her chalk across the page without even looking at what she was doing. She refused to slow down and think about what she was doing. "I got no time for that," she would exclaim. Riane worked with a reckless abandon that was somewhat intimidating to her peers in the group. A cloud of chalk dust swirled around her and she seemed to have little concern for the kids who worked beside her.

At first, I encouraged Riane's efforts. Her work seemed to be cathartic for her. But after awhile I began to have misgivings about her style. I saw her handling of the chalk as erratic and unpredictable. Her refusal to take her time and respect the space of her peers in the group seemed to be resistive and defensive. She often left her area in the group room a mess and I would end up having to spend extra time cleaning up after her.

After several sessions passed with no observable change in Riane's engagement in the materials and no noticeable alteration in her style of interacting with her peers in the group, I decided to alter my approach with Riane.

As the group members gathered for the next session, I approached her, "Riane, I think it would be helpful if we made some changes in what you do in the group."

"I like things just the way they are. I don't want any help."

"I don't agree with you, Riane. I think that you do need some help and I really want you to try slowing down some."

She went about the tasks of taping her paper to the wall and gathering chalk.

I said, "You won't be needing the chalk today, Riane. I've been thinking about you a lot. You seem like somebody who could have good skills, but you don't make an effort to use them."

She looked at me, "What are you talkin' about?"

"Riane, today I'd like for you to try using oil pastels. They have really intense color and you might be able to get some great effects."

As I handed her the box of craypas, I could see other adolescents in the group breathe a sigh of relief.

Reluctantly, she accepted the media.

After the group had completed its check-in ritual, I said, "Step one today is to cover your paper with brown and red. Try not to let any of the paper show through.

Riane glared, "That'll take forever with these things" (Figure 21).

Figure 21. Riane's covered page.

"It may take awhile, but I have faith that you can do it."

And so Riane's lessons in engagement with materials began. She learned to blend the craypas, and to overlay. For several sessions, she used the craypas until she had a good grasp of what they could do. During that same time period, other adolescents in the group were working to master drawing basic shapes. Still others were learning to make shadows and highlights.

The change in media allowed Riane's peers to work beside her without fear that she would damage their work. This, of course, made it possible for them to form a relationship with her. As Riane's skills improved, her peers in the group praised her work and she loved the attention. Over time, Riane got better while in the group. Her self - esteem improved, she developed positive relationships with her peers and she learned to struggle with quality in her work.

Art therapists who work with adolescents should take the quality of patient's artwork seriously. Expression is not the only goal for adolescent art therapy groups. It is important to encourage adolescents to express their feelings, but it is also important to develop artistic skills as well. When attention is given to masterful involvement with materials, adolescent patients sense that real caring is being shown by the art therapist.

ART MAKING AS EXISTENTIAL EXPRESSION

Adolescence is pervaded by angst, and so the work in art therapy groups is always tied to the metaphoric and creative struggle with core issues of meaning, isolation and freedom. Art therapists working with teenagers often hear expressions like:

"That isn't fair."

"I don't want this pain anymore."

"I am so alone."

"It isn't my fault."

Art therapists work to engage the patient in a creative struggle with the ultimate concerns of human existence. Artistic expression leads to mindfulness, which leads to creative anxiety, which leads to change/action, which fosters expression, which deepens mindfulness.

* * *

When Joslyn entered the art therapy group, she was seventeen years old. During one session she told me that the last time she could remember feeling happy was when she was in elementary school. "I don't know what's wrong with me; I never feel good."

Joslyn had been in the adolescent art therapy group for a few sessions when an image of a crystal appeared on her paper. Initially, she drew it as part of a bleak and otherwise empty cave. Drawn in white with blue sparkling emanations, this crystal became a regular feature of Joslyn's work.

The crystal image recurred over a period of three weeks, though when one of her peers asked her about it, Joslyn said, "I just like to draw it. I don't know why, I just do."

On one such occasion, I told Joslyn that I believed that images are always trying to tell us something. "I think images come to us because they have something to say, or something to teach us."

She looked at me skeptically.

"Hmmm. Maybe the crystal is telling me that my boyfriend is picking out my diamond right now." This brought a round of light laughter from her peers in the group, but she did not smile.

Billy, another adolescent in the group, spoke, "I think it looks cool, you know, like one of those magic crystals Merlin or somebody would have."

Jenny added, "I think that would be one huge engagement ring."

Marla said, "Joslyn, it always looks sort of cold to me."

Billy chimed in again, "Crystals are cool, because they are formed by heat and pressure." As these words left Billy's mouth, Joslyn's expression changed abruptly.

"Joslyn," I asked, "do you want to say anything about the drawing.

She shook her head and said, "No."

Joslyn's crystal appeared again during the next session. This time it was depicted as dangling from a chain, suspended above a blazing fire. The fire was in a cave-like room that had dark and rough walls. When it came to her turn to talk about her image, Joslyn said, "I've been thinking about this crystal ever since our last group. If it has a message for me, Bruce, I don't get it, and I'm not sure I want to."

"Joslyn, sometimes the things we most need to hear are the ones we least want to listen to," I said.

"Yes, I know," she replied. "But I don't like what the crystal is saying to me." Tears welled in her eyes. Marla asked, "What is it, Joslyn?"

"I'm not sure, but every time I think about this thing...I..." Tears ran down her cheeks.

Billy asked, "What's the matter?"

She sobbed, "It's...it just reminds me of something."

Jenny put her arm around Joslyn's shoulders. "It'll be alright, Jos'."

"No, no it won't!" she sobbed, "It won't. I thought I'd gotten over all this! "All what?" Billy asked.

I said, "Billy, it is okay for Joslyn to keep things to herself. What is important in this group is that we make art about our feelings. We don't always have to talk about them.

She wept, "I hate that crystal" (Figure 22).

Figure 22. Josylyn's crystal.

Joslyn was in the adolescent art group for almost two months. The crystal was too. Sometimes she would give the crystal a voice and let it speak. The dialogue always revolved around metaphoric themes of loneliness and vulnerability. Although I often wondered just what the crystal represented for her, she never volunteered the information, and I did not ask.

ART MAKING AS PERSONAL METAPHOR

In adolescent art therapy groups it is important to remember that metaphors are not just words, but images and actions as well. The purposes of action and image metaphors are to express and define their maker. Our capacity to see and respond to the visual and action metaphors of adolescents is an extraordinary aspect of art therapy. I am committed to the premise that images can, and should, just be. They must be regarded as having lives of their own. We should not allow them to be dissected or "imaginally" autopsied.

* * *

When Kenny came to the art therapy group he was thirteen years old, an overindulged boy who experienced severe panic attacks, especially whenever his parents planned to be away from home. Kenny's father was a very successful lawyer who regularly traveled and often asked his wife to accompany him. These trips were frequently disrupted by some intolerable acting-out behavior on Kenny's part. In the months preceding his hospitalization, Kenny had escalated his behavior and his actions had become increasingly destructive and dangerous. On one occasion, he broke into his father's liquor cabinet, got drunk and climbed out of his bedroom window onto the roof. He slipped and fell off the roof.

As Kenny participated in the art therapy group, I often felt angry at his obnoxious and entitled manner. He behaved as if he was a preppy snob who was too good to be in the company of the others in the group. At one point, he sneered at me, "My dad could have you fired this afternoon if I wanted him to."

Somewhere along the way, however, I began to really listen to the stories he told as he described his drawings. During one session, it struck me that the reason his arrogance and snobbery was so irritating to me was that it recalled feelings of rejection and exclusion that I had lived through during my own adolescence. How dare he make me remember!

An image Kenny often drew was of a brick wall with graffiti on it. When I asked him about this image, he would shrug his shoulders and say that it was just something he liked to draw. Rather than push him for an explanation of the wall, I decided to respond metaphorically to it. I began the next session by telling this story:

"Once there was a man who had a garden. He really loved his garden. He tended the soil, fertilized, weeded and watered his plants. It was a beautiful garden. Every autumn he was always the envy of his neighbors because his harvest was so large and bountiful.

So, you can imagine how dismayed he was when one morning he discovered that some wild animal had gotten into his garden and eaten many of the vegetables and even some of the flowers.

He decided to build a fence around his garden. After several days of construction he was pleased when, at last, his fence was done. He was sure that now no animal could get in to harm his plants.

The next morning, he was outraged when he went to his garden and saw that some wild animal had somehow broken into the garden and eaten his vegetables.

He immediately began to draw up plans for a brick wall, ten feet high. It took him most of the summer to build his wall, and though it was true that he neglected his gardening most of that summer in order to focus on the wall, when he finally finished it he breathed a sigh of relief. Now, he thought to himself, now no animal will ever get into my garden again. The fact that the year's harvest was woefully meager did not overly distress him, for he was sure that next year would be better.

All that winter the man planned his garden. He made drawings of how he would lay out the rows and lists of the supplies he would need. That spring he went about tilling the soil and planting with a renewed vigor. Imagine the rage he felt when late in the summer he discovered that somehow a wild animal had managed to get over the wall and begun to nibble at his beans and zucchinis. Utterly furious, he decided then and there to build a roof over his brick wall. And that is what he did.

Unfortunately, within no time at all, all of his plants died. This bothered the man, but he took some comfort in the realization that at least the animal would never get into his garden again."

I then asked the group to draw their responses to the story. Kenny drew the wall and covered it with angry epithets directed toward "the stupid animal." As we talked about the drawings, Kenny blurted out, "I hope that damned animal is happy!"

Another patient in the group turned to Kenny and said, "How about the stupid guy who built the wall?"

He fumed for a moment, and then he just sat there in silence. He had discovered the meaning of his recurrent drawings of the wall.

Metaphorically, the image of the wall had been trying to get the message to Kenny that it was time to grow up, even if growing up meant not always having his parents all to himself. Kenny's drawings did not immediately change his life, but he did begin to let go of his stranglehold on his parents (Figure 23).

Figure 23. Circular wall.

By responding to his metaphor with a similar metaphor of my own, I helped Kenny to see himself in the mirror of his drawings. I do not mean to imply that this was all there was to Kenny, nor was there only one meaning to be found in his image of the graffiti wall. There was much more to him than his dependence on his parents, just as there was more to the wall than one brick.

In this encounter, I did not make an interpretation of his image. I engaged in imaginal interpretive dialogue that allowed Kenny to participate with the metaphor. I believe that had I attempted to make a literal or clever analysis of his drawings, he would have withdrawn from me and from the group and he would not have been helped.

ART MAKING AS RELATIONSHIP

Adolescents' feelings are intense. Art therapists working with these intense feelings must always contend with the question of how to hold the adolescent in the group in such a way as to promote healthy expression of feelings and the development of relationships. I believe that the most effective way to form a therapeutic alliance with adolescent patients is through making art, rather than through discussion. By making art, the adolescent takes images from within and spreads them in the world. This is an act of acknowledgment of the "others" beyond the boundaries of the self. The others are the beholders, the audience, the peers in the group.

The experience of loneliness is extremely painful for most adolescents. Hence, the importance of working in groups. Personal meaning can be found only in the context of relationship. The creative process is most clearly manifested in the context of relationships.

By making art, an adolescent offers his view, his unique response to the world. The community of the art group beholds the product of the artist's imagination. The others in the group give witness to the uniqueness of the adolescent artist. The artist creates, the community responds, the artist makes again and the community attends. Art making is relating.

* * *

Mandy's drawing seemed harmless enough. She had used oil sticks on a large sheet of tag board to portray a vibrant landscape A red dog howled at a bright moon shining in the turbulent sky. In the distance there was an adobe-like building (Figure 24).

Figure 24. Red dog howling.

The group, consisting of eight adolescent girls, had been a tough one. It was one of those days when I knew that I wasn't being paid enough. One of the girls had been in restraints in special care (seclusion) the night before. Another was all hyped up, in anticipation of a family therapy session. Other girls in the group were explosive, angry, depressed and resistive.

Mandy had worked independently and had caused no problems that session, so her drawing had not seized much of my attention. When it came her turn to talk about her drawing with the group, she said quietly, "Mmm, I'm not sure I want to say anything about this to you guys. It's hard for me to look at."

"You don't have to say anything, Mandy," I said.

"Yes, I know that," she replied. "You always say that."

"It's most important to me, Mandy, that you did the art. Talking is okay, but it's not the main thing."

"I said, I know that." She paused. "I guess I'd like to hear what everybody else thinks about this picture. Is that okay?"

"Sure," I replied. (This is a technique of engagement with images that I often use in adolescent groups. I ask group members to react to the story that they see in the image.)

Beth, one of the other girls, spoke, "When I look at your drawing, Mandy, the thing that really hits me is the wind. I mean, it looks really stormy there."

Malinda said, "There is something sort of eerie about that building. It looks dark inside. I don't think I'd want to go in there."

Sharon added, "I like dogs, but I can't tell if that one is friendly, or if it is a wolf or something like that."

As Mandy listened to these responses to her image, she began to cry.

I stood up and got the box of tissues from the cupboard and offered it to her.

She said, "I don't know about the dog either, Sharon. I know that you guys all know about why I am here...my dad and stuff. When he found out that I had told my counselor at school...he (more tears) he called me a bitch and told me that no man would ever want me again. Oh God, it makes me sick. But I still love him."

"Oh Mandy," Beth said.

Malinda moved her chair close to Mandy's, and Sharon dabbed at her own tears. For a few moments there was silence in the room.

After a couple minutes, I said, "There are times in this group that I am amazed by what happens here. It is an honor to be with you."

Mandy said, "That poor dog has no place to go. She can't go back to the house, and it is going to rain."

"Mandy, I think that our drawings are sort of like self-portraits. But I also believe that the picture can be changed, if that's what you want to do."

She looked at me but didn't respond.

"You can change the image, Mandy. You don't have to be the dog anymore. You can get out of the storm."

Beth said, "Well, if I was that dog, I think I'd go hunting and tear someone apart." In turn, each of Mandy's peers in the group shared their reactions to Mandy's story and in so doing they let her know that she was not alone.

ART MAKING AS STRUCTURE AND CHAOS

Making art involves a process of continually moving back and forth between order and disorder, spontaneity and composition, chaos and structure. In this way making art is an allegory of the adolescent journey toward adulthood in that the individual is unceasingly moving between the order and security of the family and the capriciousness and experimentation of the peer group. Making art in a group provides an essential action metaphor of the way life is for adolescents.

* * *

Doug was fourteen years old when he came into the art therapy group. After I had given instructions to the group about the drawing task, he just stood there looking at the 3' x 3' empty paper for several minutes. It was as if he was overwhelmed by the possibilities. He could make no decision, bring no order or limits to the chaotic potential of the drawing he had not yet started.

Doug suffered from Obsessive Compulsive Disorder. He had been abandoned by his biological parents when he was a few months old. He had lived with a foster family until he was adopted, at the age of two.

When I met him, he told me that he did not want to be in the art group. "I don't like hobbies, and I am not interested in getting to know other kids." I had very little information to go on in terms of treatment planning for Doug's involvement in the group, but I decided that I would begin by trying to help him to artistically develop a sense of control in his life. That is to say, that I would look for ways to encourage him to make choices and be in charge of his work.

He stood, staring at the empty paper, as the others in the group worked all around him.

"Doug, having a little trouble getting started?" I asked.

"I told you I don't want to be here."

"Yes, I know you did. But, for the moment you are here and I'd like to help."

"I don't need your help."

I did not respond to his rejection. I stood beside him and looked at his empty paper. "Yowsa," I said. "This is a big piece of paper."

He sneered, "Too big."

"Well, let's make it smaller," I said.

"Can ya' do that?"

"Sure, what size do you think you would like it to be?"

He shook his head. "I don't know. Maybe about half that size."

"Okay," I replied. "Help me take the tape off of it and we'll fold it in half." When that was done, I gave Doug the roll of masking tape and I held the paper against the wall as he taped it up. "Now Doug, I think it would be helpful to you if you would only use two pieces of chalk. What is your favorite color?"

"Blue," he replied.

"Okay, you can use blue. Do you want your picture to be peaceful looking or should it look like there is a war going on?"

"Like a war," he said, and smiled.

"All right. Then let's have you use orange as the other color."

"Why orange?" he wanted to know.

"Orange is the opposite of blue on the color wheel, and so it is good to use with blue if you want a lot of clashing colors" (Figure 25).

Figure 25. Doug's War.

In the sessions that followed, Doug gradually became more comfortable in the group. I worked continually to help him structure his artistic work so that he would not be paralyzed by his obsessive considering of endless possibilities. At the same time, I limited his involvement with peers by insisting that he choose one of two positions and chairs in the group room. This structured his selection process and made it possible for him to make a simple choice rather than be overwhelmed by multiple possibilities.

By structuring his artistic work and his social encounters, Doug was able to bring order to his world. As he became more secure in the environment, I gradually transferred the structuring responsibility to him. Through his involvement with art processes and relationships in the group, he was able to deal with his own inner chaos. He made decisions and brought order and limits to his life.

Artists structure the chaos of possibilities in order to create products. This is powerful medicine for adolescents who feel at the mercy of the staggering turmoil of their lives.

ART MAKING AS EMPOWERMENT

The adolescents who come to art therapy groups bring a troublesome sense of inadequacy and powerlessness. They have no faith in their personal power and they have been emotionally wounded. Art therapy groups are an ideal milieu in which adolescents can work to develop their own power.

In order for an adolescent to transform a disempowered stance, words are not enough. Empowerment is not a process that can be enacted through language alone. There have to be experiences that promote the development of power within the individual. Empowerment is a process of transformation from the position of the victim to that of the heroine, and from a passive to an active engagement with the world.

The empowering nature of art therapy group work with adolescents is found in its capacity to accept and embrace distress, not in its desire to rid the patient of it. The arts bring our deepest fears, loneliness and anguish to our attention. Rather than "cure" these discomforting aspects of life, art therapy enables the adolescent to live with them courageously.

* * *

Shannon's mother had heard about the outpatient art therapy group from a friend. When she called, she told me that she felt "a little weird" about calling me to see if her daughter could join the group. I asked what she meant. She explained that she wasn't sure that Shannon's problems really required any professional help. "I think that she's just feeling sorry for herself," she sighed. After I had explained the group to her, Shannon's mother said that she wanted Shannon to come to the studio to meet me. I told her that it was important that Shannon feel as if she had some say in the decision of whether or not to be in therapy. I said that I was willing to meet with her in order to give her a chance to make up her mind.

The difficulties of Shannon's life, that her mother felt a little funny about seeking therapy for, revolved around the recent death of Shannon's father.

When Shannon and her mother arrived at the studio the next week I was immediately struck by how in control the mother was, and how passive and submissive Shannon seemed to be. The mother was in her early fifties and as she introduced herself and Shannon to me, she established steady eye contact easily. There was a firm assuredness in her eyes that was in stark contrast to her daughter.

The mother said, "I'm still not sure if we should be here, Mr. Moon."

"I don't know exactly why you've come to me either, or if I can be helpful to Shannon. Maybe it would be a good idea if Shannon and I spend some time together alone," I said.

"I don't think Shannon would be comfortable with that."

I responded, "Well, let's get started on the right foot here." I turned to Shannon, "What do you think, Shannon?"

Shannon looked toward her mother and said, "It doesn't matter what I think."

This brief interaction helped me to understand some of the dynamics that were at work between mother and daughter. After a half hour interview, I told Shannon and her mother that there were openings in the adolescent art group but that I thought they should talk it over, and if Shannon decided that she wanted to be in the group that she should give me a call later that week. The mother objected to this, "I think we should just sign her up right now."

I restated my desire that they talk it over and that Shannon call if she wanted to enter the group.

A week went by before I received a phone call from Shannon. "Mr. Moon,

I think I'd like to be in your art group."

So, the next session Shannon entered the group. She introduced herself to the other kids by sharing that her father had died suddenly, a couple months earlier. She told the group that she felt lost, hurt and lonely. "I always got along with him; Dad was cool."

It so happened that one of the other members of the group, Angela, had also lost her father within the last year. Angela said, "You'll like this place. The art stuff really helps."

The art task for that day was an open-ended one. I said to the group, "Our theme today is, I am..... You can use any material that you want. Let's work for about an hour and then we'll have a few minutes at the end to talk about what we have made."

Shannon looked at me hesitantly. I said, "Go on, take a look around and see what we have. You can use whatever you want." And so began Shannon's art therapy group journey. By making images, she was able to metaphorically portray her struggle with letting go of her dad and getting on with her life. She transformed her painful lost-ness into images that she was able to share with the group. Shannon and Angela became very good friends. This did not make the pain go away, but it did make it bearable. Shannon needed a place where she could be in charge of her grieving process, a place not controlled by her mother. She needed to experience the feelings of loneliness and loss in her own way. In the adolescent art therapy group, she was able to use them as the source of her creative work. This enabled her to live with her loss and to share it with others, especially with Angela. The drawings and paintings that she made while in the group became a sort of metaphorical journal. Her images helped her move from being a passive child caught in an overwhelming and senseless emotional storm, to a young woman standing apart from her mother as they looked out at a rolling ocean surf. She did not portray the sea as calm, but neither was it overwhelming. As Shannon discovered the healing power of making art and sharing her work with others, she was also able to discover the power she could have over her own life.

ART MAKING AS REPARATIVE EXPERIENCE

Adolescent art therapy groups offer many opportunities for reparative experiences. As adolescents make art in the context of the therapy group, they create a social microcosm. Problematic relating skills that contribute to the adolescents' difficulties almost immediately emerge in the group. The adolescent quickly displays his dysfunctional behaviors in the group setting. There is no need for him to tell the group about his maladaptive patterns, because these will surely be acted out within the group. The inherent tensions within a group provide opportunities to repair the trauma of past experiences by transforming maladaptive behavioral reactions into artistic working-through activity. Such transformations occur when the members feel safe in the group and when there is honest reflection on the images that are made during the session.

One such transformation was seen in the case of Jeremiah, a fifteen-year-old African-American boy. Jeremiah had been remanded to the hospital by juvenile court authorities for a psychiatric evaluation prior to sentencing. He had been convicted of assault and vandalism. He entered the group with a sullen swagger that seemed intimidating and aggressive. When my cotherapist and I had discussed our plan for the group earlier in the day, we had talked about our hunch that Jeremiah would use his smouldering interactive style as a way to keep others at a safe distance from him.

It was not surprising that in the early moments of the session Jeremiah made a very hostile and devaluing remark toward one of his peers. My cotherapist intervened by saying, "Jeremiah, there is nothing to be afraid of here. You don't have to impress anyone."

The drawing topic that day was an open-ended one—draw something that has been on your mind. Jeremiah drew a cartoon that showed him posed with a chain saw about to cut through a woman. He labled the drawing, "What I'm gonna do to you."

Keeping in mind that we always work from the premise that everything we make is a partial self-portrait, my cotherapist and I did not outwardly react to this threatening and violent image. From this perspective, Jeremiah's drawing was not about intimidation of my cotherapist, but rather, it was about his own self-destructive energies. When it came time for the group to focus its attention on Jeremiah's angry image, my cotherapist looked at the drawing for a long while without saying anything. The air was thick with tension in the room and I am sure that the other patients in the group expected an unpleasant confrontation to ensue. However, as she turned away from the picture and looked at Jeremiah, there were tears in her eyes. She said, "Oh Jeremiah, you must have been hurt a lot. I ache when I look at your drawing."

He was taken aback by this response, but he quickly resumed his typical stance and said with a sneer, "You better believe it would hurt."

The tears gently eased down her cheek. She said, "Somebody must have really been mean to you."

This time Jeremiah was visibly shaken by her gentle response. "What'sa matter with you woman? Don't you get it!"

Dramatically, my cotherapist looked to his drawing, then back at him, and then again to the drawing and back once more. She said, "I understand, Jeremiah."

Jeremiah's hostility crumbled. In the two weeks that he was in the group, he portrayed several violent scenes from his life. He drew out the emptiness, the anger and the bewilderment he felt regarding his father's abandonment of his family. He almost always entered the room with his gang-banger braggadocio but would quickly settle into a different way of being in the art group room. Clearly, the gentle and sensitive interactions with my cotherapist, in concert with the expressive content of his images, and the presence of others in the group, combined to provide Jeremiah with reparative emotional experiences.

ART MAKING AS SELF TRANSCENDENT HOPE

If there is no hope, there can be no therapy. The same can be said of art, that where there is no hope, there will be no art. The art therapist must have hope for the adolescent patient, and the patient must hope for herself. Making art is a symbolic expression of hope.

* * *

Julianne entered the group room quietly, 17 years old, but looking closer to 30 than 17. Her eyes were listless. I knew, from having read her medical chart, that she had been using drugs on a daily basis and that she described herself as an alcoholic. The report also said that she had recently begun to snort cocaine. She had told the admitting physician that Grace Slick, of the Jefferson Airplane rock group, was her role model. She had a worn and hardened look about her.

Julianne's mother had brought her to the hospital for admisison. They just showed up early one morning at the Emergency Services door where the mother told the clinician, "Either you admit her right now or I am afraid that she might be dead by tomorrow!"

She came into the art group room, her eyes doleful, her hair greasy and disheveled looking. I welcomed her into the group. She sat in a chair in the corner farthest away from me. As I introduced her to the other members of the group, she stared at the floor and said nothing. The art task that day was to create an image of a wish. As her peers gathered materials and began to work, Julianne sat motionless. I approched and asked, "Is something wrong, Julianne?"

She looked up irritably. "This is so lame," she replied.

"I'm not sure I understand," I replied.

"You wouldn't," she sneered.

"Is it the making art that you don't like?" I asked.

"No, that has nothing to do with it."

"Then why is it lame?"

She looked at the floor. "Man, if you had any clue about me, you'd know that I don't have any wishes." A few moments of silence fell between us.

I said, "Well then, why don't you just do whatever you'd like to do, Julianne.

Whatever you do will be all right."

She glared at me. "Yeah right, I doubt that." She stood up, selected a piece of black charcoal from the chalk tray and made one quick slashing movement across the page (Figure 26).

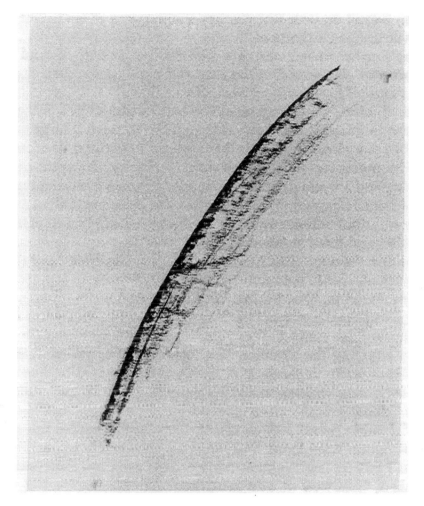

Figure 26. Julianne's slash.

Later in the session, as the group members shared their thoughts and feelings about the images they had made, Julianne withdrew into her corner and refused to interact with her peers.

The next several group sessions followed much the same course for Julianne. She participated minimally in the art-making process and not at all in the discussion of the images that were made.

A turning point for Julianne came on the day that the group was working with the theme, "The Book of My Life." Group members were asked to imagine that someone had been hired to write a book about their life. In the instructions to the group, I said, "...and since you are an expert on your life, you have been asked to create the title and a cover image for the book."

Julianne's cover image was of a dark landscape with a road that ended abruptly. At the end of the road she portrayed a danger sign. The title that she gave her book was, "Dead Ends."

Instead of asking the group members to talk about their images, I asked them to imagine that they were walking through a large bookstore and to talk about the books that somehow captured their imagination. The members of the group quickly got into the spirit of this role playing and a lively period of discussion ensued. Commenting on Julianne's book, Ella said, "This one really intrigues me. When I look at the cover, I think this is a mystery and that there will be lots of unexpected twists and turns in the story.

Greg added, "Yeah, I think it is going to be a book about hard times, but I think it all comes out okay in the end."

Lauren chimed in, "No, I think it is a tragedy."

I turned to Julianne and asked, "Do you have any idea what some of the chapter titles might be?"

Clearly enjoying the attention and interest of her peers, Julianne said, "I didn't really think about it, but I suppose they'd be like road signs. Maybe one chapter would be called "Road Work." Another might be "Yield."

"Well," I said, "when I think about your title, it makes me think about how when I see Dead End signs when I am driving around, I know that I have to take another route or go a different direction."

Ella asked, "Juli, how do you think the book ends?"

"I don't really know. Either I die, or I change directions. I know I can't keep going the way I am."

The group then turned its attention to another book that was in our imaginary store that morning.

* * *

Without hope, there can be no art. The session described above in many ways marked the beginning of Julianne's hard work in therapy. Although in the earlier sessions she had maintained a stance of isolated disinterest, the fact that she had made drawings indicated that there was reason to hope. I had faith that as long as she was willing to make a mark, then she was also, at some deep level, willing to engage with others and in life itself. Art therapists who work with adolescents often encounter young people who are so angry, so defiant, so withdrawn, or so disillusioned with the world that it is difficult to see reasons to hope. But the simple act of making a mark is a dramatic indicator that all hope is not lost. Making art in the company of others is a symbolic expression of hope.

ART MAKING AS A WAY OF BEING WITH ADOLESCENTS

The work of being with adolescents in art therapy groups is complex. It requires intense focus and concentrated energy on the part of the art therapist. The art group leader must simultaneously pay attention to her own artistic work, to the individual adolescent and to all of the images that arise within the group. It is important for the group leader to always maintain a consistent involvement with his or her own art making. There must also be a constant effort to maintain an attitude of concern for the adolescents and for their feelings, and a genuine willingness to be with them. The adolescent who needs art therapy will always bring with her the pain and the struggles of her life. In the context of the expressive art therapy group, art therapists encourage adolescents to use art as a way to find meaning in their lives. We work to be with the patient as he discovers the point of his journey. We do this through our own artistic efforts in the group, through how we act toward adolescents, and through the things that we say during the session. In a multitude of ways, art therapists exude faith that the suffering, anguish and insecurities of the adolescent patient are important. Our work enables the adolescent patient to be healed through making art in a group setting.

* * *

When I first met Jeff, he was a defiant, angry and hostile sixteen-year-old who had recently been admitted to the short-term adolescent unit at the hospital. He had been in out-patient therapy for nearly a year, and had been admitted to two other treatment programs during that time. He had been discharged, against medical advice, from each of those programs. Jeff's history included violent behavior at home, vandalism and truancy. He was failing at school. He had been arrested several weeks before after having caused a scene at the restaurant where he had worked as a dishwasher. Jeff had become angry at a supervisor when he had been given orders to speed up his work. This episode led to his being fired from the job.

The psychiatric team leader's referral note said that Jeff was very uncooperative in individual psychotherapy and that little or no progress was being made. In discussion with Jeff's individual therapist, I learned that the team leader's note was somewhat euphemistic. In fact, Jeff had been refusing to attend individual therapy sessions.

As I thought about Jeff's entry into the expressive arts therapy group, I paid close attention to the therapeutic interventions that had been tried and failed. A common theme seemed to be efforts to coerce, or control him. I decided that I would make every effort to avoid power struggles or confrontations with Jeff, and that I would try to engage Jeff through the metaphors of his images and the images of others in the group. Jeff was entering a group that consisted of five adolescents: three girls, two boys, and me.

The first session that Jeff attended began with all of the members sitting in a circle. I asked everyone, "So, how are you starting out today."

Shelby said, "Cool."

Allen said, "Don't ask."

Tony said, "Fine!"

Kathleen said, "It's been a terrible morning."

Sandy said, "Okay"

Jeff stared at the floor.

I said, "We have a new member starting with us today. Jeff, you are in expressive art. In this group we use art as a way of expressing feelings. You don't have to be Picasso or Michelangelo, or anyone like that. Whatever you do will be fine. I do ask that when someone else is speaking that we all pay attention. I know that everyone in here has a long history of people not taking their feelings seriously. I promise that in here, we will always take you seriously. Welcome to the group, Jeff. I am glad that you are with us." Jeff continued to stare at the floor and he yawned.

I then asked the group members to cover their entire 3' x 3' piece of brown craft paper with a color that, for them, would express the feelings they came into the group with. Shelby, Allen, Tony, Kathleen, Sandy and I immediately gathered chalks, moved to a place at the wall and began to work. Jeff remained seated, but I could see out of the corner of my eye that he was looking around himself, checking out what everyone was doing. After a couple minutes had gone by, I overheard Sandy comment to Jeff, "It looks like you want brown to be your color," she giggled.

Jeff looked up, "I don't play with crayons."

Tony said, "Actually these are not crayons. They are chalk."

Sandy added, "C'mon Jeff, it can be fun sometimes."

Jeff sneered, "Oh yeah."

At that point, I intervened. "Jeff, as I told you earlier, whatever you do here will be okay. You know, I am really interested in performance art. So far you are making an interesting artistic statement."

Shelby laughed, "Bruce, you always see the good side."

When all except Jeff had completed covering their pages, I asked them to think about this as a background. "Now, I'd like you to imagine some object that would look right on this background."

Allen asked, "You mean like a thing?

"Yes, anything you want. Just look at your background for a moment and see if an idea comes. When you have something in your imagination, go ahead and draw it onto the page."

Before I returned to my work, I moved toward Jeff and sat in the chair beside him. "Yowsa, Jeff. When I look at your brown empty page, I see a kazillion possibilities."

He turned to face me. "I don't see anything."

"Nothing?"

Jeff looked away, shook his head and muttered something under his breath.

"What?" I asked.

He put his head in his hands. "Nothing."

"Oh," I said. "I thought I heard you say shit." Although the other adolescents were working on their images, I could tell that they were paying close attention to this interaction. I went on. "If I did hear you say that, Jeff, I do want to ask you to please not use language like that while you are in this group. You know I try to maintain a very safe atmosphere here and swearing doesn't help. Now, if you wanted to draw that, it would be fine."

He looked up at me. "You mean I can draw shit, but I can't say it."

"I mean, I don't allow swearing here, but if that is what you see when you look at your page, by all means draw it." This idea seemed to capture Jeff's interest. He stood up, went to the counter and gathered two different shades of brown and a couple sticks of black chalk. He then proceeded to draw his rendition of a pile of excrement. Internally, I celebrated for I know that once I can get an adolescent to use artistic materials, usually something good will come out of it.

After approximately forty minutes, everyone in the group had completed their drawings and returned to the circle of chairs. I asked if anyone would like to share their images.

Shelby volunteered. For her "Cool" image she had covered the page with a dark blue. The object that she portrayed was a large iceberg. She said, "I think I'd like to hear people's reactions to this first, before I tell you what I was thinking about."

Tony spoke, "When I think of icebergs, I think about the Titanic, how it sunk when it hit one."

Kathleen added, "It reminds me of a story my dad used to tell me when I was little. Something about a polar bear who lived on an iceberg and he tried to paint it so that there would be color in his life."

Allen said, "It sure does look cold."

Sandy said, "Doesn't look like a very comfortable place to be."

As Shelby listened to these reactions to her iceberg, her facial expression changed from a smile, to a rather somber look. "You guys are all mostly right," she said. I was thinking about how they say that most of an iceberg is under the water, that you can't see it. I guess that's how I feel, but you are right Sandy, it isn't a great place to be."

The group sat quietly for a few moments, reflecting on Shelby's image. I then said, "Shelby, since you were brave enough to start things off, is there anybody else's image that you'd like to hear about?"

She looked around the room. "Yes, I wanna hear about Sandy's picture."

Sandy had covered her page with orange and drawn what appeared to be a green park bench on the left side of the paper. Above the bench there was a purple sun. She looked at her drawing. "I don't know if this one means anything or not. It's sort of blah, really."

"Sandy," I said, "I notice that all of the colors you used are ones that combine other colors."

"What?"

"You know, orange is in between red and yellow, green is in between blue and yellow, and puple is in between blue and red."

Kathleen chimed in, "...and Sandy is in between mom and dad." Sandy's mother and father were in the midst of a painful divorce.

Sandy responded, "that's me, always in the middle."

From the out of nowhere, Jeff said, "Sucks big time, doesn't it?"

Sandy turned toward him. "Yes, it sucks."

Jeff replied, "Sounds familiar." An uneasy silence fell upon the group. Finally, Allen spoke. "Sandy, your picture would be real different if you drew it in red, yellow and blue, or even in just black and white."

"Yes, it would," Sandy said. "But for now, this is the way it is."

A few moments later, I said, "Sandy, it must be hard being in-between. I admire your strength."

"Thanks," she replied.

"Is there anyone else's image that you'd like to hear about?"

Sandy looked around her. "Uh huh, let's talk about Allen's.

Allen had covered his paper with black. The object he depicted was a battered

"Stop" sign.

"Allen, you've really drawn this well," I said. "It looks like this sign has gotten run over though."

"Yea, it's been beat to hell. Now can we go on, I don't want to say anything else."

"Sure Allen, that's always okay here. Talking about our pictures is just the icing on the cake. What is most important is that you did the work. Whose drawing to you want to hear from?"

Allen rubbed his stubbly beard and said, "Let's take a look at Kathleen's."

Kathleen had covered her page with an intense red. Superimposed on the red were two yellow rings. One of the rings was intact while the other appeared to be broken. As the group focused its attention on Kathleen's drawing, tears began to form in her eyes and her nose got red. I sensed that she would have difficulty beginning a discussion of her work, and so I asked if she would like to hear how her drawing made others feel. She nodded her head.

"Shelby, what feelings come to mind for you when you look at Kathleen's drawing?"

"Hurt and angry!"

"Allen?"

"Betrayed."

"Tony?"

"Screwed over."

"Sandy?"

"Shocked?"

I added, "Disappointed, and broken. Kathleen," I said, "how about you."

"That about says it all," she sobbed. "Last night, my boyfriend and I broke up. I can't believe it. I feel so stupid, so ashamed."

Shelby said, "Oh Kathleen, do I know how that feels."

Sandy added, "Me too."

"But I thought we'd always be together. If I had known, I never would have...." Kathleen's words dissolved into her tears.

The members of the group sat quietly, waiting for Kathleen. After a minute or two she said, "Let's look at Jeff's drawing. Jeff's body seemed to tense up, but he kept his eyes downcast toward the floor. Kathleen said, "I remember what it was like here on my first day, Jeff. Your drawing seems to sum it up pretty well." He glanced toward her.

Tony said, "I think we've all been there."

Jeff looked at his drawing. "Are you guys putting me on? This isn't anything."

"Oh Jeff," I said. "I disagree. I think your drawing is important. It lets us know how you feel, and that is the whole point of being in this group."

He grimaced, "Whatever you say. You are the boss."

"No, Jeff. I am not the boss. I am on your side here...I am not your enemy."

An uncomfortable silence filled the room. Finally, Tony said, "Can we move on now? I wanna talk about my picture."

I asked Jeff, "Is there anything else you'd like to say about your drawing?" He returned his gaze to the floor but said nothing. I said, "You did fine, Jeff. Welcome to the group. Okay, Tony, let's take a look at your work."

Tony had covered his paper with a light, sky blue. He had added a yellow kite with an unattached string floating in the air. "Like I said at the beginning today, I feel fine."

Shelby asked, "What's up, Tony?"

"What can I say? Things are goin' good. They say that I can leave next week. My mom and dad trust me again, and everything's cool."

"Tony," I said, "Does that mean that today will be your last day in the group?

"Uh, no. I think I'll be here one more time."

"That's good," I said. "We'll want to pay special attention to saying good-bye."

Shelby said, "It must feel good to be going home."

"Yeah, but I'll miss some things about this place."

At this, Jeff looked up from the floor and said, "You gotta be kidding. I want outta here as quick as possible."

I responded, "Jeff, you know that reminds me of a story."

Once there was a Zen Master who had a new pupil.
On the pupil's second day of training, the old Master
took him to a place where there was a huge cardboard box.
The Master said, "For today's lesson, I want you to spend
the day contemplating how you could get out of this box."
And so the new pupil spent hours thinking of ways to get out.
When the Master returned he asked his pupil what had been
learned. The pupil recited all of the many ways he had devised
to get out of the box. The pupil told the Master that he could
use a saw to cut his way out, or he could use a match to set fire
to the box, or he could build a ladder to climb out, and on and on.
Finally the Master raised his cane and struck the pupil on the head.
He said, "No, young one. In order to get out of this box one must
first get into it."

"So Jeff, if you really want to get out of here as quickly as possible,
I suggest that you really get into it as quickly as possible."
Jeff did not respond.
At the close of every art therapy group session I always ask each
member to sum up what they have gotten from the experience. This
provides both a cognitive and an emotional transition away from the
images and feelings that have been the focus of the group. In a sense,
this provides a ritual ending of our time together.
"Shelby, what are you leaving the group with today?."
"I am going to be thinking about icebergs, and how I keep so much
to myself."
I replied, "Shelby, I am struck by how much you participated today.
That is clearly one way to let people know more about you. Good
work!"
"Thanks."
"Allen, how about you? What are you leaving with?"
He pulled at his whiskers and said, "I'm leaving with a beat up stop
sign."
"It's a hard road that you've been on, Allen." I replied. "Thanks for
letting us come along. Tony, what are you taking with you today?"
Tony said, "I'm fine, just fine!"
"Wow, Tony. I am going to have to get myself ready for saying good-
bye to you next week. I will miss you."
"I'll miss you too, Bruce."

"Kathleen, what are you leaving with?"

She said, "I still feel terrible, but at least I know I am not the only one who ever felt that way."

I said, "That is a good thing to know, Kathleen."

"Sandy?"

Sandy said, "Okay, but I have to ask Jeff something. Jeff, when I was talking about my drawing you said that being in the middle sucks big time. I just wondered if what I said about my parents was like your family, or something."

Jeff looked up from the floor. "Not really, my old man took off a long time ago, but I still remember what it was like before he split."

Sandy replied, "I just wanted you to know that I heard what you said, and if you ever wanna talk or something, just let me know."

"Jeff," I asked. "This was your first time with us. What is your first impression of the group?"

He thought for a moment. "I don't wanna be here, in the hospital I mean. But, I guess this thing is okay"

"It is not easy being in the hospital," I said. "It is hard work, Jeff, but really, the quickest way out is to really get in. You are welcome here."

Kathleen spoke up. "And what are you leaving with today, Bruce?"

"Hmmm. I am leaving with a sense of awe at all these pictures. I will be thinking about icebergs and kites, rings and stop signs, manure piles and park benches all day. It really is an honor to be with you folks.

* * *

Jeff was in the art therapy group for several more sessions. My encounters with him were always focused on encouraging him to make art as a way to find meaning in his life. As I reflect upon Jeff's work in the expressive arts therapy group I know that the gains he made were due in part to my efforts to avoid coercion and control issues with him. I made every effort to stay out of power struggles and negative confrontations with Jeff. I focused on engaging him through the metaphors of his images and the images of his peers in the group. I did this through my own artist efforts in the group, through story telling and through my behavior toward each adolescent during the session. In many ways, I exuded a sense of faith that the pain, anguish and success of each patient was important. Whether expressed in the image of an iceberg, a free flying kite or a pile of excrement, the work enabled Jeff and his peers to heal themselves through making art in a group setting.

Chapter XIII

ART AS THERAPY WITH ADOLESCENT'S FAMILIES

Achieving independence and establishing a healthy sense of self as separate and distinct from the family are some of the primary tasks of adolescence. The principle focus of this text has been on the crucial role that art making plays in the successful treatment of young people who experience emotional and mental disturbances as they make their way through the difficult transition from childhood to adulthood. However, I would be remiss if I failed to acknowledge the impact of the adolescent period on the family unit. Not only does the individual face many complex challenges brought on by the biological, psychological, social and spiritual changes that occur during adolescence, but parents and other family members also must confront a plethora of formidable tasks during this cycle of family life. Landgarten (1987) notes, "...the two generations are simultaneously grappling with the conflict of dependence versus independence" (p. 179). The result of this concurrent struggle often stimulates ambivalence in both the adolescent and his or her parents leading to unclear expectations of one another, confusing and conflicted feelings about one another and mixed messages to and from one another.

The process of entering into psychotherapy of any kind for an adolescent is nearly always a process that is loaded down by years of gradually escalating conflict. Entry into art therapy implies that the adolescent can no longer manage his or her feelings and behavior amid the many stresses of normal life. The commencement of the art therapy relationship means that, in most cases, the parents, guardians or some other authority in the adolescent's world feel inadequate to meet the adolescent's needs. They have sought the art therapist for help. Although often disguised and almost never openly acknowledged, both the family and the adolescent patient harbor profound feelings of guilt, failure and anger as a result of such a situation. As has been noted at length earlier in this text, much of an adolescent's early behavior in art therapy expresses metaphoric themes of resistance to the therapy process. It is important for art therapists to know that the adoelscent is not the only one in the family system who is resistive. Rinsley (1980) suggests that in relation to inpatient hospital treatment, "before the patient can move into definitive treatment, the parents must come to grips with their own resistances to the meaning and implications of their child's [treatment] hospitalization" (p.25).

Art therapists who are working with adolescents must always keep in mind that the adolescent individual is a member of a very complex social system, a family. Within the family there are always sets of communal rules, roles for each member and both overt and covert power structures. Perhaps it goes without saying that the adolescent patient has been deeply influenced by the family's rules, roles and power relationships, both positively and negatively. Likewise, it is a safe assumption that the adolescent's entire family unit has been ardently affected by the adolescent, both positively and negatively.

Art therapists who are motivated to pursue the study of family art therapy in relation to adolescents should refer to the writings of Kwiatkowska (1978), Landgarten (1987), Levick & Herring (1973), Linesch (1993), Riley & Malchiodi (1994), and Wadeson (1976).

I would suggest that in addition to reviewing the above authors' works, it may be helpful to think of the family as a group. To be sure, such a group has a long history, and treating them as a group does present particular difficulties, but I believe that the curative principles of group art making that were described in the two previous chapters apply equally well to family groups. Art can surely become a safe language for adolescent families. The process of engaging with materials can help to diffuse the intensity of conflicted feelings and clarify communications among family members. Art making provides families with a way to explore and express their ultimate existential concerns. Art making provides opportunities for families to explore both personal and communal metaphors. Shared art making enhances relationships through the processes of doing things together. Art making helps families experience and reflect on their own structures and, in some instances, helps them to begin to create structure out of their own chaos. Making art together empowers each member of the family and offers reparative experiences in which old patterns of behavior can be overcome. Collective art making encourages families in crisis by providing experiences that uncover hopeful visions of how the family can be. Finally, art making provides the family with new ways of being together. Since for most families the process of making art together is a new experience, it can provide avenues for being with one another that are not as easily contaminated by past encounters.

Chapter XIV

LAST THINGS

As I near the completion of the writing of this book, *The Dynamics of Art As Therapy With Adolescents*, in the early summer of 1998, I am well aware that this is a difficult time in our national history of mental health care for teenagers. Economic pressures brought on by insurance companies and H.M.O.'s seem, in my view, to be strangling mental health services for children and adolescents. There have been radical changes in the insurance industry that have resulted in profound changes in health care service delivery systems. Health care in the United States has become a divisive political issue during the past decade and although there have been many proclamations and much discussion, there has been little in the way of progress. The well-being of individual adolescents has been reduced to corporate statistics measured in dollars and cents. The treatment of emotionally disturbed kids seems to have been labeled a bad investment and resources have been allocated elsewhere.

Still, I believe that art therapy is one of the most significant treatment options for adolescent patients. Despite the economic trauma that has afflicted the health care industry, art therapy continues to be an effective and crucial modality that is growing in demand and popularity. Over the past few years, I have encountered many art therapists who are working with adolescents outside of the established health care institutions. Art therapists are treating adolescents in their own private practice offices, in public school settings, community studios and a host of other nontraditional environments. This is happening both out of necessity and in response to demand for services from consumers.

In this age of slick electronic media designed to sell commodities rather than tell good stories or explore truth, I am more convinced than ever that Nietzsche was correct when he asserted that only artists dare to show us the human being as he or she really is. The central task of art therapists working with adolescents is to engage with teenagers without the aid of disguises or make-up. We must be who we are without trickery or beguiling intent. We must make our art in the company of adolescents as we encourage them to make art as we attend. As we look for the particular and genuine self of our patient, often scarred or hidden deep within, we cannot help but encounter our own scars and hidden qualities.

The task of all art is to depict what is genuine and true about life. All art has an existential quality. The intent of art, and art therapy, is to get beneath the surface of things. It is the responsibility of the artist to express the way things feel. In a very real sense, the facts of an adolescent's life may be irrelevant if the images and the feelings associated with the images are true. The anguish, zest and untamed intensity of existence is the essential subject of inquiry for art therapy.

As a practicing artist, my work comforts me in times of turmoil and afflicts me in times of comfort. I look at my own paintings and those of my adolescent patients and I am awed by the bravery and honesty I see. At other moments, I am shocked by the painful open wounds that stare back at me. The quandary I face as an artist, and an art therapist, is that I know that there is no hiding from the angst these images show. There is no retreat.

I know that as these words appear on the screen of my computer monitor, they inevitably fail to convey the depth of my passion for working with adolescents. I fear that I have taken you only into the shallows. Art as therapy with adolescents is a subject that in some ways defies academic exploration. You must make art in the company of hurting children in order to really understand this book. Still, I hope that the stories and ideas I have shared here will excite your interest. If I can do this skillfully and with integrity, perhaps you will be drawn into the work with adolescents as I was so many years ago.

As I have written this book, I have felt a deep responsiblity to each of the adolescents I have worked with, to their art and to myself. As I sit before the computer, or stand before the blank canvas, I am intensely aware of the seriousness of this effort. I feel very alone. The canvas surface reminds of inner realities that must be addressed. The computer screen dares me to write about the way I feel in the studio. The canvas and the screen call out to me, asking to be freed from their emptiness. As my fingers move on the keyboard and as my brush slides across the tension of the canvas, deep things within me tremble.

I regard my work with adolescents as sacred. Every time an angry kid dips his woundedness in paint he finds nourishment and courage that his life's journey demands. The therapy is not found in helping adolescents get rid of their suffering; it is found in helping them immerse themselves in the creative flow. I think my faith in the power and goodness of art making is contagious. I don't have to tell adolescents that I believe in this. My faith is exhaled in the air I breathe. They see this faith with their own eyes. They smell it in my sweat. Adolescent patients do not fear that I will abandon them in the midst of their journey. They know that I will be with them, and welcome them in the studio. They know that we will make art.

"Come with me," I tell them. "Let's dye our wounds with paint and decorate our lives with the strength and courage we need to continue our journeys."

It is presumptuous to expect that this book has completely explored the complexities of art as therapy with adolescents. But I know that presumption is an act of imagination. If that is so then I will conclude that I have adequately presented a text which touches the major themes and issues of working with adolescents in art therapy. It is my deepest hope that this might become an important book in my profession, and that students new to the field will be the better for having read about adolescent art therapy as I practice it. I am hopeful that the strengths of this text are in my continual references to art-making processes. It is my desire that readers will finish this book with a good feeling about working with adolescents and their images. I fantasize them laying the book aside and saying, "Art therapy is the treatment of choice for suffering teenagers." If this fantasy is true at all, I have succeeded in creating the text I set out to make.

I do not present the reader with systematic theories of symbolic interpretation, nor do I provide scientifically verifiable statistical information regarding the diagnostic use of art. I could not and would not write about things that I do not believe. Yet, there are surely some who will regard this as a deficiency in my work. So it goes. I know that the basic tenets of art as therapy with adolescents that I have presented here are applicable to hurting kids, and so I will leave the writing of art therapy books about systematic interpretation and diagnostic applications to others in the profession. I have little interest in such pursuits.

Our journey through this book is nearly complete. We have walked a path littered with images, broken hearts, metaphors and mysteries. I hope you have enjoyed the walk and I pray that you have felt the deep passion and joy that I have for working with adolescents. I have been blessed by being an art therapist. I confess, I love what I do.

I would like to end this book by sharing one more brief story. Not long ago, my wife Cathy and I went to see the movie *Good Will Hunting*. During the hour- long drive home through the mountains of Northeastern Pennsylvania, we shared about our reactions to the movie. The story stirred up memories of a relationship I'd had with an adolescent boy several years ago. As I talked about that relationship tears welled up in my eyes. I hadn't thought about him for quite some time and I wondered how he was doing. Now, by no means was that boy, Bobby, a genious like the character portrayed in Good Will Hunting. Still, there was something about the relationship I had with Bobby that was brought back to the surface as I watched the movie. It was something about love.

Later that evening, I sat down with my guitar and wrote a song for Bobby.

Bobby Wouldn't Speak

Back when I met Bobby
he wouldn't even look at me at all
He'd stand with his hands in his pockets
and he'd lean against the wall
The doctors said that there
was really nothin' they could report
I guess they gave him to me
thinkin' I was just the last resort

He was seventeen years old
and he still hadn't passed the seventh grade
he's the only kid in junior high
who really had to shave everyday
he drew a picture of himself
with a broom stuck where it don't belong
then he shoved it across the table
as if to say, hey tell me is that wrong

and Bobby wouldn't speak, there was nothin left to say
hell he musta' figured it wouldn't matter anyway
all the things his uncle did were locked up deep inside
I guess no one ever noticed 'cause Bobby never cried

Well no one gave him much of chance
They figured he was really a lost cause
he was almost an adult and he still
believed in Santa Claus
But the thing about him was that though he
wouldn't talk - you should'a seen him draw
And during two long years, my Bobby
he showed them, he drew it all

> and I never will forget the last time that we met
> he had tears in his eyes and his cheeks got so wet
> he opened up his mouth and the words finally came
> he said I love you Bruce and he said it without shame

Back when I met Bobby
he wouldn't even look at me at all
he'd stand with his hands in his pockets
and he'd lean against the wall

I have no idea where Bobby is at the time of this writing. I don't know where most of the adolescents I have cared for are today. I suppose some of them have never made another drawing since they left therapy. But, I hope that right now somewhere in the world, Bobby, or one of his peers, is working on a painting. I have faith that adolescents are better off because of the time they spend making art.

B.L.M., August, 1998.

REFERENCES

Alexander, F. & French, T. (1946). *Psychoanalytic therapy: Principles and applications.* New York: Ronald Press.

Allen, P. (1992). Artist in residence: An alternative to "clinification" for art therapists. *Art Therapy: Journal of the American Art Therapy Association, 9,* 22-28.

Allen, P. (1995). *Art is a way of knowing.* Boston: Shambhala.

Ansbacher, H.L. (1956). *The individual psychology of Alfred Adler.* New York: Basic Books.

Arnheim, R. (1967). *Toward a psychology of art.* Berkeley, CA: University of California Press.

Ault, R. (1986). *Art therapy: The healing vision.* (Video tape) Topeka, KS: Menninger Foundation.

Beres, Block, Copeland, Newell, and TroKylaowski. (1996). *Sister Hazel - Somewhere More Familiar.* CD. Crooked Chimney Music Inc. New York: Universal Records, Inc.

Berne, E. (1964). *Games people play.* New York: Grove.

Berry, P. (1982). *Echo's subtle body: Contributions to an archetypal psychology.* Dallas: Spring Publications

Champernowne, H. (1971). Art and therapy: An uneasy partnership. *American Journal of Art Therapy. 10,* 142.

Chapin, M. (1993). The art therapist as exhibiting artist. *Art Therapy: Journal of the American Art Therapy Association, 10,* 141-147.

Clark, D. & Davidson, L. *Catch Us If You Can.* Epic Records.

Cohen, B., Hammer, J., & Singer, S. (1988). The diagnostic drawing series: A systematic approach to art therapy evaluation and research. *The Arts in Psychotherapy, 15,* 11-21.

Cohen, B., Mills, A., and Kijak, A. (1994). An introdution to the DDS: A standardized tool for diagnostic and clinical use. *Art Therapy: The Journal of the American Art Therapy Association. 11,* 105-110.

Cohn, R. (1984). Resolving issues of separation through art. *The Arts in Psychotherapy, 11,* 29-35.

Corbin, H. (1979). Avicenna and the visionary recital. Dallas: Spring Publications.

Dracknik, C. (1994). The tongue as a graphic symbol of sexual abuse. *American Journal of Art Therapy. 11,* 58-61.

Duritz, A. (1993). Anna Begins. *August and Everything After.* CD. Los Angeles: EMI Blackwood Music Inc. / Jones Falls Music / Knucklevision Music / Puppet Head Songs / Siren Says Music BMI.

Elkind, D. (1967). Egocentrism in adolescents. *Child Development, 38,* pp. 1025 - 1034.

Erikson, E. (1963). *Childhood and society.* (2nd Edition). New York: Norton.

Feder, E. & Feder, B. (1981). *The expressive arts therapies.* New York: Prentice-Hall.

Feen-Calligan, H., & Sands-Goldstein, M. (1996). A picture of our beginnings: The artwork of art therapy pioneers. *American Journal of Art Therapy. 35,* 43-53.

Feldman, S. & Elliott, G. (1993). *At the threshold: The developing adolescent.* Cambridge, MA: Harvard University Press.

Frankl, V. (1955). *The doctor and the soul.* New York: Alfred A. Knopf.

Frankl, V. (1959). *Man's search for meaning.* New York: Washington Square Press.

Franklin, M. & Politsky, R. (1992). The problem of interpretation: Implications and strategies for the field of art therapy. *The Arts in Psychotherapy, 19,* 163-175.

Franklin, M. (1992). Art therapy and self esteem. Art Therapy: *The Journal of the American Art Therapy Association. 9,* 78-84.

Freud, A. (1958). Adolescence. *Psychoanalytic study of the child. 13:* 255-278.

Gannt, L. (1987, October). *Symbolic expression. Making tangible the intangible.* Keynote address presented at the Buckeye Art Therapy Association Annual Symposium, Columbus, OH.

Gussow, A. (1971). *A sense of place.* San Francisco: Friends of the Earth.

Haeseler, M. (1989). Should art therapists create artwork alongside their clients? *The American Journal of Art Therapy, 27,* 70-79.

Henley, D. (1986). Approaching artistic sublimation in low-functioning individuals. *Art Therapy: The Journal of the American Art Therapy Association 3,* 67-73.

Henley, D. (1987). Art assessment with the handicapped: Clinical, aesthetic, and ethical considerations. *Art Therapy: The Journal of the American Art Therapy Association, 4.* 65.

Henley, D. (1997). Expressive arts therapy as alternative education: Devising a therapeutic curriculum. *Art Therapy: The Journal of the American Art Therapy Association. 14,* 15-22.

Hillman, J. (1975). *Re-visioning psychology.* New York: Harper and Row.

Hillman, J. (1988). *Archetypal psychology, a brief account.* Dallas: Spring Publications.

Hillman, J. (1989). *A blue fire.* New York: Harper & Row.

Huestis, R. & Ryland, C. (1990). Outcome after partial-hospital treatment of severely disturbed adolescents. *International Journal of Partial Hospitalization,* Vol. 6 (2).

Jones, D. (1983). An art therapist's personal record. *Art Therapy: The Journal of the American Art Therapy Association,* 1, 22-25.

Jourard, S. (1968). *Disclosing man to himself.* New York: Litton Educ.

Jung, C.G. (1958). *Psyche and symbol.* New York: Doubleday.

Jung, C.G. (1964). *Man and his symbols.* New York: Doubleday.

Kapitan, L. (1996). In Moon, B. (1996). Preface to *Art and soul: Reflections on an artistic psychology.* Springfield, IL.: Charles C Thomas.

Kielo, J. (1991). Art therapist's countertransference and post-session therapy imagery. *Art Therapy: The Journal of the American Art Therapy Association,* 8 (2), 14-19.

Kopp, S. (1976). Guru. New York: Bantam Books.

Kwiatkowska, H.Y. (1978). *Family art therapy and evaluation through art.* Springfield, IL.: Charles C Thomas.

Kramer, E. (1958). *Art therapy in a children's community.* Springfield, IL.: Charles C Thomas.

Kramer, E. (1971). *Art as therapy with children.* New York: Schocken.

Kramer, E. (1979). *Childhood and art therapy.* New York: Schocken.

Lachman-Chapin, M. (1983). The artist as clinician: An interactive technique in art therapy. *American Journal of Art Therapy, 23,* 13-25.

Lachman-Chapin, M. (1987). A self psychology approach to art therapy. In J. A. Rubin (Ed.), *Approaches to art therapy* (pp.75-91). New York: Brunner Mazel.

Landgarten, H. (1987). *Family art psychotherapy.* New York: Brunner Mazel.

Levick, M. (1983). *They could not talk and so they drew: Children's styles of coping and thinking.* Springfield, IL: Charles C. Thomas.

Levick, M. & Herring, J. (1973). Family dynamics as seen through art therapy. *Art Psychotherapy, I* (1), 45-54.

Levine, E. (1995). *Tending the fire.* Toronto: Palmerston Press.

Levine, S. (1992) *Poiesis.* Toronto: Palmerston Press

Linesch, D. (ed.) (1993). *Art therapy with families in crisis: Overcoming resistance through non verbal expression.* New York: Brunner Mazel.

Linesch, D. (1988). *Adolescent art therapy.* New York: Brunner Mazel.

Lopez-Pedraza, R. (1977). *Hermes and his children.* Dallas, Spring Publications.

Lowenfeld, V. & Brittain, W. (1970). *Creative and mental growth.* (5th ed.). New York: Macmillan.

Lusebrink, V. (1990). *Imagery and visual expression in therapy.* New York: Plenum Press.

May, R. (1975). *The courage to create.* Toronto: McLeod.

McConeghey, H. (1986). Archetypal art therapy is cross-cultural art therapy. *Journal of the American Art Therapy Association. 3,* 111-114.

McMahon, J. (1989). An interview with Edith Kramer. *American Journal of Art Therapy, 27,* 107-114.

McNiff, S. (1982). Working with everything we have. *American Journal of Art Therapy, 21,* 122-123.

McNiff, S. (1988, October). *The problem of interpretation in the arts therapies.* Keynote address presented at the Buckeye Art Therapy Association Annual Symposium, Columbus, OH.

McNiff, S. (1988). *Fundamentals of art therapy.* Springfield, IL: Charles C Thomas.

McNiff, S. (1989). *Depth psychology of art.* Springfield, IL: Charles C Thomas.

McNiff, S. (1993b). *Art as medicine.* Boston: Shambhala.

McNiff, S. (1995). Keeping the studio. *Art Therapy: The Journal of the American Art Therapy Association. 12,* 182.

Mills, A. & Cohen, B.M. (1993). Facilitating the identification of multiple personality disorder through art: The diagnostic drawing series. In E.S. Kluft (Ed.), *Expressive and functional therapies in the treatment of multiple personality disorder.* Springfield, IL.: Charles C Thomas.

Moon, B. (1996). *Art and soul: Reflections on an artistic psychology.* Springfield, IL.: Charles C Thomas.

Moon, B. (1995). *Existential art therapy: The canvas mirror* (2nd. ed.). Springfield, IL: Charles C Thomas.

Moon, C. (1994). Mystery: The guiding image. *Art Therapy: The Journal of the American Art Therapy Association, 11* (1), 18-22.

Moore, T. (1992). *Care of the soul.* New York: Harper Collins.

Moustakas, C. (Ed.). (1956). *The self: Explporations in personal growth.* New York: Harper.

Moustakas, C. (1995a). *Existential-psychotherapy and the interpretation of dreams.* New York: Jason Aronson.

Moustakas, C. (1995b). *Being-in, being-for, being with.* New York: Jason Aronson.

Peck, S. (1978). *The road less traveled.* New York: Simon and Schuster.

Pfeiffer, J. & Jones, J. (1981). *A handbook of structured expereinces for human relations training.* La Jolla, CA: University Associates.

Richter, J. P. (1973). *Horn of Oberon.* (M. Hale, Trans.). Detroit: Wayne State University Press.

Riley, S. (1994). *Integrative approaches to family art therapy.* Chicago: Magnolia Street Publishers.

Rinsley, D. (1980). *Treatment of the severely disturbed adolescent.* New York: Jason Aronson Inc.

Robbins, A. (1982). Integrating the art therapist identity. *The Arts in Psychotherapy, 9,* 1-9.

Robbins, A. (1988). A psychoaesthetic perspective on creative arts therapy and training. *The Arts in Psychotherapy, 15,* 95-100.

Robbins, A., Cooper, B. (1993). Resistance in art therapy: A multi-modal approach to treatment. *Art Therapy: Journal of the American Art Therapy Association, 10.* 208-219.

Rosenburg, H., Ault, R., Free, K., Gilbert, J., Joseph, C., Landgarten, H., & McNiff, S. (1983). Visual dialogues: The artist as art therapist, the art therapist as artist. *Proceedings of the 1982 Annual AATA Conference. Art Therapy: Still Growing.* (pp. 124-125). Baltimore, MD: AATA.

Sandburg, L., Silver, R., & Vistrup, K. (1984). The stimulus drawing technique with adult psychiatric patients, stroke patients, and in adolescent art therapy. *Art Therapy: Journal of the American Art Therapy Association. 1,* 137-140.

Simon, L. (1986). *Cognition and affect: A developmental psychology of the individual.* Buffalo, NY: Prometheus Books.

Simon, P. (1983). *Cars are cars. Hearts and Bones.* (LP). New York: Warner Brothers Records Inc.

Spaniol, S. (1989). *Art Therapy: The Journal of the American Art Therapy Association, 6,* (3).

Ulman, E., & Levy, B. (1984). Art therapists as diagnosticians. *The American of Art Therapy, 23,* 53-55.

Unger, E. (1995). One thousand penises: Working with adolescents. *The American of Art Therapy, 12,* 132.

Wadeson, H., Landgarten, H., McNiff, S., Free, K., & Levy, B. (1977). The identity of the art therapist: Professional self-concept and public image. *Proceedings of the 1976 Annual AATA Conference: Creativity and the Art Therapists Identity* (pp. 38 - 42). Baltimore, MD: AATA.

Wadeson, H. (1980). *Art psychotherapy.* New York: Wiley & Sons.

Wadeson, H. (1987). Pursuit of the image. *The Arts in Psychotherapy, 14,* 177-182.

Wadeson, H. (1976). The fluid family in multifamily art therapy. *American Journal of Art Therapy, 13* (4), 115-118

Watkins, M. (1980, Oct.). *Six approaches to art therapy.* Paper presented to the annual meeting of the New England Association of Art Therapists, Cambridge, MA.

Wolf, R. (1990). Visceral learning: The integration of aesthetic and creative process in education and psychotherapy. *Art Therapy: The Journal of the American Art Therapy Association, 7* (2), 60-69.

Yalom, I. (1980). *Existential psychotherapy.* New York: Basic Books.

Yalom, I. (1985), *The theory and practice of group psychotherapy.* New York: Basic Books.